AF247527

WONDERS
OF THE
STEREOSCOPE

WONDERS
OF THE
STEREOSCOPE

John Jones

Alfred A. Knopf
New York 1976

To Gabriela, Rachel and Nicolette

THIS IS A BORZOI BOOK
PUBLISHED BY ALFRED A. KNOPF, INC.

ISBN 0 394 40882 9

Library of Congress Catalog Card Number 76–19125
First American Edition

A list of credits
appears on page 128 of this volume

CONTENTS

FOREWORD

The popular crazes and household trivia of one generation are the rare curios of the next. It is remarkable how quickly a familiar, commonplace object can become extinct.

From the 1850s to about 1920 the stereoscope was well known even by people who did not own one, and hundreds of millions of pictures were made for it. Yet, today, when told the subject of this book, many qualified their enthusiastic smiles with puzzled frowns.

The aim of this book is not simply to erase the frowns, but to survey the history of the stereoscope and broadly indicate its enormous range of subjects; and, with the aid of a special viewer and reproductions of original stereo-views, to let readers experience the fascination which made this scientific toy so popular for nearly a hundred years.

Even those who have encountered stereoscopy before are sometimes confused about the words stereo*scope* and stereo*graph*. A stereograph is a pair of photographs mounted side by side, one showing an object as seen by the right eye and the other showing it as seen by the left eye. When a stereograph is looked at in a special viewer which helps direct each eye to its proper half of the pair, the object photographed appears in three dimensions. This viewer is called a stereoscope.

Except for the reproductions of two paintings from the Tate Gallery, London (on pages 86 and 88), all the pictures in the book are from my own collection, which has been put together with more luck than expertise. For what special knowledge I have I am primarily indebted to that fountain of information, Helmut and Alison Gernsheim's *The History of Photography,* and to William Culp Darrah's *Stereo Views,* an exemplar of the researcher's craft. Sir David Brewster's *The Stereoscope* is the ancestor of all informed writings on the subject, and volumes of the *Art Journal* published in the nineteenth century provided insights into the critical frame of mind with which the early stereographs were received.

Finally, I would like to express my gratitude to Margaret Lawrence for converting my crossings-out into typewritten pages of great clarity.

JOHN JONES

AN
INTRODUCTION
TO STEREO-VIEWS

THE POWER OF OLD PHOTOGRAPHS

All photographs are a trifle mysterious, if we stop to think about them. There is something uncanny about a scene 'frozen' before the eyes in such vivid detail. In 1839 the experience was so compelling, archives tell us, that people talked about nothing else for months. What excited everyone was the 'truth' of the image.

Today we may have reservations about the veracity of the camera. In another context, Jean Cocteau wrote, 'A plaster cast is exactly like the original except in everything,' and we might say the same about a photograph; its stillness is so *un*like the original. This could be a clue to its fascination for us: that it seems to have escaped our own subservience to time's flow.

Apart from this idea, which is true of all photographs, there is nothing very important about the view, opposite, of the *Old Mill on the Avon*: a bearded man sitting on a bench looks at his hands and a boy stares into the water. It is a non-event on a no-particular day. The only thing we can be sure about is that it actually happened – the camera *can* lie, but why should it lie about anything so trivial? If we let our attention wander over its details, it is possible to feel drawn into the scene. As our gaze absorbs such intimate trivia as the dent in the man's hat, the actuality of that winter's day over a hundred years ago suddenly becomes more immediate. A fleeting instant from the past merges with the present. Devotees of old photographs dote on this intensification of the lost anonymous moment.

Great as may be the power of old photographs, stereographs are just that bit more potent. Compare, for example, the plate opposite with the same view seen through the stereoscope (Card No. 1). Quite literally, stereographs have a clarity and immediacy which our everyday perception lacks.

SEEING DOUBLE

Because we have two eyes we see everything double, and almost everything out of focus. But because our eyes can scan and change focus at great speed, and our brain is able, no less rapidly, to assimilate and interpret what we see, we are hardly ever aware of these peculiarities of vision. We perceive the scene before us in clear focus and in three dimensions. That we do so arises, paradoxically, from our inability to focus very much at any one time. To see how small that area of focus is, just look fixedly at one word on this page. Even the words next to the one you have chosen will be difficult to read; the rest of the page will be virtually illegible.

In practice our eyes scan a scene very quickly, gathering focused clues, as it were, which the brain instantly jigsaws together. The areas surrounding these small points of focus are blurred and, to put simply what is a very puzzling phenomenon, the mind blots them out. If this were not so, and the eye could simultaneously focus everything before it, as a camera does, vision would still be impossibly confused. This is because our eyes are about three inches apart and each sees a different image; the scene is the same, but we see it from two viewpoints.

It is easy to demonstrate our 'double vision'. Hold a thin book, closed and upright, its

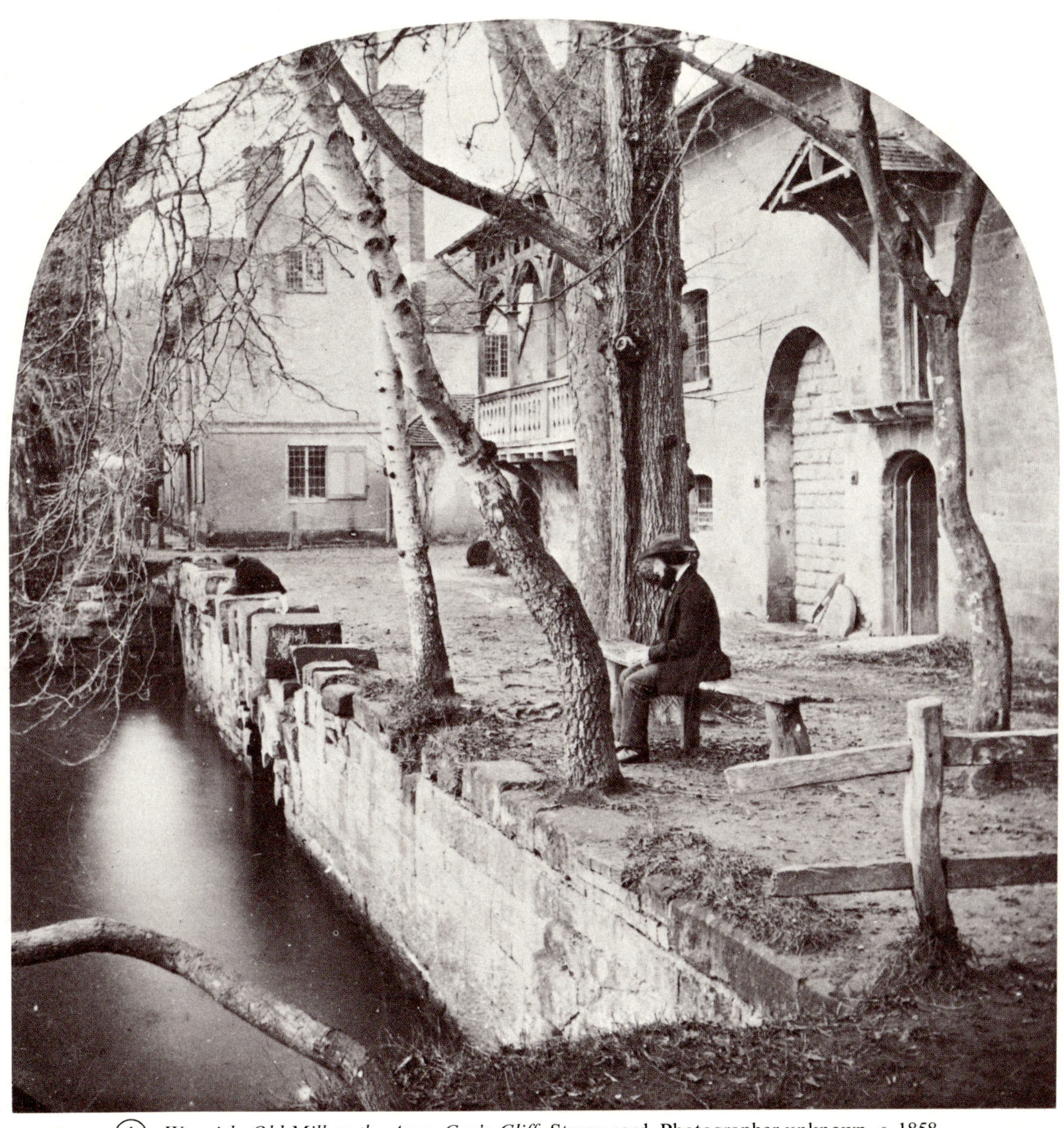

① *Warwick. Old Mill on the Avon, Guy's Cliff.* Stereo-card. Photographer unknown, *c.* 1858.

spine towards you, about a foot from your nose. Close your left eye and you will see a little of the front of the book, then close your right eye and you will see a little of the back. Open both eyes and, although focus may be a little difficult, for the reasons given above, you will see both back and front of the book at once. Now, in place of the book, hold up a finger and look past it at something yards away; the finger will be seen twice. Focus on the finger, and distant objects, although blurred, will appear double.

I have left out one obvious but important consideration. In normal vision the eyes are doing two separate things which it is easy to confuse: focusing and being directed at the focused area. These two muscular actions are synchronized but independent; it is the latter which produces the double vision. In looking at an object, each eye is aimed along a line of vision from itself to the object, where the two lines of vision meet. Only there do the images received by the two eyes coincide – or almost coincide. The distinction is critical to understanding the principle of stereoscopy. For even at that point where focus and lines of vision come together, the eyes do not both see quite the same thing. Because the lines of vision approach from different angles, two viewpoints are superimposed – as happened with the back and front of the book in our example. This minimal double vision is what allows us to perceive the third dimension.

PHOTOGRAPHY AND ITS INVENTORS

It is convenient to preface any account of stereoscopy with a brief history of the invention of photography, since the progress of both are intimately connected.

The *camera obscura,* from which all photographic cameras developed, was a drawing aid for artists. It consisted of a box with a lens at the front, an inclined mirror inside, and a ground-glass screen at the back. Light from the scene under observation entered through the lens and was reflected by the mirror on to the glass screen, where it could be brought into focus to form an image of the scene which an artist might trace or copy. The mirror was not an essential part of the *camera obscura,* but without it the image on the glass was inverted.

A box-form *camera obscura.* From *The Cyclopedia of Photography*, edited by Bernard E. Jones (1911).

It occurred to many people that if a light-sensitive material, one which darkens or lightens according to the amount of light falling upon it (like skin tanning or dyes fading), could be substituted for the glass screen, the image might be retained permanently. Several materials were tried out with varying success, the principal obstacle being to arrest the action of the light once the image was adequately formed.

In 1826 a French physicist, Nicéphore Niepce, exposed a pewter plate covered with a layer of bitumen in a mirrorless *camera obscura* for eight hours. Light makes bitumen insoluble, so that the parts of the bitumen layer which had not received light could be dissolved, leaving an image of undissolved bitumen adhering to the pewter. Niepce called this image a 'heliograph', the name given for a time to all early photographs.

Three years later, to experiment further along these lines, Niepce formed a partnership with an artist and compatriot, Louis Daguerre. When Niepce died in 1833, the partnership was maintained by his son, Isidore; and in 1838 Daguerre discovered by accident the process that bears his name. A sheet of silver-plated copper exposed to iodine fumes formed silver iodide on its surface and became sensitive to light. After about thirty minutes in the camera, a latent image formed on the surface which, when exposed to mercury fumes, 'developed'. A solution of common salt or sodium hyposulphite 'fixed' the image, which was then washed to remove any remaining light-sensitive iodine. The dark parts of the picture were the bare silver, the light parts a film of mercury which the least touch would wipe off. To protect it, the 'daguerreotype' was sealed under glass.

Very soon, chemical alternatives were found which speeded up the process to a matter of seconds, made the image clearer and preserved it longer. Daguerreotypes do not fade in sunlight but the metals involved can tarnish; the image is back to front unless a mirror is used in the camera, which increases exposure time, and copies can only be made by repeating the whole process.

In England during the 1830s Henry Fox Talbot experimented with paper soaked several times alternately in common salt and silver nitrate. He then placed the subject to be recorded, usually leaves or lace or a butterfly's wings, on the paper and exposed it to sunlight. This produced a light image of the subject on a dark ground. Fox Talbot fixed the image, which he called a 'photogenic drawing', with common salt or potassium bromide or iodide. From these beginnings he developed the process which he named the 'calotype', but which others called the 'talbotype'. Working in a dark room, he placed in the *camera obscura* paper which had been soaked in silver nitrate and potassium iodide and brushed over with a solution of silver nitrate and acetic acid mixed with gallic acid. Exposure took about six minutes, after which the image was developed in the gallo-nitrate of silver mixture (as above) and fixed with potassium bromide. The result was a negative from which any number of prints could be taken.

These two kinds of photograph, the daguerreotype and the talbotype (calotype), were employed in many improved forms by the early stereographers until the 1850s when a new process, 'wet collodion' (see below), superseded both. For his pioneering work Louis Daguerre was awarded a pension by the French Government, who announced that his discoveries would not be patented but 'given to the whole

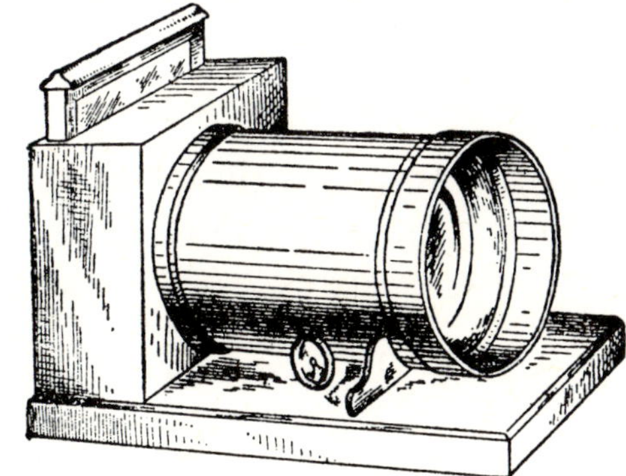

Engraving of Louis Daguerre's first camera. From *The Cyclopedia of Photography*, edited by Bernard E. Jones (1911).

world'. (In fact, before they said this, Daguerre had taken out a patent in England.)

At the time there was understandable rivalry between Talbot and Daguerre and several other claimants for the title of 'inventor of photography'. A patent is a way of establishing primacy and Daguerre's was the first photographic patent ever. Talbot did not patent his calotype until 1841. Daguerre also sold a licence to Antoine Claudet, who worked in England, and instructed him personally in the daguerreotype process. Such restrictions and permits led to many disputes and legal actions in England, and here is not the place to resurrect the *longueurs* of those controversies. But the granting of a licence to Claudet was an important event in the history of stereoscopy, since he was to be one of its most creative practitioners.

The daguerreotype had two disadvantages: copies could not be made from it without repeating the whole process, and special lighting conditions were needed for its bare metal surface to be seen clearly. The calotype process had neither of these problems but it was, one might say, no better than the paper it was printed on; that is, a great deal depended on the texture and quality of the paper negative through which the light had to pass when a print was made. Thus neither metal nor paper were wholly satisfactory. Even a waxed-paper process introduced by Gustave Le Gray, which made paper more translucent, could not compete for clarity and definition of image with glass, which superseded the metal and paper plates.

In Niepce's early experiments, glass had been tried out with some success; Daguerre followed up his work, and in 1839 Sir John Herschel invented a method of photographing on glass which was acclaimed for the delicacy of its picture. They all, however, encountered problems which probably had to do with the difficulty of making the image adhere to the glass during the washing and processing stages. Several inventors deserve recognition for their creative contributions to the solving of this problem, but particular credit must go to Nicéphore Niepce's cousin, Abel Niepce de Saint Victor, who persisted with glass supports and in 1847 succeeded by incorporating a layer of albumen (white of egg) in the preparation of the plate. (Four years earlier, in America, Alexander Wolcott had tried coating glass plates with white of egg, but he had abandoned his efforts after limited success.)

During this period Fox Talbot displayed an eagerness to preserve his monopoly of negative-positive processes by modifying and then patenting every new idea that appeared; he quickly refined the albumen process sufficiently to justify taking out a patent on it, thereby adding to the mass of restrictions on photography in England. In America John A. Whipple of Boston patented the process in 1850, but he seems to have been using it for several years previously, as had the Langenheims of Philadelphia, who patented an improvement in the same year. The combination of albumen and glass, both eminently transparent, later prompted the Langenheims to apply it to the making of magic-lantern slides to which, after 1864, they devoted their entire business. However, in 1850 they printed positives on glass and paper from albumen negatives and exhibited their results, which they called 'hyalotypes', in the Great Exhibition of 1851. An *Illustrated London News* reporter saw them there and wrote: '. . . no description of them is given in the present catalogue. They are labelled "specimens of the hyalotype, by Mr Langenheim" but, if we mistake not, are identical with a specimen executed by Mr P. V. Fry, of the Calotype Club by one of Mr Horne and Thornthwaite's camerae.' He was mistaken. Fry's specimen was one of the first examples of the most important new development in photography since its invention: the wet collodion process.

Fry was not responsible for the invention of the collodion process. When guncotton, discovered in 1846, was dissolved in sulphuric ether, it produced a sticky substance, collodion; this, spread thinly and allowed to dry, formed a transparent, strongly adhesive water-proof 'skin'. In 1850 Frederick Scott Archer combined collodion with light-sensitive iodides and applied it to the surface of a glass plate. It was then dipped into a silver nitrate bath and, *still wet*, introduced into the camera and exposed. Immediately after exposure it was developed with pyrogallic acid or ferrous sulphate and fixed with sodium hyposulphite or potassium cyanide. At first the by then relatively sophisticated albumen prints were better, but the collodion process had the great advantage of reducing the exposure time, in the case of portraits to as little as two seconds. Archer was a modest, generous man, who shared his findings with anyone who showed an interest. Peter Fry called on him and learned the new process quickly, and with Archer's help produced the photograph shown at the Great Exhibition.

Although his process had already been made generally available, Archer in 1851 published a detailed account in his manual *The Collodion Process on Glass*, and in a second edition, of 1854, he acknowledged the work of others whose experiments and suggestions had led him to his own discovery, which he declined to patent. A court case was brought in 1853 by Fox Talbot who wished to establish that the collodion process was covered by his calotype patents, but the jury found that the use of Archer's process did not infringe them. As a consequence, Talbot began to release his patents that year. Daguerre's patent expired about the same time. Neither process, however, had much of a future for, despite the skill required to practise it and the vast amount of apparatus required, the collodion became for several decades the most popular process.

The glass negative made by the collodion process could be used to print on paper or glass. One possibility was to make an 'ambrotype', an application which in fact had a considerable vogue. Ambrotypes derive from the nature of the collodion negative: its light areas are bare glass and its dark tones degrees of silver deposit. Held against the light the image is in negative, but placed on a black ground, the essential feature of the ambrotype, the silver reflects light and the bare glass becomes dark, converting the image to positive. Mounted in decorated cases against a black velvet or paper background, or simply painted with black varnish, ambrotypes were very popular for portraits (see *Portrait of a Young Lady* on page 34).

ORIGINS OF THE STEREOSCOPE

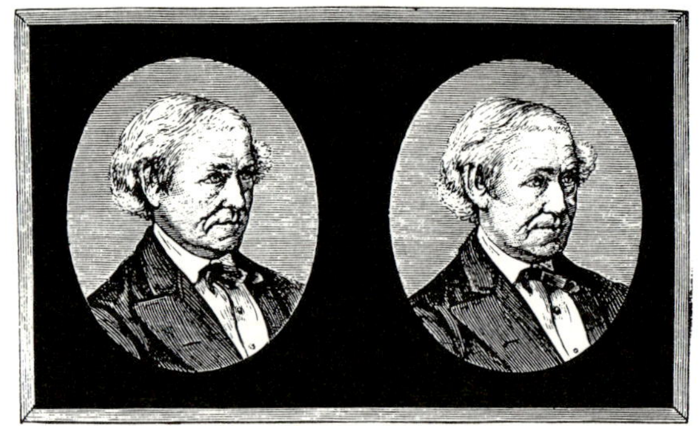

Engraved stereo-portrait of Sir Charles Wheatstone, inventor of the stereoscope.

It is surprising that the facts of binocular vision did not lead to the invention of some form of stereoscope centuries ago, since they were commented on by many early scientists, the earliest being Euclid in about 280 BC. In his treatise on painting Leonardo da Vinci calls attention to the subject, implicitly regretting that painting cannot render volume as convincingly as the eyes experience it. He points out that conventions of perspective and chiaroscuro, however deployed to create the illusion of depth, can never quite surmount the main obstacle, the flat surface of the painting.

It is sometimes thought that stereoscopy was kept waiting in the wings for photography to make its entrance. In fact this is not so. Sir Charles Wheatstone, for many years Professor of Experimental Philosophy at King's College, London, and a prolific inventor (the linear motor, submarine telegraphy, the concertina, etc.) was the first man to expound the principles of stereoscopy. He formulated the idea that, by making two perspective drawings of a solid object from points of view about three inches apart and presenting one to the left eye and the other to the right, the normal experience of vision would be simulated and the brain would 'see' a solid.

When, in the 1850s, the Scottish physicist Sir David Brewster contested Wheatstone's claim to have invented stereoscopy, evidence was produced which suggested that Wheatstone had had a stereoscope as early as 1832, and there are subsequent references to it in scientific papers of the 1830s. The first time the apparatus was publicly shown and a descriptive paper about it published was at a meeting of the Royal Society in 1838. A diagram of Wheatstone's apparatus was published with his paper. In it two mirrors (A′,A) placed at ninety degrees to each other, reflect the drawings which are mounted to left and right (E′,E). When the nose is placed against the point where the mirrors meet, each eye sees only one reflected drawing, but the illusion is that both eyes are looking straight ahead at a 'solid' image.

The date of Wheatstone's paper preceded by several months the first public announcements of discoveries in the field of photography; hence the first versions of the stereoscope were demonstrated with the aid of drawings, one of which is illustrated opposite. These stereoscopic drawings were always

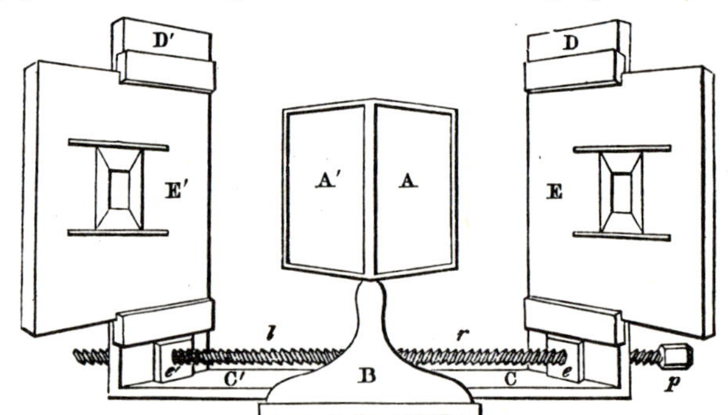

Diagram of Wheatstone's stereoscopic apparatus. Two mirrors at A′,A reflect the drawings at E′,E and produce a 'solid' image when viewed simultaneously from very close range. From *The Stereoscope*, by Sir David Brewster (1856).

simple since few artists had the skill to make pictures of any complexity that would render accurately the slight differences that occur in a three-inch change of viewpoint. Later, in 1852, when photography was established, Wheatstone wrote:

'What the hand of the artist was unable to accomplish, the chemical action of light, directed by the camera, has enabled us to effect.

'It was at the beginning of 1839, about six months after the appearance of my memoir in the *Philosophical Transactions*, that the photographic art became known, and soon after, at my request, Mr Talbot, the inventor, and Mr Collen (one of the first cultivators of the art) obligingly prepared for me stereoscopic Talbotypes of full-sized statues, buildings, and even portraits of living persons. To Mr Fizeau and M. Claudet I was indebted for the first daguerreotypes executed for the stereoscope.'

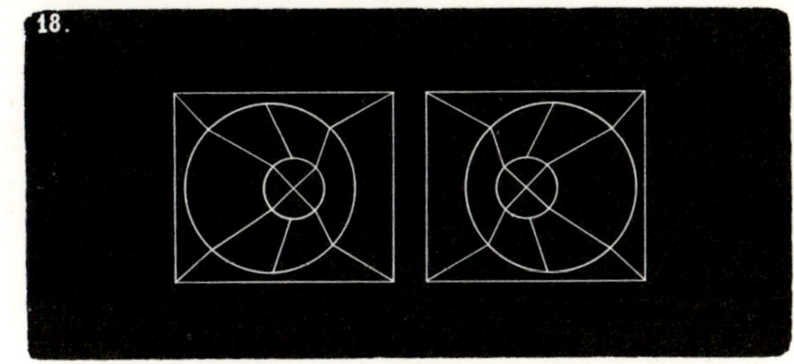

A drawn stereo-card made before the invention of photography to demonstrate Wheatstone's stereoscope.

Claudet and Wheatstone explored the commercial possibilities of the stereoscope, but seem soon to have dropped the idea. One reason may have been that with Wheatstone's viewer it was difficult to illuminate the two photographs evenly, still more so when the photographs were daguerreotypes, which have a shiny surface.

The daguerreotype, as we have seen, is made on copper, which is silver-plated. The dark part of the image is simply a bare metal surface; this, being highly polished, acts like a mirror. To see a daguerreotype clearly one must hold it so that the shiny part reflects as little as possible; light should fall on it obliquely. If the person looking at the image is wearing pale-coloured clothes, he may see more of his own reflection than of the photograph. By placing the daguerreotype in a dark box, however, and viewing it through a peephole, the problem is all but eliminated, except for the fact that *some* light is necessary for the picture to be seen at all.

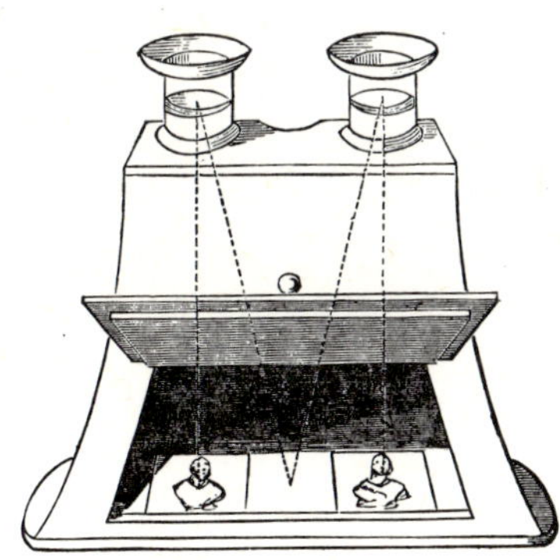

Brewster's refracting or lenticular stereoscope. From the *Illustrated London News* of 24 January 1852.

One solution to this viewing problem is to insert a flap in the side of the box, faced with mirror, which can be manipulated to bring light to fall glancingly on the surface of the photograph. Two lenses, one for each eye, form the peephole, allowing each eye to see one half of the stereograph, and to see it magnified. The clarity and detail of a stereoscopic daguerreotype so viewed is astonishing. The apparatus just described, a box with lenses and flap, is in fact the essential stereoscope. It was designed in 1849 by Sir David Brewster specifically for the characteristics of the daguerreotype, the latter being introduced into the viewer through a slot at the side.

Brewster identified his apparatus with the name *lenticular stereoscope*, ie a stereoscope with lenses, as opposed to Wheatstone's *reflecting stereoscope*, which used mirrors. The two lenses

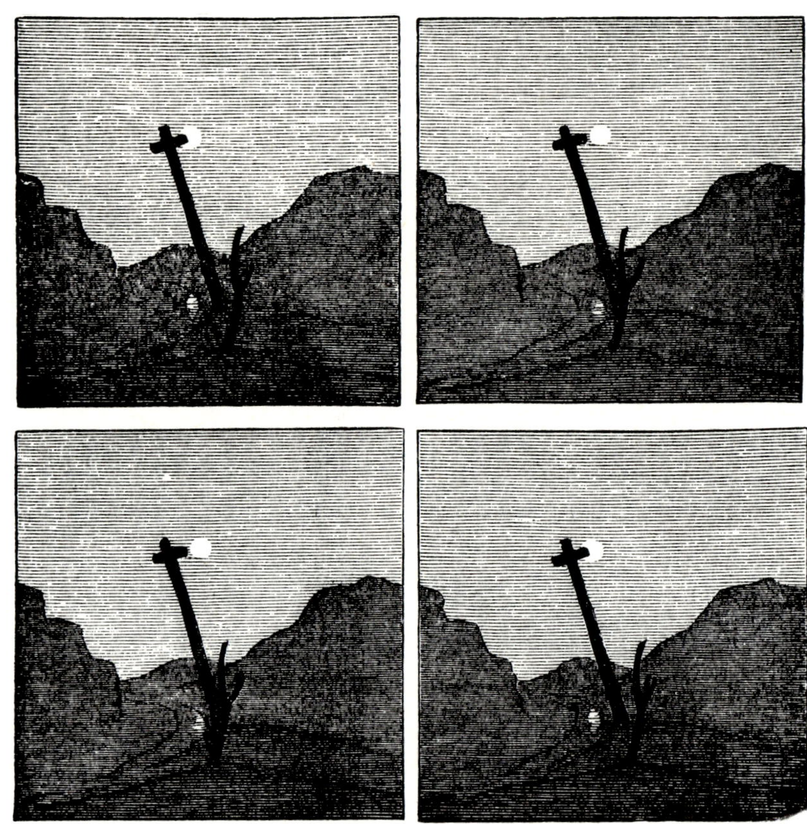

Elliot's 'ocular' views, devised in the 1830s, which made it possible to see the stereo effect with the naked eye. Two alternative methods are shown here: in the upper pair, the eyes should look past the picture and then slowly bring the focus nearer; in the lower pair, the eyes should be crossed, the right eye looking at the picture on the left, the left eye looking at the picture on the right. Illustrations from *The Stereoscope*, by Sir David Brewster (1856).

were made by halving a larger one and trimming the halves to fit the eye-holes of the stereoscope. They were, more precisely, wedge-shaped prisms which, when placed with their thinner edges together, refracted the light from the stereograph to the eyes in such a way as to produce the illusion that one image was being looked at rather than two. Hence Brewster's apparatus is also called a *refracting stereoscope*.

Brewster had difficulty in finding an instrument manufacturer in England who would produce his stereoscope for public sale, so in 1850 he took a prototype constructed for him by Loudon of Dundee to a French optical instrument-maker, Soleil. He, with his partner and son-in-law, Jules Duboscq, agreed to make the stereoscope commercially in Paris. They produced some excellent stereo-daguerreotypes to go with the viewer, and in so doing can be credited with setting stereoscopy on the road to international popularity.

Brewster's name was of course associated with the success of the apparatus, and his

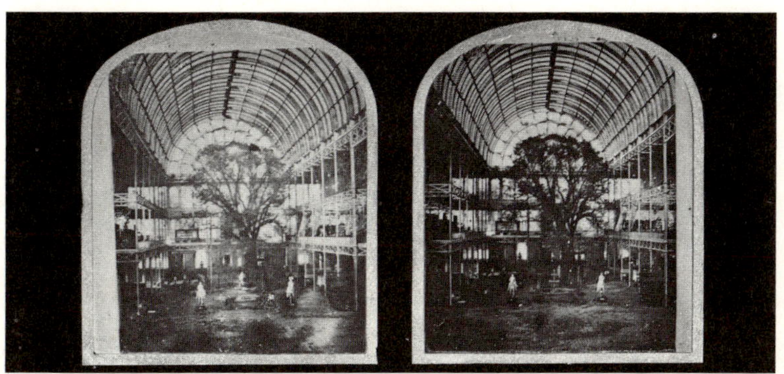

Stereo-daguerreotype by Jules Duboscq of the elm tree in front of which the Great Exhibition of 1851 was opened. Queen Victoria was delighted with a presentation set of Duboscq's views, and her enthusiasm created a huge fashionable demand for three-dimensional photographs.

celebrity, already substantial in other fields, was enhanced. Success did not bring out the best in him, certainly not in his treatment of Wheatstone. As we have seen, the basis of Brewster's design had been mooted by Wheatstone as early as 1832, and jealousy may well account, in part at least, for the obsessive way Brewster applied himself to robbing Wheatstone of the credit for being first with the idea. In 1856 Brewster published a book, *The Stereoscope*, which described binocular vision, a variety of stereoscopic apparatus and methods of providing pictures for them, and speculated exhaustively on the applications of stereoscopy to art, science, education, etc. The excellence of the book is marred by a large section devoted to pointing out Wheatstone's errors of theory, the ambiguity of his written expositions, the short-comings of his optical devices, and, in effect, to question his right to the title of inventor of stereoscopy. The same theme was taken up in disputatious correspondence in *The Times* and in his lectures.

Whilst Brewster clearly implied that the bulk of recognition should go to himself, he offered James Elliot as the earliest exponent of the stereoscopic principle. In fact Elliot's efforts, both in theory and practice, came after Wheatstone's, as Elliot himself admitted. Elliot had, during the 1830s, devised a small gadget without lens or mirrors which helped to direct the eyes separately to their respective 'dissimilar pictures', but it was hardly more than an aid to squinting. Some people have little difficulty in fusing two paired pictures without any form of mechanical aid, either by gazing past the stereograph and slowly bringing the focus nearer, or, alternatively (if the position of the two pictures is exchanged) by simply crossing their eyes. Elliot produced pictures for his experiment which are reproduced opposite, and the reader may care to practise this 'ocular stereoscopy', as Brewster called it. (A card placed vertically from the mid-line of the drawings to between the eyes is sometimes a help.)

At the Great Exhibition of 1851 in London, Jules Duboscq showed the stereoscope and pictures which he had produced for Brewster. Queen Victoria was captivated by them. Duboscq responded by making a special viewer and a set of stereographs which Brewster

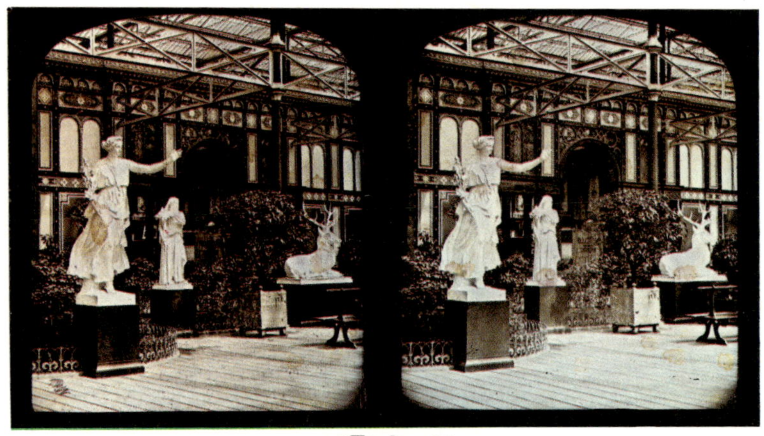

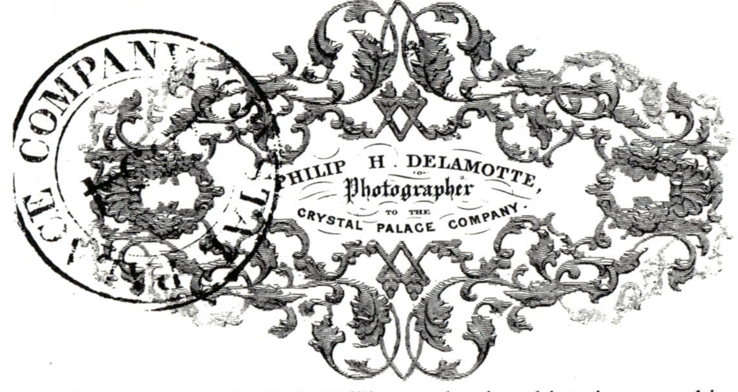

Stereo-daguerreotype of Crystal Palace by T. R. Williams, who signed it twice, scratching his monogram on the plate and pencilling his signature on the black mount. The label on the back of the view shows that it was taken for Philip Delamotte, official photographer of the Crystal Palace Company.

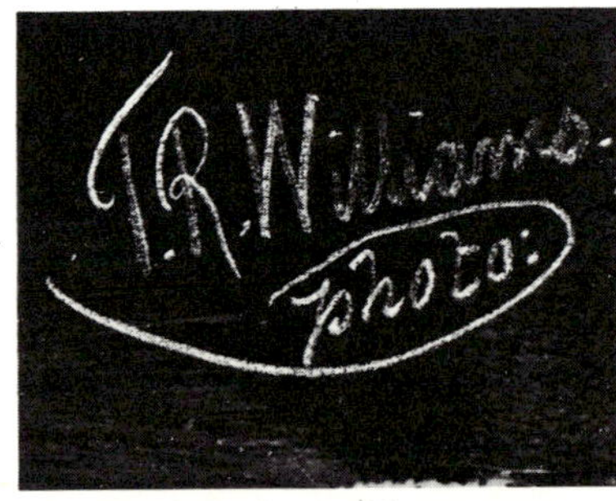

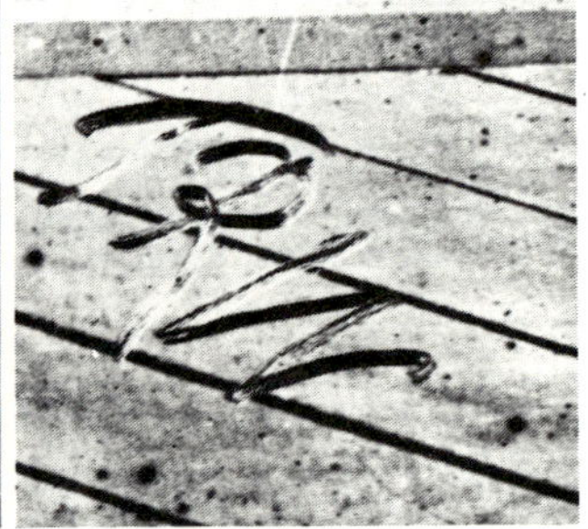

presented to Her Majesty. The view (on page 17) must be one of the earliest bearing the 'Duboscq & Soleil' trade mark: it shows the great elm tree in front of which the opening of the Exhibition took place. Duboscq was subsequently overwhelmed by a huge popular demand for stereo-views.

London's principal photographers also rose with eagerness to the challenge. The Crystal Palace Company gave a concession to the firm of Negretti and Zambra to publish views of the Exhibition, the concession running for several years to include the site at Sydenham to which the Palace was removed in 1854. Inevitably a large number of early stereographs, thousands in fact, were of the Crystal Palace itself. Commercial considerations

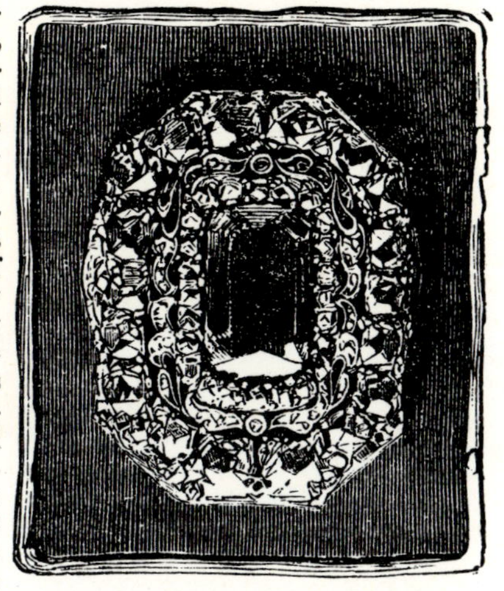

STEREOSCOPIC DAGUERREOTYPES.

THE Emperor of Russia has recently transmitted to M. Claudet, the eminent photographer, of Regent-street, a magnificent diamond ring, in acknowledgment of the p'easure which his Majesty has experienced in examining by the aid of Mr. Wheatstone's ingenious invention, called the Stereoscope, a series of Daguerréotype views of the Great Exhibition, taken by M. Claudet, and forwarded by him to St. Petersburg for the Emperor's inspection. The present is accompanied by a very complimentary letter, in which it is stated that the Emperor has been enabled, by these views, and by the marvellous phenomenon of plane surfaces producing representations of objects in perfect relief, " to form a correct idea of the Great Exhibition." It is also stated that the present is made in acknowledgment of M. Claudet's " constant endeavours ever since 1839 to improve the interesting art of photography."—*Times*.

RING, PRESENTED BY THE EMPEROR OF RUSSIA TO M. CLAUDET.

An account of Antoine Claudet's enterprise in sending stereographs to the Emperor of Russia. From the *Illustrated London News* of 3 April 1852.

apart, the lighting conditions of the Palace, which was in effect a large glass studio, must also have stimulated photography. Several photographers were employed to provide subjects for engravings which appeared in such publications as the *Illustrated London News* and exhibition records and catalogues; here the same names recur – Delamotte, Claudet, Mayall, Kilburn, Beard and T. R. Williams – and often it is not clear who worked for whom. One view by T. R. Williams, illustrated here, bears his unmistakable monogram scratched into the plate itself, and his signature is pencilled on the black mount; but the label on the back of the view is that of Philip Delamotte, official photographer of the Crystal Palace Company.

Claudet, displaying the same initiative that had obtained him a licence direct from Daguerre twelve years before, sent a collection of stereographs to the Emperor of Russia. This had the agreeable result reported, above, in the *Illustrated London News* of April 1852.

The range of Claudet's original ideas, his improvements to the inventions of others, his projects, exhibitions and enthusiasm for every new development of photography make him the outstanding representative of the era of the daguerreotype, which he initiated in England and was the last to abandon. His innovations in stereography include refinements to Brewster's viewer (1855), a revolving stereoscope holding a hundred stereographs and a 'stereomonoscope', intended to allow several people to view stereographs together without the use of lenses.

19

VARIATIONS ON THE STEREOSCOPE

The essential stereoscope remained the same for the rest of the century, although variations of every kind were played on the basic theme. 'Improvements' affected their optical efficiency only slightly, the main differences reflecting changes of furniture styles and degrees of affluence. One of the most spectacular was an American viewer about the size of a small piano, patented in 1854 by Southworth and Hawes in Boston, the 'Grand Parlor and Gallery Stereoscope', which employed Wheatstone's mirror principle; twelve pairs of daguerreotypes, $6\frac{1}{2}$ ins $\times$ $8\frac{1}{2}$

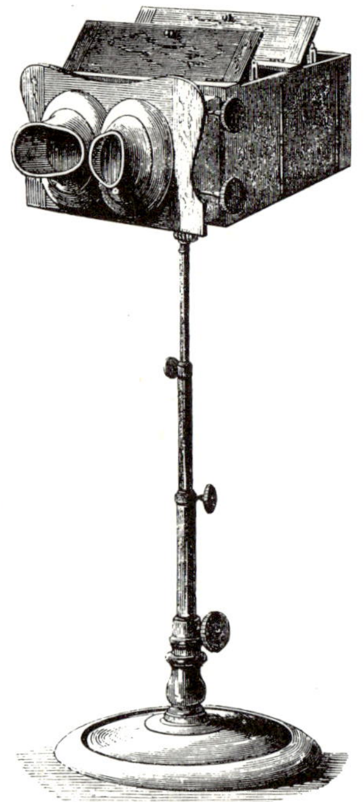

Engraving of G. C. Cooke's viewer, patented in 1858. From the *Art Journal* (1858).

ins, framed and in magazines, could be brought into view in turn by cranking a handle. At the other end of the range a small tin viewer, the Rotoscope, appeared in the early part of the twentieth century for use with stereographs the size of cigarette cards. Many stereographic cigarette cards were later published for which various cheap but efficient mini-viewers were designed.

Of the others, Knight's Cosmorama (1854) increased the lens size; Claudet's model introduced adjustable lenses (1855), and in 1858 George Colleton Cooke patented the viewer here illustrated which attempted to cater for every kind of eyesight and so eliminate all the snags in existing apparatus. Its 'trumpet-mouthed' eye-pieces cut off all light except that coming from the stereograph, but the major optical addition was a choice of movable lenses for people with defective sight. By manipulating the knobs at the side of the apparatus, four types of lenses could be brought into position as well as a magnifying glass which required that the stereoscope be placed nearer the eyes (hence the double mirror flap). A *passe-partout* or frame gave uniform size to every stereograph and eliminated light 'spill' from its margins. There were also coloured glass components to tint the view. In the same year Claudet described his stereomonoscope, mentioned earlier, and a prototype was probably made, but it does not seem to have been widely adopted.

The problem in stereography has always been to arrange for each eye to see the half of the stereograph intended for it, and not both halves. In 1858 a Frenchman, J. C. d'Almeida, projected the two halves on to a screen where they were superimposed. Projection was by two magic lanterns, one with a red glass filter and the other a green one. The spectator then placed a red glass in front of one eye and a green glass in front of the other. The eye covered with green saw only the red picture, because through green glass a green image is virtually invisible, and the other eye, covered with a red glass, saw only the green picture. This system was patented by Louis Ducos du Hauron in 1891, and has been used many times to solve the problem of showing pictures in relief, in books for example, where the flimsiest kind of red-green spectacles effect the desired result. The same principle was employed in the cinema for three-dimensional films until quite recently.

At the same time as he proposed his two-colour stereoscopic pictures, called 'anaglyphs', d'Almeida put forward another idea which has strong cinematic connections. Again two magic lanterns projected the two halves of the stereograph onto a screen, where they were superimposed. In addition, in front of each lantern was a spinning disc with holes in it, the holes placed so that the two images alternated with each other very rapidly, only one being on the screen briefly at a time. A similar perforated disc, synchronized with the first, span before the eyes of the spectator. While one eye could see its half of the stereo pair, the other eye could not see its half at all, and the spectator had the sensation of seeing an uninterrupted image in relief. This method avoided the darkening of the picture common to anaglyphs, and coloured pictures could have been shown with it, but the complexities involved in setting up a spinning-wheel apparatus in front of each spectator made it impractical.

The most practical device for viewing cards and by far the most popular was the invention of Oliver Wendell Holmes, whose enthusiastic writings about stereoscopy in the *Atlantic Monthly* typified and stimulated the popularity of the stereograph in America, which increased during the 1860s while in Europe it was declining. Holmes's viewer was manufactured from 1861 by his friend the photographer Joseph L. Bates.

A folding device which combined magnifying glass and stereo-viewer, the graphoscope, was common in many European homes for the rest of the century. And in 1896 a Frenchman, Jules Richard, introduced a stereo camera called the Verascope which took glass negatives ($1\frac{3}{4}$ ins × $4\frac{1}{4}$ ins) from which glass positives were made. To view them Richard designed the Taxiphote (1900), an elegant mechanism with ingenious refinements. Twenty-five views in a magazine were placed inside the machine which at the touch of a lever presented them in turn for viewing. Particular views could be pre-selected by turning a dial. Another lever brought a magnifying glass into play for looking at detail and a third produced the title of the view. When twenty-five views had been looked at, a bell rang to indicate that the magazine must be changed; others were housed in a storage cupboard which formed the pedestal on which the apparatus stood. The eye-pieces could be adjusted to suit all types of vision. In 1924 Richard introduced a camera that took pictures on 35-mm film. Although twentieth-century stereoscopy is not our main concern here, mention must also be made of the excellent Stereo Realist camera and viewer and the popular 'Viewmaster', which have preserved the popularity of stereoscopy to the present day.

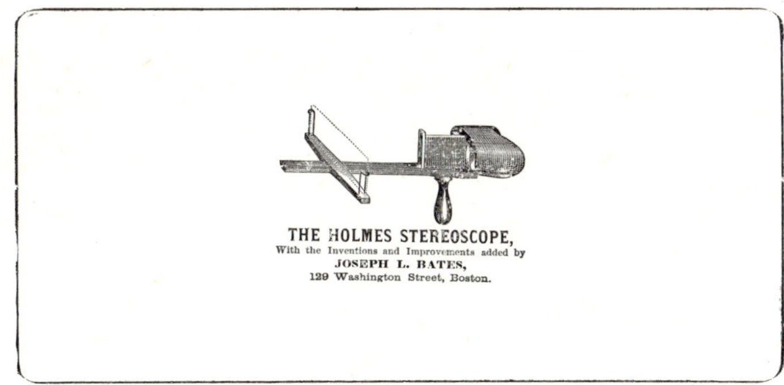

The Holmes viewer, illustrated on the back of a stereo-card published by Joseph L. Bates of Boston, Mass.

French viewer with large glass slides, each containing ten views. The slides were stored in the base. Early twentieth century.

Revolving table stereoscope which two people could view at once. The label reads: 'The Stereoscopic and Photographic Company, 108 & 110 Regent Street. "Adjusting Achromatic Revolving Stereoscope".'

Richard's Taxiphote ('Stéréo-classeur. Distributeur auto-matique'). Made for glass slides, 4·5cms x 11·5cms. The slides, in cassettes, were housed in trays in the base.

A table graphoscope–a large magnifying glass and stereoscope combined.

Hand viewer for glass slides measuring 6cms x 13cms.

Knight's Cosmorama. The label reads: 'Cosmorama Stereoscope Registered Sept. 15th 1854. Knight. Foster Lane. London.' 1854.

Refracting stereoscope. A late form of Sir David Brewster's invention. 1850s.

lisplayed the most significant types in circulation between the
ifty views to the pocket Rotoscope, foreground right, designed for use with stereographic cigarette cards.

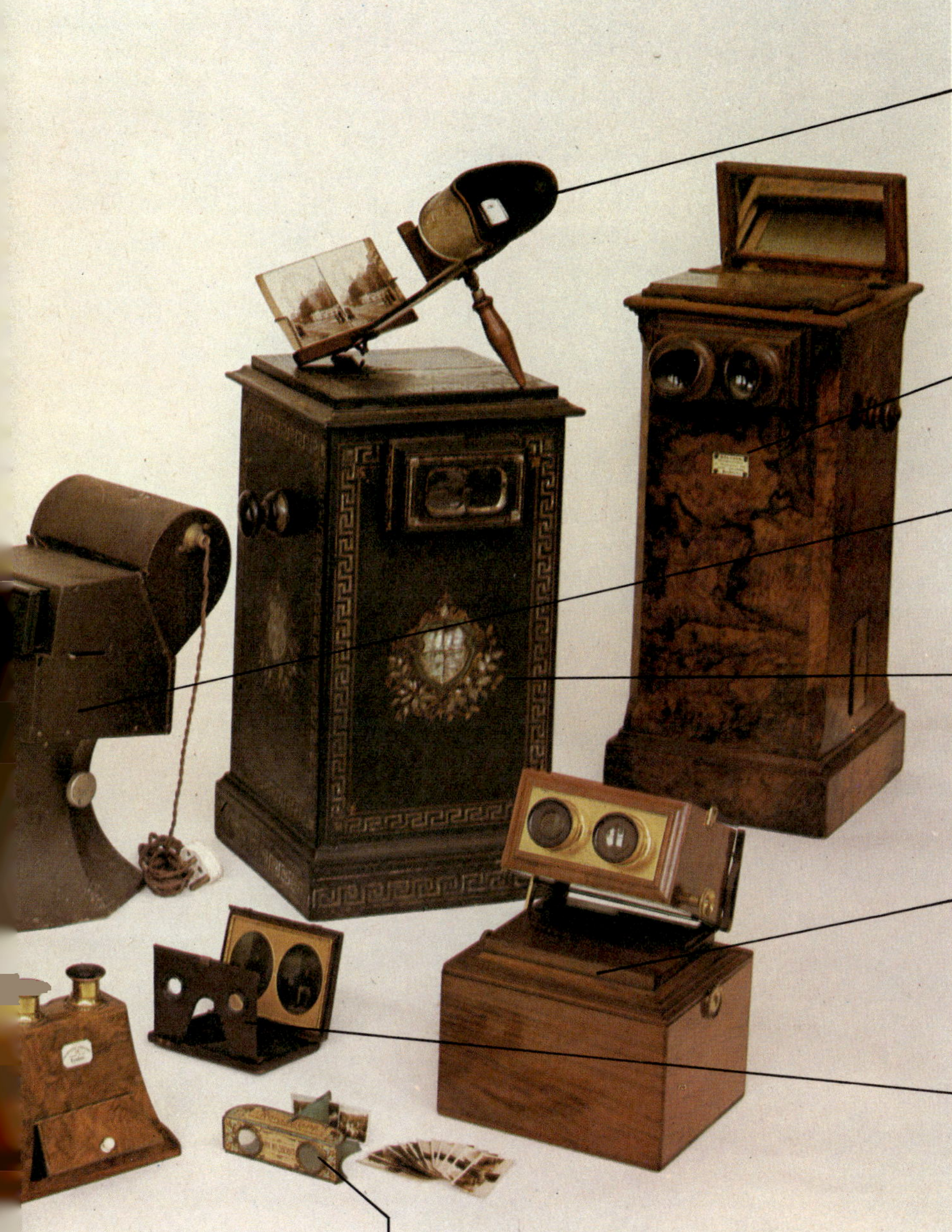

A 'Holmes' viewer. Its metal hood is engraved with the words 'Sun Sculpture' (the Underwood & Underwood trademark). 1901.

Revolving table stereoscope designed to contain fifty cards. The label reads: 'Meagher. Manufacturer. 21 Southampton Row. High Holborn. London W.C.' c. 1860.

Gaumont viewer, made for glass slides (6cms x 13cms) by L. Gaumont & Cie, Paris. The slides were in cassettes. c. 1930.

Revolving table stereoscope. Made in papier mâché and inlaid mother of pearl, with gilt painted decoration. c. 1860.

A Beck achromatic stereoscope, contained in a mahogany case which becomes its stand. The brass eye-pieces are marked: 'Achromatic Stereoscope. Smith, Beck and Beck. 6 Goleman St., London.' c. 1860.

A folding pocket stereo-scope of the kind designed by Kilburn and modified by Claudet. The photographs are ambrotypes. 1850s.

Refracting stereoscope with adjustable eye-pieces, an improvement by Antoine Claudet. The label reads: 'Carpenter and Westley. 24 Regent St. London.' 1850s.

The Rotoscope, a portable folding stereoscope, with small stereo-cards. Made in Germany for the Rotary Photographic Co. Ltd, London. Early twentieth century.

THE STEREO-CAMERA
AND INSTANTANEOUS PICTURES

The earliest stereographs were taken with one camera, which was moved sideways in a small arc between the two exposures, half a plate being taken at a time. A base was soon devised with slots in it so that the sideways movement of the camera could be controlled and standardized. The principal disadvantage of this method was that the subject had to remain still for both exposures. Two cameras placed side by side achieved the same result, although involving problems of alignment. Exposures were made by removing the caps of both lenses simultaneously; this reduced the time needed and the chance of the subject changing position.

A. Quinet of Paris produced the first binocular camera (having two lenses) in about 1853. Also at this time J. B. Dancer of Manchester made a prototype of a highly esteemed camera which was produced in 1856. Dancer's camera carried several sensitized plates within it which could be moved into position for exposing by a simple internal mechanism. A lens-opening device made certain that both halves of the stereograph were taken simultaneously and with equal exposure time. A feature of the binocular camera was that the position of the two separate pictures is reversed in the negative. Prints made from it had to be cut in half and the left and right halves changed about before being stuck on the card. This was a time-consuming process and some photographers preferred to divide the negative and reverse its halves before printing, so that on the final card the two pictures were not divided but constituted a single print. With little modification a single-lens camera could be used to make stereographs. This was done by substituting a front with two lenses for the single one.

Lenses for early binocular cameras had a short focus, that is, the foreground and background of the picture could be kept in clear focus without closing the aperture, as was necessary with landscape cameras. The picture, dictated by the distance between the eyes, was small. These two factors meant that even moving objects might be photographed because small movements did not show; more important, a picture taken with a large aperture requires a shorter exposure time. When the chemistry of the plate was fast enough this produced what were called 'instantaneous' photographs. In 1854 the first instantaneous stereo-views were taken. They were of Paris streets and the photographer, André Disdéri, worked from some distance, which served to diminish the effect of small movements. Helmut Gernsheim, the eminent historian and collector, regards the photographs that G. W. Wilson made of Edinburgh in 1859 as the first truly successful pictures to 'freeze' movement, because they relied less on the position of the camera to render small movements invisible. Also in 1859 the great American photographer Edward Anthony produced instantaneous views of Broadway, New York. As early as 1856 Wilson had made remarkable stereographs of a boat on the Loch of Park, in which moving clouds and ripples on the water are clearly distinguishable.

During the 1860s the many stereographs of arrested movement caused considerable debate, much of it concerned with their 'truthfulness'. Because they rendered visible moments of action which the naked eye could not normally grasp, they were thought by some to be 'untruthful'. Moreover, artists argued that figures caught in 'accidental' poses often seemed ungainly and off-balance, and to represent them so was unconvincing. Nevertheless the influence of photography on the art of the time is now beyond question. Degas's innovatory figure compositions owe much to it, and the pictures of the Impressionists that render the fleeting effects of light, echo the instantaneous photographs of Paris streets.

The stereo camera's ability to function in reduced lighting conditions produced some interesting interior photographs in the 1860s, and its speed was used by the British War Office in 1858 to record the trajectory of shells from experimental weapons. A more entertaining use was the study of athletes in action such as that of Miss Ward, below.

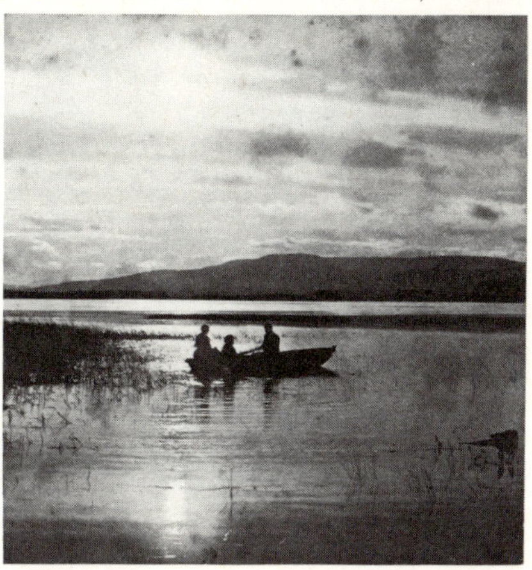

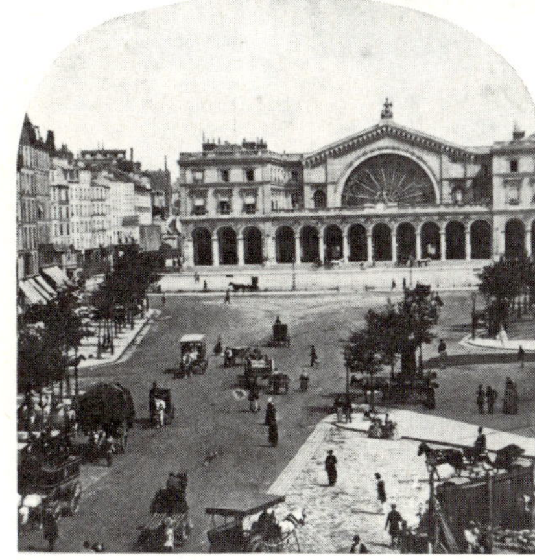

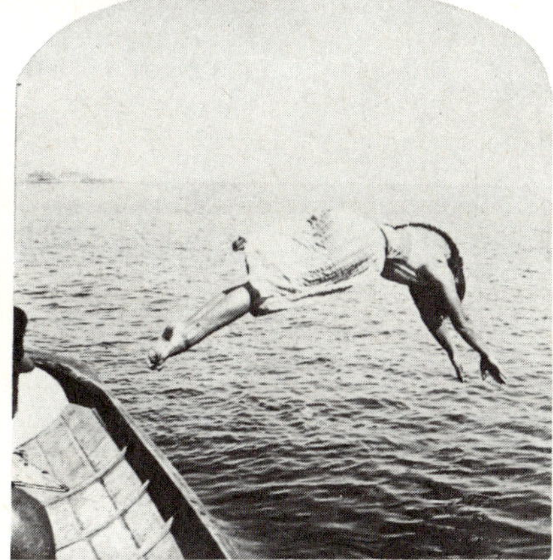

(TOP) *The Loch of Park, Aberdeenshire*, one of the first instantaneous stereographs, made in 1856 by G. W. Wilson. (BOTTOM LEFT) *Gare de l'Est*. Photographer unknown. A Paris street scene is used to demonstrate the then novel technique of arrested movement. 1860s. (BOTTOM RIGHT) *Miss Ward, the Greatest Lady Diver*. Published by Underwood & Underwood. 1889.

THE PUBLISHERS

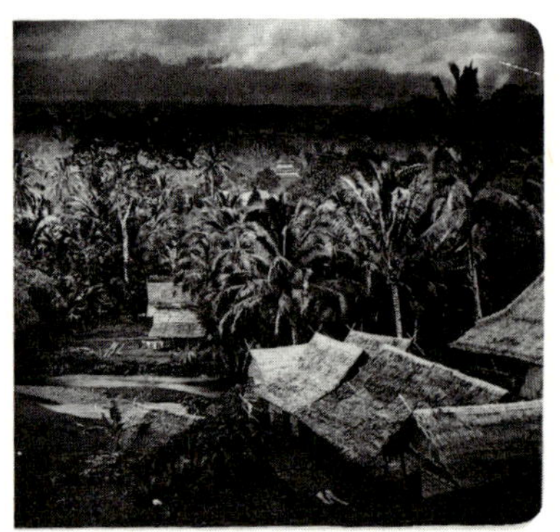

Village of Buitenzorg (Java). Glass stereo-view by Francis Woodbury.

The firm of Negretti and Zambra was founded in 1850 by Henri Negretti, who took the first photographs of London from a balloon, in 1863. As official photographers to the Crystal Palace they were responsible for the first large series of stereographs, and their sponsorship of Francis Frith's photographs in Egypt established them as pioneers in England of stereoscopic publications, in particular of examples taken outside Europe. A rarely seen series issued by them is the work of Francis Woodbury, an Australian explorer and photographer working in Java during the 1850s and '60s. Still in business today, Negretti and Zambra have produced most types of photograph and every kind of photographic apparatus.

The London Stereoscopic Company was created to manufacture stereoscopes only. It soon began to produce stereographs as well, some on glass, the majority on paper. Throughout the 1850s their premises displayed views of all types of subject, but they came to be specially associated with a particular kind of comic, sentimental or idealized image of everyday life. Opposite is an example, *The Happy Homes of England* (with, on this page, its country cousin bearing the same title). The idea of landscape painting prominently occupying the centre of the Victorian home is seductive, but a more authentic feature of *The Happy Homes of England* is perhaps the stereo-viewer on the table near the window. Several versions of this card and thousands of similar groups in contrived postures were made by the London Stereoscopic Company in the 1850s and '60s. Founded in 1854, the company published stereo-views made by its own staff photographers, notably William England, James Elliot and Alfred Silvester, and handled the photographs of many others. In its first two years the company sold half a million stereoscopic viewers, and in 1858 its advertised stock numbered 100,000 different views. The company's slogan, 'No home without a stereoscope', in fact went some way to being realized.

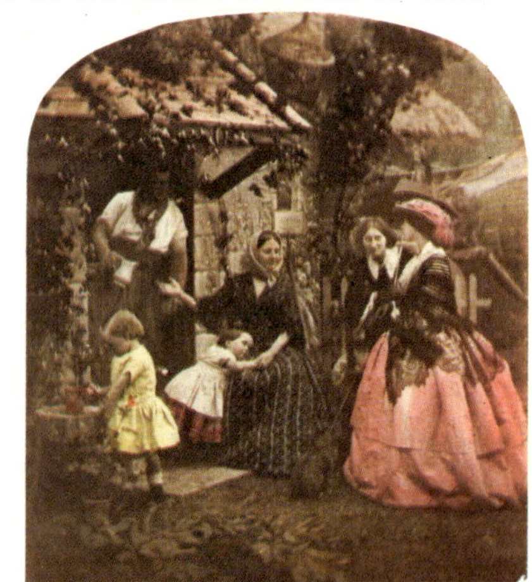

The Happy Homes of England. A cottage scene, companion to the drawing-room view opposite. Hand-coloured card. Published by the London Stereoscopic Company.

The stereograph was introduced into the USA by the Langenheim brothers, William and Frederick. Of German origin, they settled in Philadelphia and there experimented with the daguerreotype. In 1850 Frederick went to Paris to take lessons directly from Daguerre; on his return, however, his most successful work was with albumen on glass. In 1855 the brothers published a series of glass views of American scenery, a project

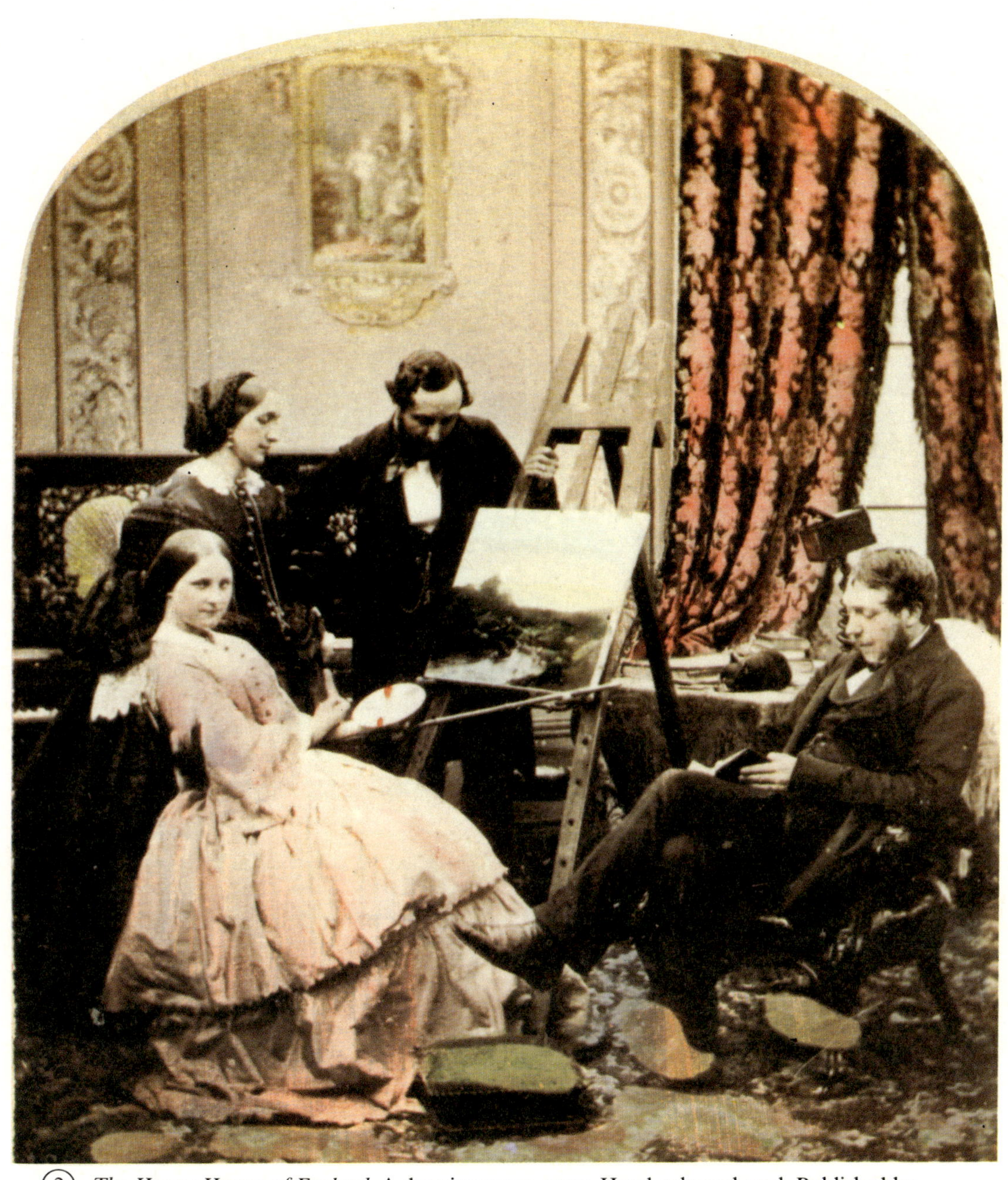

2 *The Happy Homes of England.* A drawing-room scene. Hand-coloured card. Published by
the London Stereoscopic Company.

sponsored by a group of twenty-one businessmen who in return each received a set of twelve views. During the 1850s the Langenheims published many glass views and even more of the cheaper variety produced on card. Frederick travelled to Europe, possibly to Moscow, to make foreign views which the brothers sold until 1859, when their stock was supplemented by imported foreign views, for example Frith's series from Egypt (see pages 38–41). In 1861 they formed the American Stereoscopic Company, but by 1864 they had abandoned making stereographs in favour of magic-lantern slides. By that time several firms had begun to issue stereographs in America, the most important being that of E. & H. T. Anthony of New York.

Their first views were issued in 1859 and included a set called 'instantaneous', which showed street scenes in which the movement of figures was arrested. These were taken by Edward Anthony who in 1860 went into partnership with his brother at 501 Broadway. During the next eleven years the firm of E. & H. T. Anthony became the most famous publishers of American views, moving in 1871 to 591 Broadway where they continued to publish stereographs until about 1873. Their labels, bearing the firm's current address, assist in the dating of their photographs. Collectors should nevertheless bear in mind that they published from the same negatives for many years; moreover, their method of numbering negatives was erratic and does not always reflect the chronology of their publications.

While independent photographers in small towns produced stereographs for a limited local clientele or the souvenir-seeking stranger, Langenheim and Anthony had established that stereography was big international business. A third pair of brothers, Edward and Benjamin West Kilburn, in 1865 formed a publishing partnership in Littlehampton, New Hampshire. This grew by 1873, when they built new premises, to produce more than two thousand cards a day, employing a staff of fifty-five. The Kilburns introduced the curved mount, a feature of late nineteenth- and early twentieth-century cards, which was thought to assist the stereo effect and was adopted by subsequent publishers. The company continued until 1904 when its negatives were bought by James M. Davis; he later sold them to the Keystone View Company.

At first negatives for the views were taken by the publishers themselves, but all the large firms came to buy other photographers' negatives in quantity. By about 1880, when Edward Kilburn retired and Benjamin took over the firm, the task of marketing views had taken precedence over photographing them. In 1882 another pair of brothers, Ben and Elmer Underwood, embarked on a scheme for selling stereographs from door to door. They arranged with three large firms exclusive distribution rights west of the Mississippi, and two years later they became their sole agents for the entire USA. By 1889 they had a branch in England, and in 1891 started to produce stereographs from their own negatives and from others they had purchased. By the beginning of the twentieth century they were manufacturing 25,000 stereographs a day, selling 300,000 Holmes-type viewers annually, and thousands of young men were trained as salesmen. They devised the formula of providing subjects in sets: these were sold as being either entertaining or educational, and were an unprecedented success, not only in America but via agencies all over Europe, in Russia and Japan. The card illustrated is from a

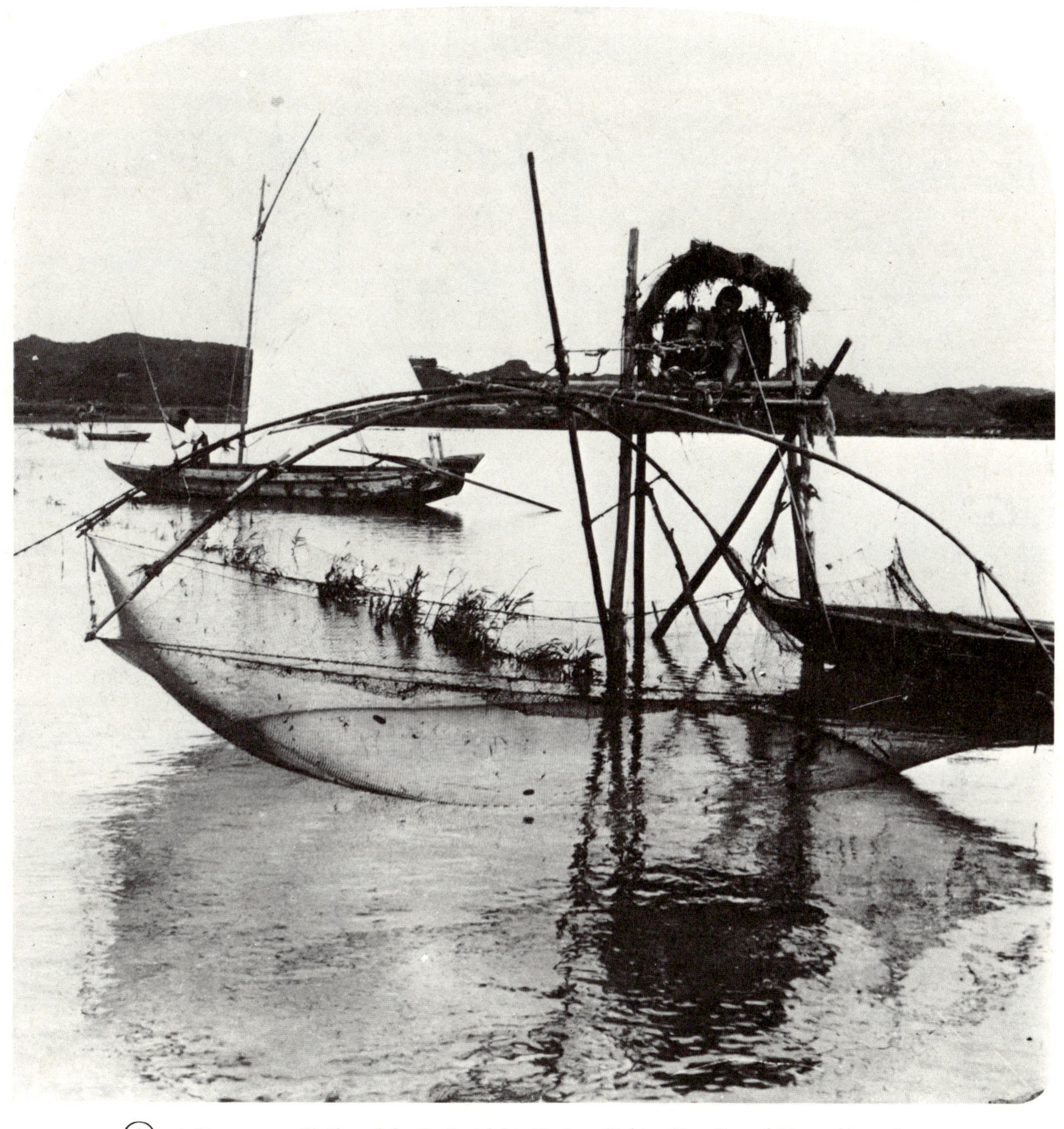

③ *A Picturesque 'Toiler of the Sea' with his Curious Fishing Net, Bay of Matsushima, Japan.*
Stereo-card. Published by Underwood & Underwood.

set about Japan, and goes beyond the educational and 'armchair traveller' aims of the series to achieve exceptional beauty as a photographic image. Three other companies copied their system: Griffith and Griffith, H. C. White and the Keystone View Company which, having bought up the Kilburn negatives from James M. Davis, did the same in 1910 for H. C. White and finally bought the stock of Underwood & Underwood itself, becoming after 1920 the only important manufacturers of stereographs in the world.

IDENTIFYING STEREO-VIEWS

Millions of stereographs were produced by amateurs, small photographic businesses and mass-production companies who did not think it necessary, any more than they do today, to put the photographer's name on every print. Identifying unsigned stereographs still offers considerable scope to an aspiring pundit with an eye for style. There is no doubt that master photographers sometimes invest their work with a style amounting to a signature, but, when no supporting documentary evidence is available, identification based on style alone is a daring thing to do. It takes a bold, not to say foolhardy, historian to do for a photograph what experts in painting failed so miserably to do in the matter of Vermeer and the Van Meegeren forgeries.

Fortunately, however, many attributions require little special knowledge. As with paintings and wine, the shortest route to connoisseurship is to read the label. Most stereographs bear a photographer's or publisher's imprint, and those that do not will often yield clues to the date and maker's name. Occasionally, in a series or group, for example, only one card will be labelled, but the others will bear such strong family resemblances that common parentage can be confidently assumed.

Even so, cards which carry imprints can sometimes leave the collector guessing. Many nineteenth-century French photographers, for instance, were curiously reticent and would divulge no more than their initials, a custom only one degree less chilling to the researcher than the bleak description, 'Anon'. Some labels are, moreover, ambiguous. A photographer-turned-publisher, *eg* G. W. Wilson, might continue to use his own label on prints made by his assistants; while publishers such as Underwood & Underwood bought up the negative stock of countless photographers and, when issuing their work, often did so without acknowledgment.

Subject matter seldom helps identification, particularly motifs like the Alps or the Piazza San Marco which have been assailed by so many photographers that one imagines them flinching at anything sounding remotely like the click of a camera shutter. Such views defy attribution to any one photographer, and hardly merit research. On the other hand some rare stereographs more than repay investigation. The plate overleaf, for example, an unsigned, undated daguerreotype, has been reclaimed from the lost-property department of the history of photography in the name of one of its most distinguished figures.

THE PLATES

Unless otherwise stated,
the illustrations in this part of the book are
half-views taken from stereo-cards.
The numbered plates (1-48)
are also reproduced in Volume 2
as stereo-cards
and may be viewed in three dimensions.

STILL LIFE WITH STEREOSCOPES

The illustration opposite shows one half of an unlabelled stereo-daguerreotype. Its subject, *bric-à-brac* carefully arranged to look like an untidy jumble in an attic, recalls Daguerre's earliest surviving work, in which a group of plaster casts, a framed picture and a wicker-covered bottle are arranged in the light from Daguerre's studio window. At that time (the 1830s) lengthy exposures made *still* life an obligatory genre, no living subject being passive enough to endure the camera shutter's fifteen-minute stare.

In trying to estimate the age of the 'stage attic' opposite, it would therefore seem reasonable to assume that the choice of subject was dictated by the need for a long exposure. Yet for several reasons the picture must have been taken much later than Daguerre's. The simple fact that it is a stereograph proves it was not made before 1851. Furthermore, among the objects in the group are several items of photographic equipment including two stereoscopes, one of which incorporates a ground-glass screen that was not a feature of the earliest models. The date would have to be still later if we could be sure that the lens tubes are of the kind that can be adjusted, an improvement introduced in 1855; but the detail is not quite clear enough to verify this. There may well be other objects in the group to which a specialist could give a firm date. In this case, however, such expertise is unnecessary, since other features of the picture provide all the evidence needed for identification.

Because each daguerreotype is unique, it is understandable that a photographer, having taken so much trouble to set up an elaborate group, would want to make more than one photograph of it. This was in fact a fairly common practice: usually the photographer rearranged the scene slightly before taking a new picture. Such related photographs are known as 'variants'. It seems probable that variants of our attic group survive, perhaps bearing the identification label which this version lacks – although I have not come across one. However,

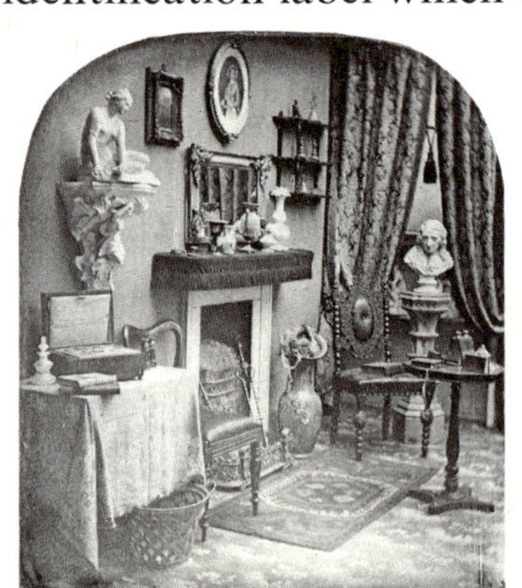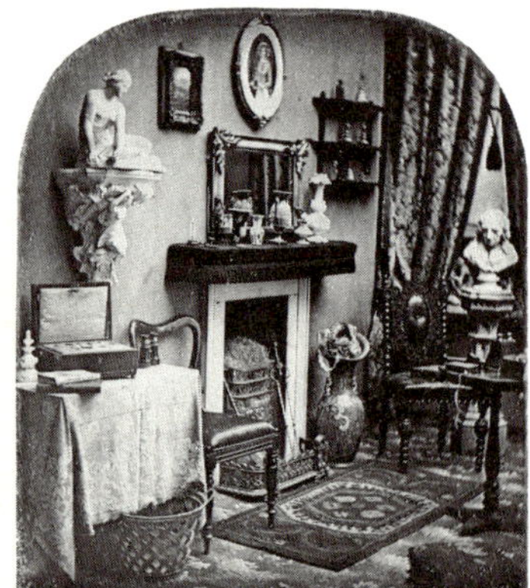

the bust at the top of the picture, the chair and the basket under it, the embroidered footstool in the foreground and several other small objects *do* appear in the unlabelled stereo-daguerreotype of a Victorian interior, left, of which a variant exists in the Gernsheim Collection of The University of Texas. The variant is mounted in its original leather wallet bearing Antoine Claudet's label and a date, 1855. From this we may conclude that all three daguerreotypes are Claudet's work of the mid-1850s.

Untitled Victorian interior. Stereo-daguerreotype by Antoine Claudet. 1855.

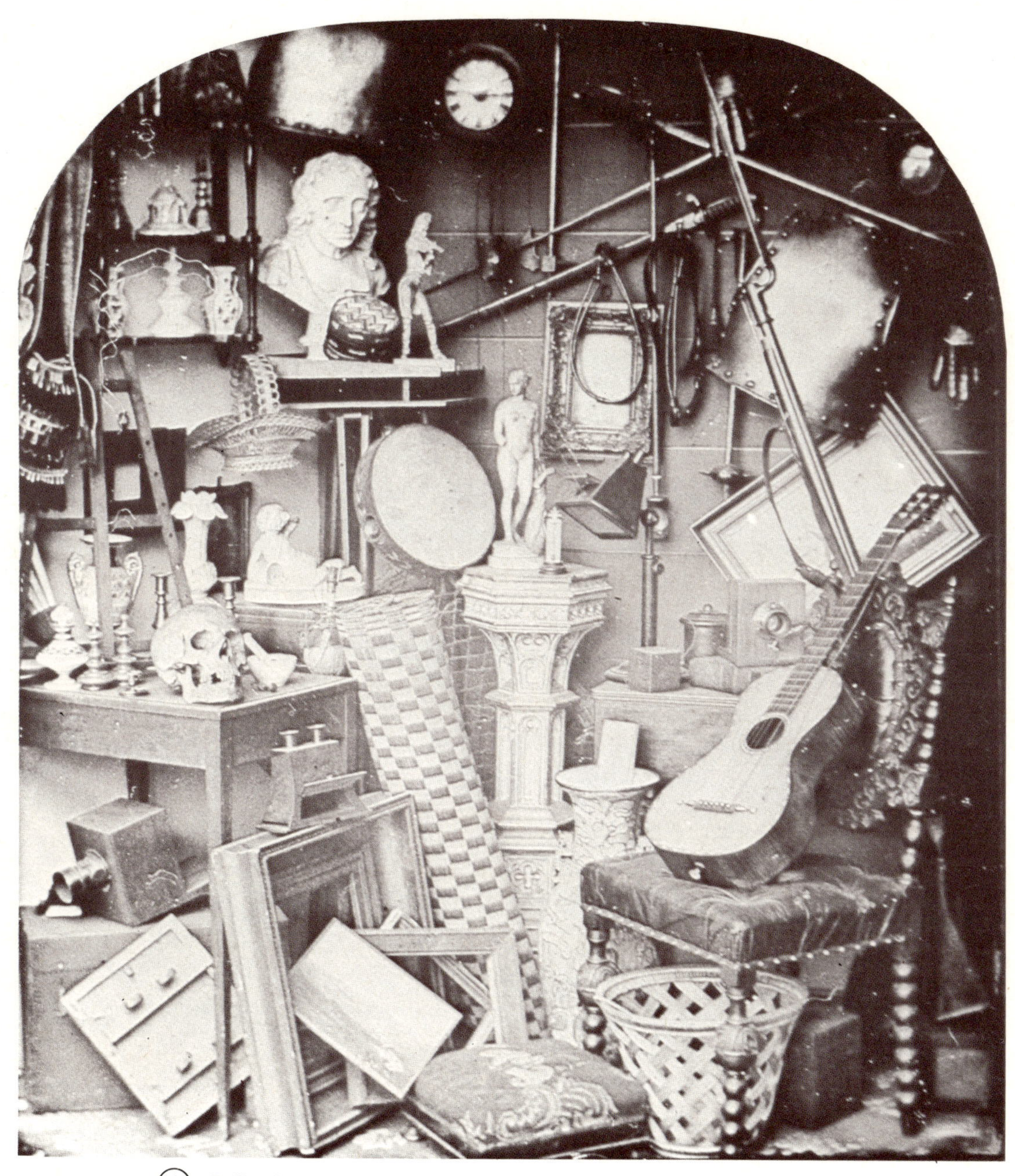

④ *Still Life in Attic*. Stereo-daguerreotype by Antoine Claudet. Mid-1850s.

FIRST SITTINGS: THE EARLY PORTRAIT STUDIOS

Antoine Claudet was born in Lyons but spent much of his working life in England, beginning there as manager of a glass manufacturing company's warehouse in London. He seems to have secured that position through having invented a labour-saving way of cutting glass cylinders, for which he was awarded a Royal Society medal. The technical aspects of photography also seem to have stimulated his flair for invention which, during his lifetime, earned him dozens of decorations including the Légion d'Honneur. Having bought a licence in 1839 from Louis Daguerre, he at first used it chiefly to take photographs from which engravings were made for book and magazine illustration.

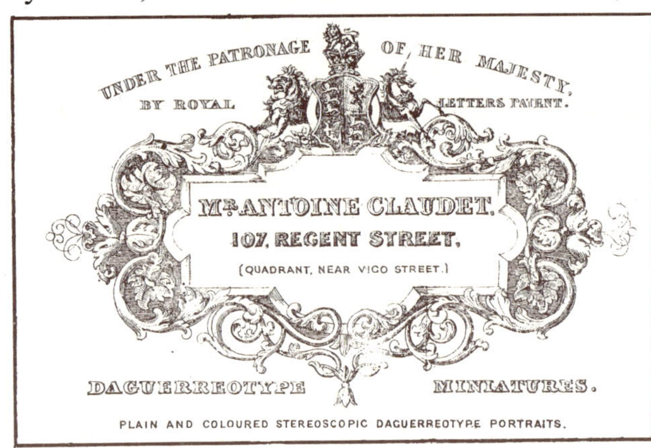

Label on the back of the Claudet portrait, opposite, bearing the address of his 'Temple of Photography' in Regent Street, London.

In the USA, meanwhile, photographers were not inhibited, as were their colleagues in Britain, by Daguerre's patent restrictions, and photography developed unhindered. A camera which incorporated a concave mirror to concentrate the light on the plate and correct the reversed image was constructed by an American, A. S. Wolcott, who offered it for sale in Europe. It was bought by a coal merchant called Richard Beard who, with expert assistance, managed to render the daguerreotype sensitive enough to reduce exposure time and make portraiture a practical proposition. Beard bought a licence from Daguerre's patent agent and opened the first photographic portrait studio in Britain, which was an immediate financial success. Soon Claudet, who had also discovered a way of accelerating Daguerre's process, opened his own portrait studio.

Claudet's earliest portraits were poor compared with Beard's but as their quality improved his clientele grew. He moved his studio several times, finally setting up a 'Temple of Photography' at 107 Regent Street, London, where the *Portrait of a Young Lady*, opposite, was made. The portrait, most delicately hand coloured, is from a family collection, and was housed in a box with a compartment for Claudet's improved stereoscope and slots for each picture. Also illustrated is another portrait of the same young lady, made three years later; this, an ambrotype, is by E. Wade of Fishergate, Preston.

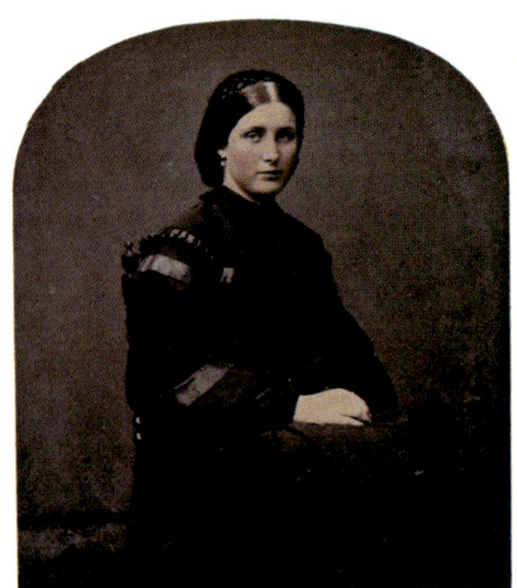

Portrait of a Young Lady.
The girl, opposite, is seen three years later in an ambrotype by E. Wade of Fishergate, Preston.

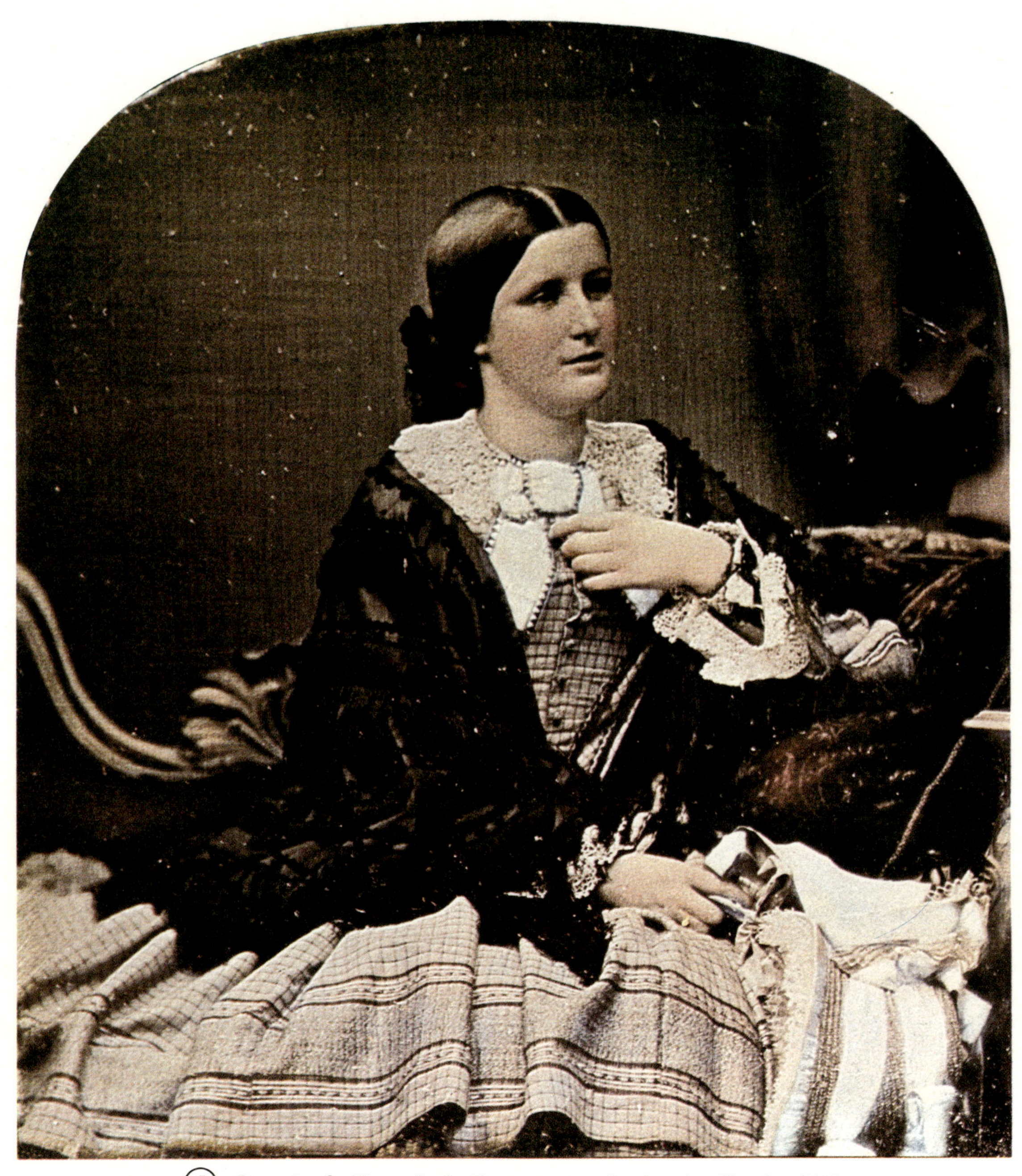

⑤ *Portrait of a Young Lady*. Daguerreotype by Antoine Claudet. 1854.

FEMALE SLAVES

In the early 1850s the problem of keeping the sitter still long enough to make stereoscopic portraits may account for the number of photographs of sculpture, but Hiram Power's *Greek Slave* would certainly have been a popular subject anyway. The idea for it, a contemporary reviewer tells us, was 'suggested by the practice of exposing female slaves for sale in the bazaar of Turkey'. Carved in marble in 1845, it became the most popular statue in the Great Exhibition of 1851, its fame stimulating and being stimulated by a large number of photographs, engravings and copies in various media and sizes. It must be one of the earliest examples of the snowball effect, familiar today, that a wide distribution of images has upon celebrity, but its success does not seem to be entirely the consequence of publicity. To have been singled out for attention from among the numerous life-size sculptures of the nude that were dotted about the Great Exhibition, it must have exerted a strong intrinsic appeal. Pre-Freudian reviewers innocently dropped hints:

'. . . it was no easy task [for the sculptor] to place a young and high-minded female in such a position without a chance of offending delicacy; but the great charm of Mr Power's work is, that it repels the very thoughts which would be likely to arise under such circumstances, and produces others totally at variance with them – sympathy and compassion for the captive; execration for those who could make merchandise of the beauty and the innocence of the fairest of God's creatures . . .' (*Art Journal,* 1851). Frederika Bremer, the pioneer feminist, described how '. . . this captive woman with her fettered hands seized upon me with unusual power, as no other statue in marble had done'.

Another statue, recorded for the stereoscope by William England, had a similar success in the International Exhibition of 1862. Following Greek precedents the sculptor, J. Gibson, RA, added flesh-colour to his marble nude subsequently known as the 'Tinted Venus'. The *Art Journal* (1863) reviewed it obliquely, ascribing to all sculptors of the female form 'the wish to give some one decisive proof of the lofty ideal to which their imaginations can soar; they desire to gather into one figure the scattered forms of beauty and love which perhaps for long have haunted their fancy'.

Modern commentary is in no doubt about 'haunted fancy' and Power's 'unusual power'. In *The Erotic Arts* (1975), Peter Webb declares that 'the impression created by the girl clutching a sheet with one hand and an apple with the other as she gazes upwards with her mouth slightly open is highly suggestive . . .' And of the *Greek Slave* he observes: 'The girl averting her face as she covers her vulva with one manacled hand and pats an extremely phallic post with the other bears close comparison with any number of today's pin-up photographs of a sado-masochistic variety.'

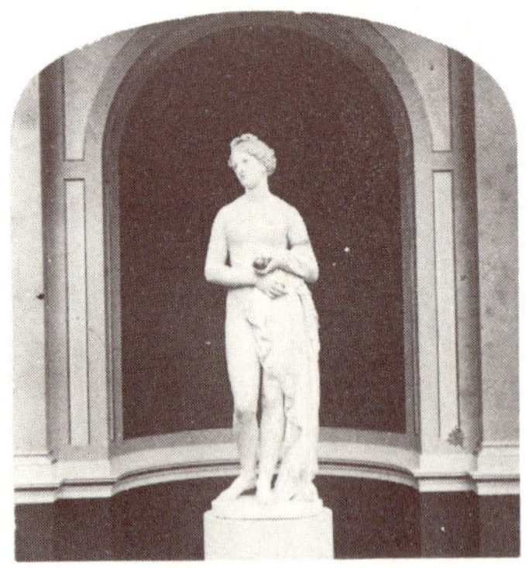

'Venus', by J. Gibson (the 'Tinted Venus'). Photographed by William England. Published by the London Stereoscopic Company as part of its coverage of the 1862 Exhibition.

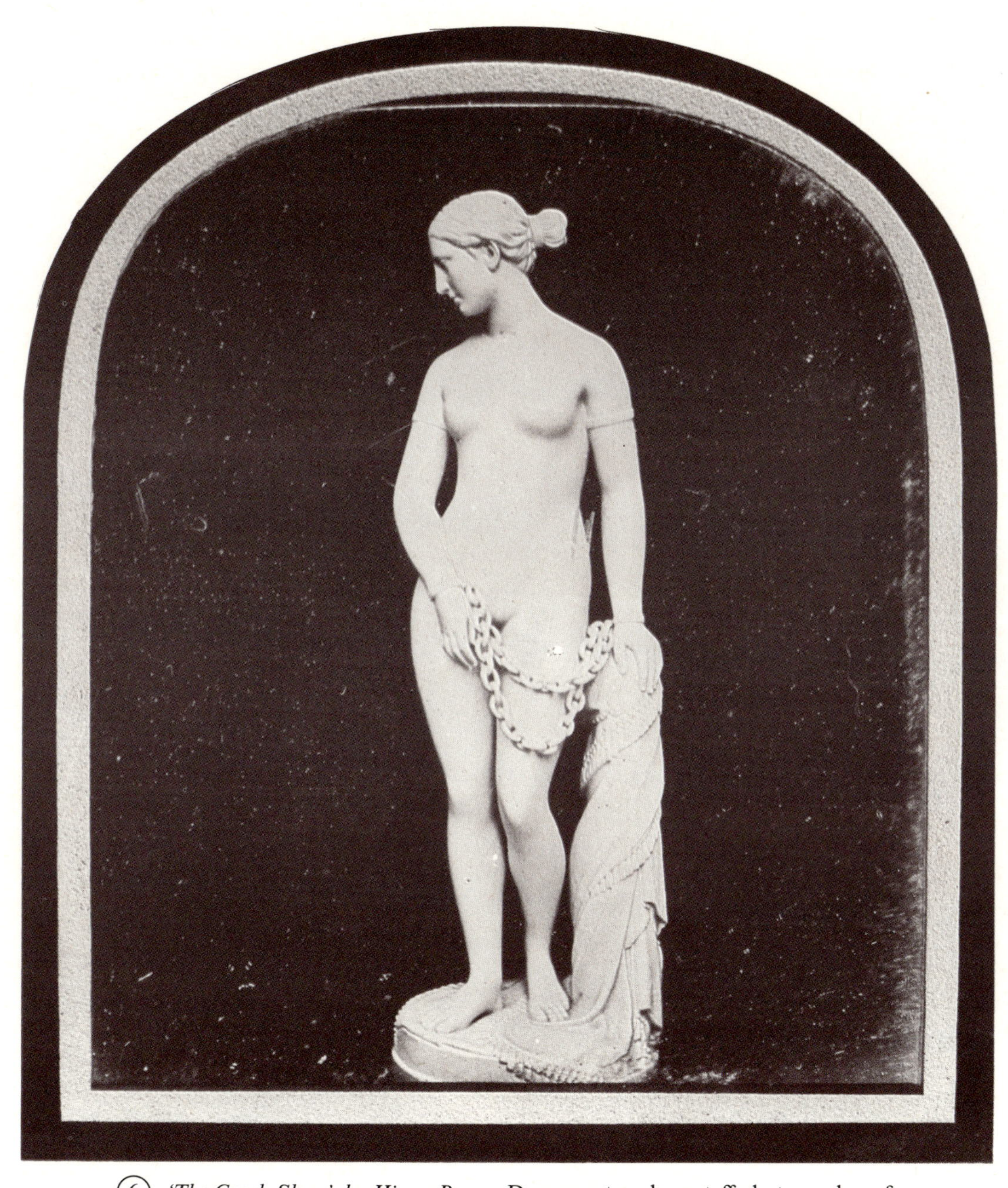

⑥ *'The Greek Slave', by Hiram Power*. Daguerreotype by a staff photographer of
the London Stereoscopic Company. 1851.

SOUVENIRS OF EGYPT

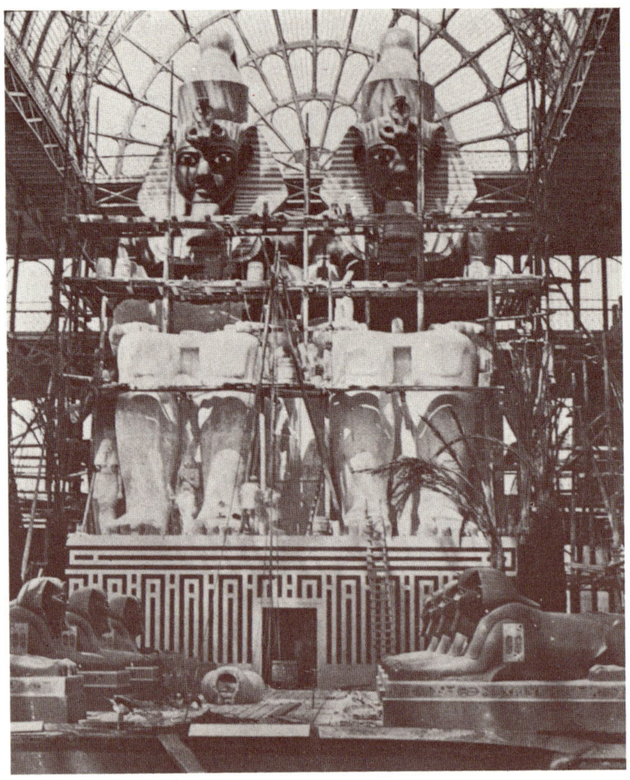

Untitled lantern slide photographed by Philip Delamotte during the rebuilding of Crystal Palace. It shows the raising of two plaster 'Colossi', facsimile portraits of Ramses II. *c.* 1854.

In October 1851 the Great Exhibition ended and during the next two years the Crystal Palace was removed to Sydenham. Philip Delamotte's photographs of its reconstruction, from the raising of the first column to the re-opening of the Palace on 10 June 1854, contain a record of the making of two 'Colossi'. These were plaster facsimiles, restored and coloured, of the portraits of Ramses II at Abou Simbel.

Appalled by their gaudy colouring, a critic in the *Art Journal* pronounced them 'monstrosities, glowering and roasting . . . their incompleteness of form being brought out by the terrific colour into a twin personification of an universal gout – head and neck, limbs, hands and feet!' He declared the originals 'infinitely grander in their native rock colour', but confessed that he had never seen them. However, he could have seen a photograph – the first ever taken of them. In 1849 Louis Desiré Blanquart Evrard devised an improved Talbotype paper negative and, to demonstrate its quality, published *Egypte, Nubie, Palestine et Syrie* which was illustrated with actual photographic prints from negatives taken for the French Ministry of Education by Maxime du Camp (travelling in the company of his friend, the author Gustave Flaubert).

This publication may have prompted the firm of Negretti and Zambra to send Francis Frith on a similar errand in 1856–57. Foreign travel, always a hazardous pastime, was made more irksome by the cumbersome baggage of pioneer photography. In choosing to work with wet collodion and to make three negatives of each view (16 ins × 20 ins, 8 ins × 10 ins and one for the stereoscope) Frith invited catastrophe. His dark room, sealed against light (and air), was the wicker-work van he travelled in – and which local Egyptians conjectured was for transporting his harem.

'It was full of moon-faced beauties, my wives all!' wrote Frith of their speculations, 'and great was the respect and consideration which this view of the case procured me.' In fact, the heat filled the interior of the van with fumes of ether, boiled the collodion as it was poured

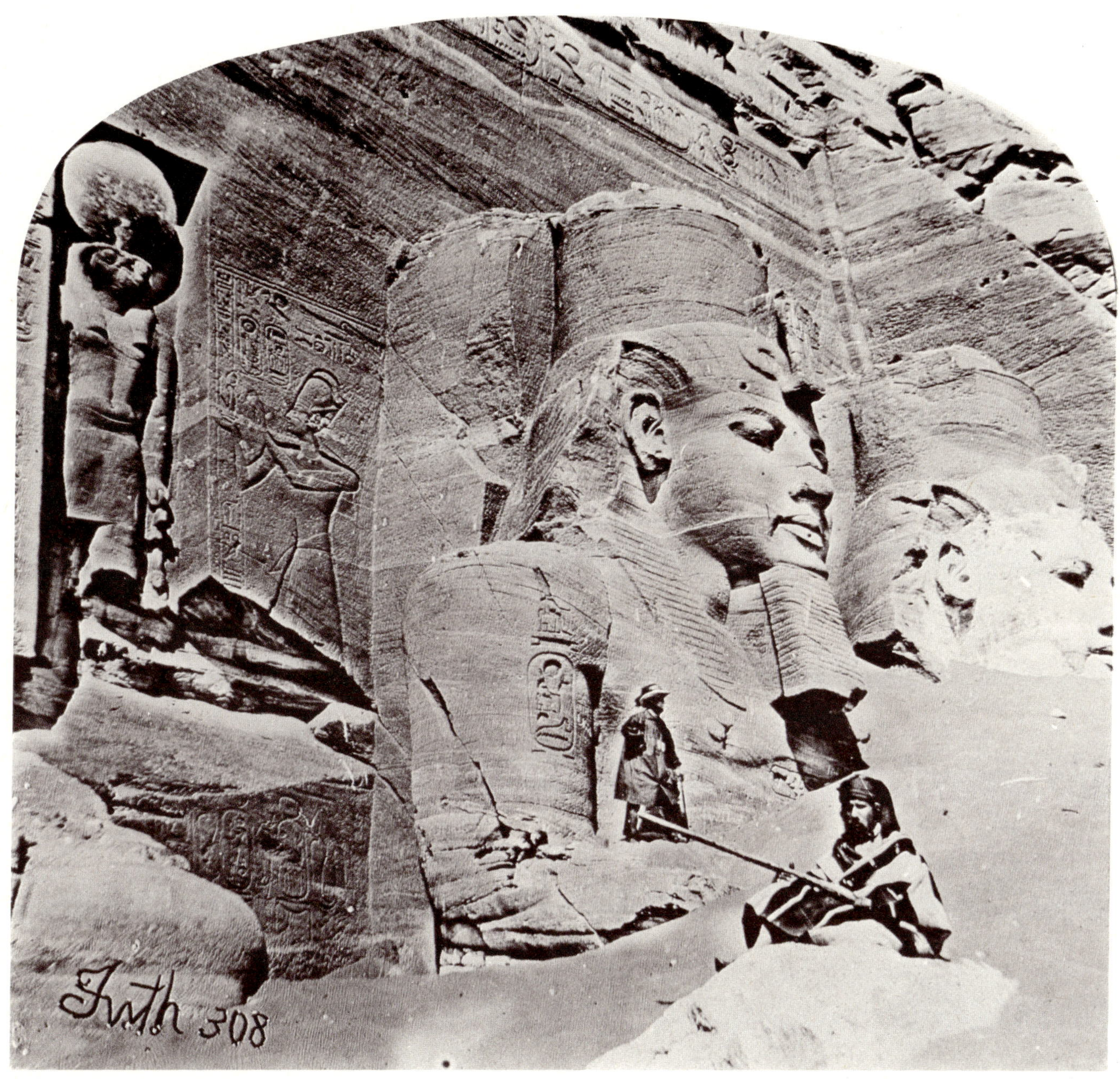

⑦ *View of the Facade of the Great Rock Temple of Abou Simbel in Nubia.* Collodion on glass by Francis Frith. Signed 'Frith' in negative and numbered '308'. The label reads: 'It was cut upwards of 3,200 years ago, in the reign of Rameses II, of whom the colossi on the façade are supposed to be portraits. These magnificent statues are 65 feet high, but only one of them is wholly exposed to view, much of the front of the temple being now buried in desert sand. It was excavated to the depth of 200 feet, and the interior is richly sculptured. It was unknown to Europeans forty years ago, and was first entered by Belzoni.' 1856.

and drove Frith to work in dark rock-tombs and caves, only to be forced back to the van because sand and dust ruined the wet plates. More bizarre tribulations are described in the text he published with the photographs: he was shipwrecked, robbed by bandits and shot at by a Turkish patrol, and had encounters with ten-foot snakes, wolves, boars, crocodiles and a panther! The Nubian women, of whose beauty he had heard, turned out to be 'severely hideous', but he noted that they wore their black hair 'stiff and shiny with a life-long accumulation of castor oil, in innumerable black twists precisely as we see the hair-dress of women represented in sculptures of three thousand years ago'. The photographs Frith brought back were excellent enough to warrant two further Near Eastern sorties.

Against the odds, Frith's skill and resourcefulness had produced stereo-photographs of which, Darrah says, 'no more remarkable series was ever issued'.* The settings seem entirely appropriate to the exotic incidents which Frith encountered; this is enthusiastically pointed out by a reviewer in the *Illustrated Times* (26 December 1851) whose down-to-earth opinion of romantic places has the flavour of present-day scepticism.

'We, looking through the lenses of the stereoscope at Mr Frith's astonishing photographs, straightway, by virtue of binocular glamour, go back thousands of years. We live in the land of Egypt, the old mysterious wonderland – not that modern Egypt . . . intersected by railways, coverted [converted?] for the purpose of canalisation by M. De Lesseps, whose pyramids are now elbowed by overland route hotels and posting houses, whose deserts are now traversed by omnibuses bearing bilious majors and "beardless griffins", and whose arid sands are strewn with soda-water bottles and the corks of byegone flagons of Bass and Allsopp's pale ale. . . .'

Frith continued to travel with his camera, visiting most countries of Europe, collecting material for several books and for the firm he established in Reigate, which became one of the largest producers of picture postcards in the world. His photographs were used to illustrate the Bible, Longfellow's *Hyperion* and, in complete contrast to his dramatic Egyptian excursions, Mr and Mrs S. C. Hall's *The Book of the Thames*.

As a footnote, it is interesting to recall that in 1866 the part of the Crystal Palace housing the two 'Colossi' burned down. No suspicion of arson seems to have fallen on the critic of the *Art Journal*, quoted above, though one might have expected him to be asked by the police to explain his odd use of the word 'roasting'. An anonymous stereographer has left us a dramatic picture of the last days of the 'Colossi'. Devastation seemed to suit them.

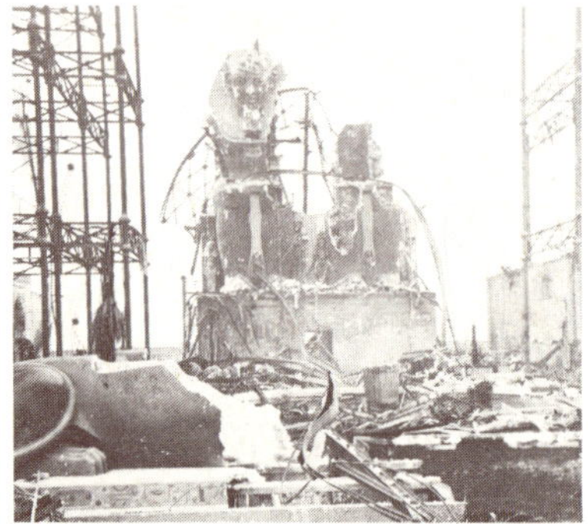
Untitled card recording the remains of the Crystal Palace 'Colossi' after the fire of 1866. Photographer unknown.

* William Culp Darrah, *Stereo Views* (1964).

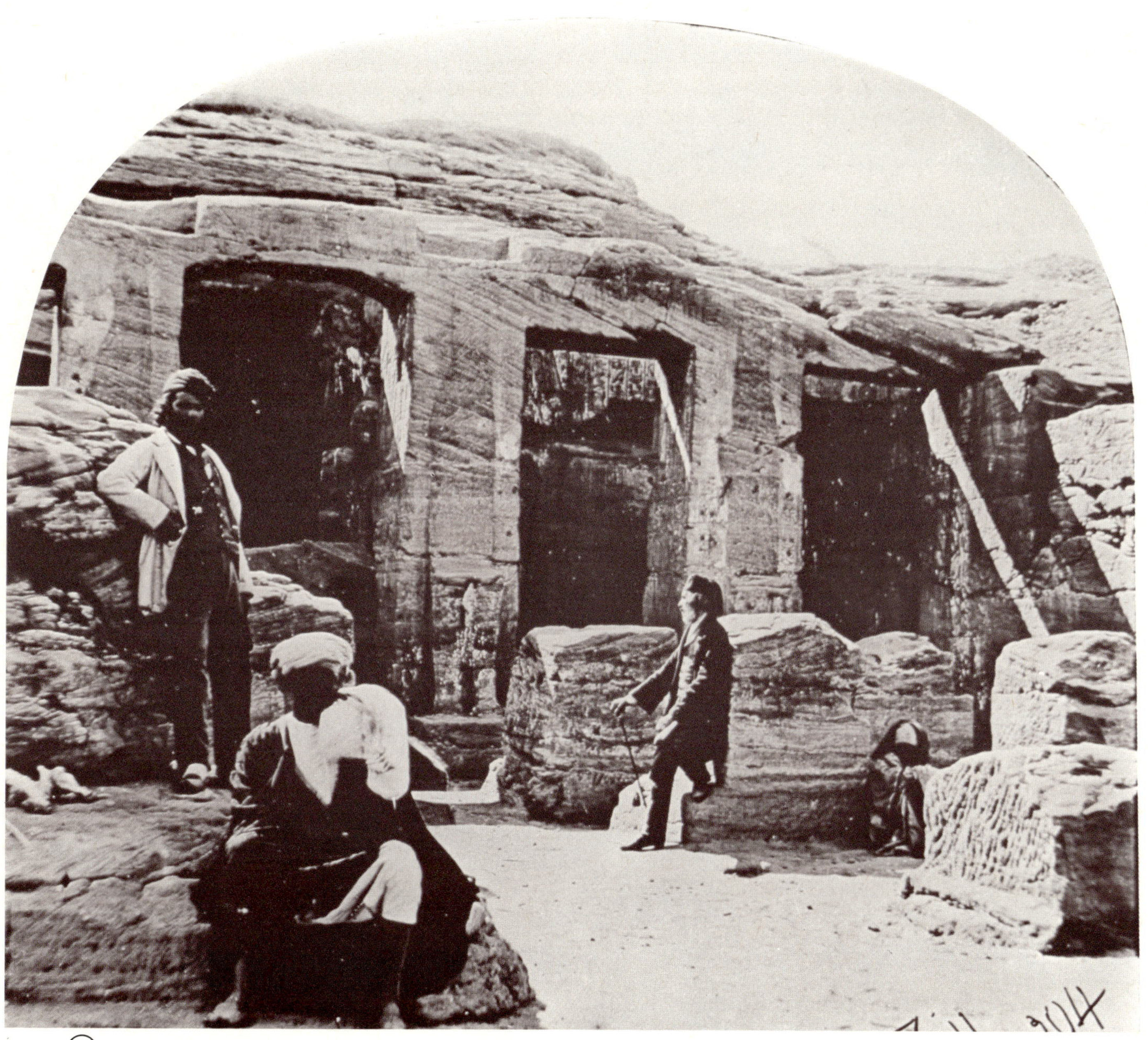

8 *View of the Rock Temple of Derr, Now the Chief Town in Nubia*. Collodion on glass by Francis Frith. Signed 'Frith' in negative and numbered '304'. The label reads: 'Of the time of Rameses the Great, in whose long and prosperous reign a very large proportion of the now existing Egyptian temples were built. This temple penetrates the rock to a depth of 110 ft; the interior walls being somewhat rudely sculptured.' 1856.

41

THE HOUSES OF PARLIAMENT

On 16 October 1834 the furnaces heating the Westminster Building, in which the British Parliament sat, were overstoked and the timber of the old building caught fire. Westminster Hall and St Stephen's Chapel were saved but the rest of the building was lost. Apart from the deep pleasure which accompanies anything that inconveniences politicians, there was a general feeling that the opportunity to build a new Palace of Westminster was a good thing. A design competition for a building in 'Gothic or Elizabethan style' was won by Charles Barry. This was something of an embarrassment to him for two reasons: first, his own stylistic preference was Classical, and second, like many architects, he had left a lot of the design work to one of his staff, the twenty-three-year-old Augustus Pugin. Four years after the new building had been started he approached Pugin to help him out. 'I am in a regular fix,' he wrote.

Pugin agreed to work with him and is responsible for the extremely complicated 'Gothic' details of the design – which did not exclude even the umbrella and ink stands. Pugin lived eccentrically, went mad and died at forty; his two passions, which he described as 'Christian architecture and boats', were on occasion combined, many of his designs for the Houses of Parliament being made whilst he was sailing.

The stereograph opposite appropriately combines water and building and may have been made just before Pugin's death in 1852. The glass slide, though unidentified, is one of a group bearing the monogram of Duboscq & Soleil, who manufactured Brewster's stereoscope for the 1851 Exhibition. Since we know that the interior decoration of the Houses of Parliament was under way in 1852, it is reasonable to assume that this picture, which shows the exterior with scaffolding still in place, might have been taken at a time when Duboscq & Soleil were responding to the enormous initial demand which their stereoscope had created. Certainly glass views were known at this early date. Gernsheim says that C. M. Ferrier produced glass stereographs in 1851 with the albumen process, and there is no reason to suppose that Duboscq could not have made this very early view.

From the same group of glass stereographs, clearly marked 'D.S.', come this view of the Seine and the roof-tops of old Paris, and another of the Hippodrome. The latter, like the Houses of Parliament, was something of a phoenix: first built in 1845, it burned down the following year. It was rebuilt and then managed to survive long enough to be stereographed, before burning down again in 1856.

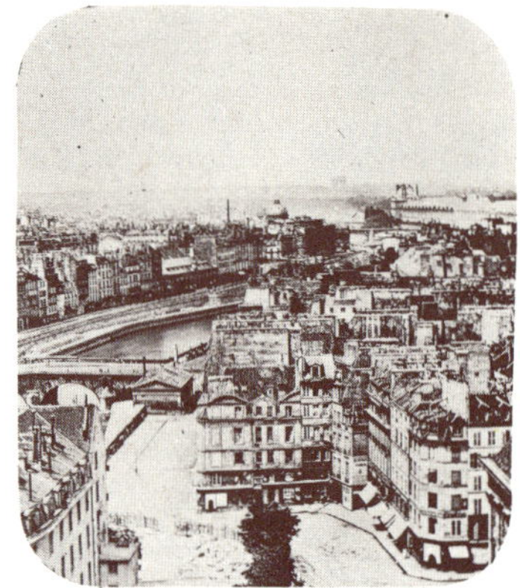 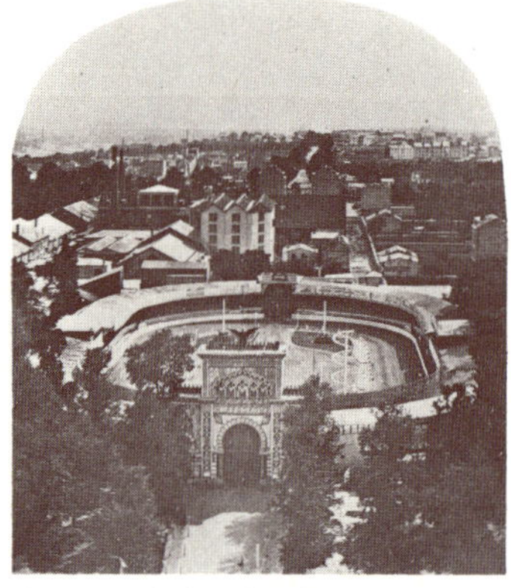

(LEFT) *View of the Seine*. Glass view, probably by Duboscq & Soleil. 1850s. (RIGHT) *Hippodrome in Paris*. Glass view, probably by Duboscq & Soleil. 1850s.

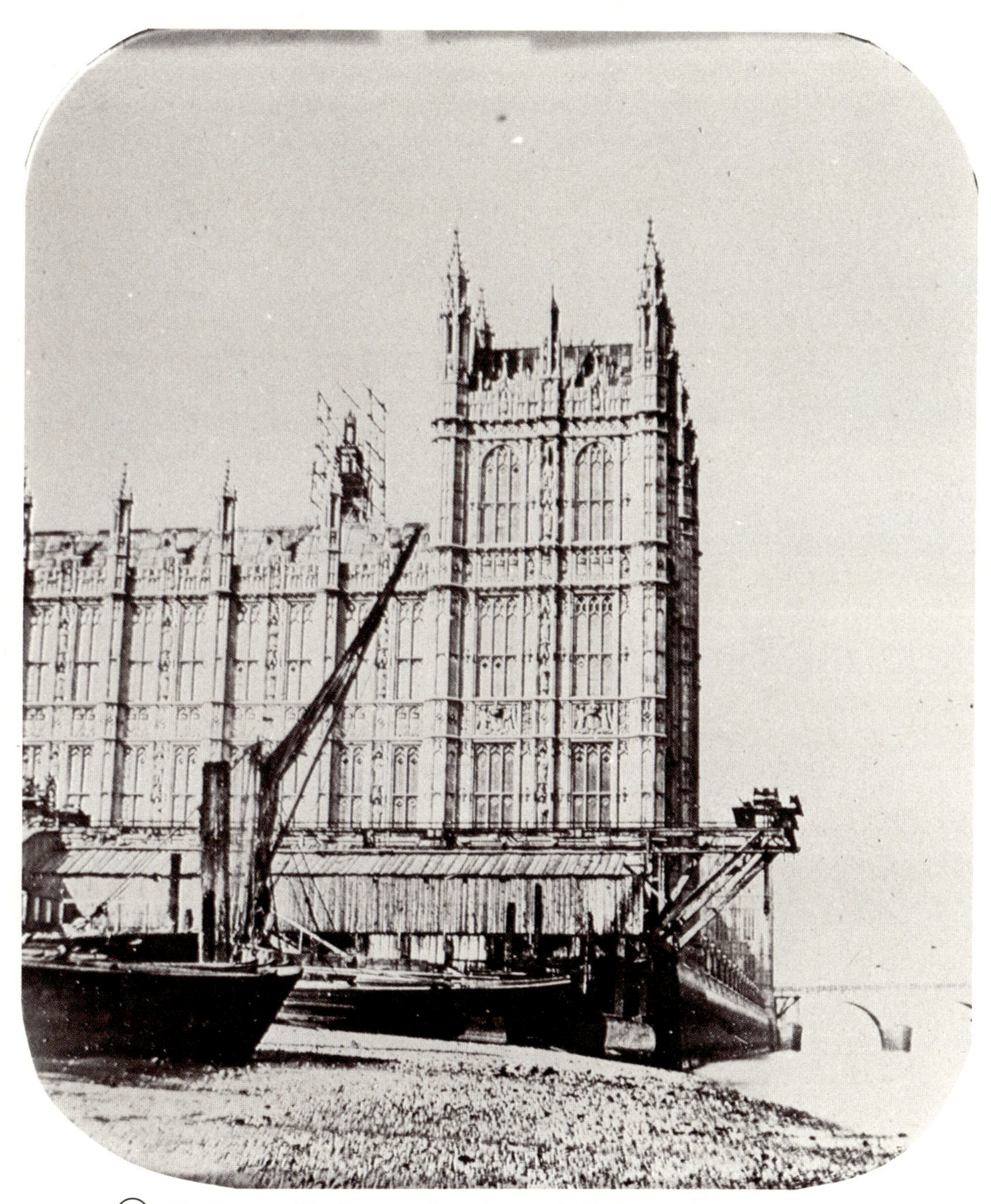

⑨ *The Houses of Parliament*. Glass view, probably by Duboscq & Soleil. 1850s.

T. R. WILLIAMS: AN EARLY MASTER

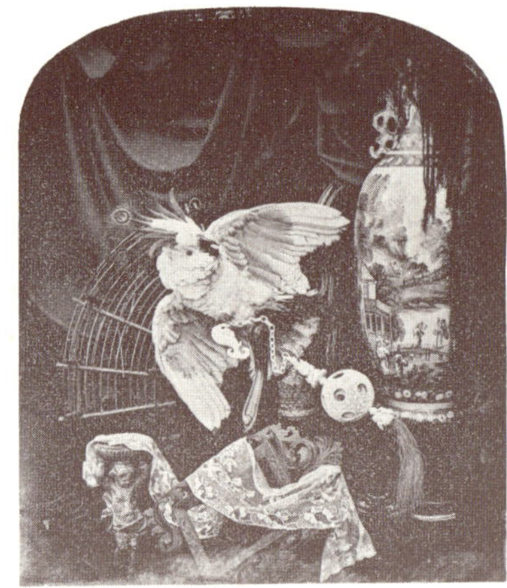

Untitled still life with parrot. Daguerreotype by T. R. Williams.

When in 1854 the Crystal Palace was re-opened by Queen Victoria at its new site in Sydenham, the supporting cast included Prince Albert and other members of the British Royal Family, the King of Portugal, three bands and eighteen hundred people singing the Hallelujah Chorus. Since the exposure time for making a daguerreotype of only one sitter was still lengthy, and the process by no means fidget-proof, the odds on photographing this assembly without it looking like a bowl of porridge were very small indeed. Nevertheless, banking on the stillness of piety, several photographers stealthily opened their lenses during the Archbishop of Canterbury's prayer. Others waited for the equally petrifying address by the Chairman of the Crystal Palace Company. The next year, during the visit of Napoleon III of France and his Empress, another large ensemble was rendered motionless by similar anaesthetics. On both these grand occasions T. R. Williams managed to bring off a picture that entered the archives as a pioneer example of news photography.

The activities of Claudet and Beard have been well documented but about T. R. Williams, who worked for both, little is known. Even a few years ago in the sale rooms, where identity is money, his initialled work was being ascribed to someone else. This anonymity is surprising because he was an inveterate signer of his works. The double signature – on picture and mount – shown on page 18 may represent an urgent plea for greater recognition, perhaps brought about because Williams was employed by celebrated people but did not feel himself to be one of them. In the still-life illustrated here, a monogram actually forms one of the group of objects; just visible in the bottom left corner, it seems to have been made of wrought wire.

T. R. Williams eventually set up his own establishment, in about 1850. He made both daguerreotypes and paper prints, one of which is the portrait, opposite, entitled *The Village Schoolmistress*. The reverse of the card bears the following anonymous verse, for whose theme the picture may have been set up.

> In life's decline, her arduous duties done,
> She loves to seat her in the setting sun;
> And, in the dreaminess of age, recall
> The long succession of each once-loved face,
> And think upon their varying fortunes, all,
> Or nearly all, within the narrow place
> Of rest; – submissively resigned
> To meet the fate prepared for all mankind.

Williams himself went to the narrow place at the age of forty-six, in 1871.

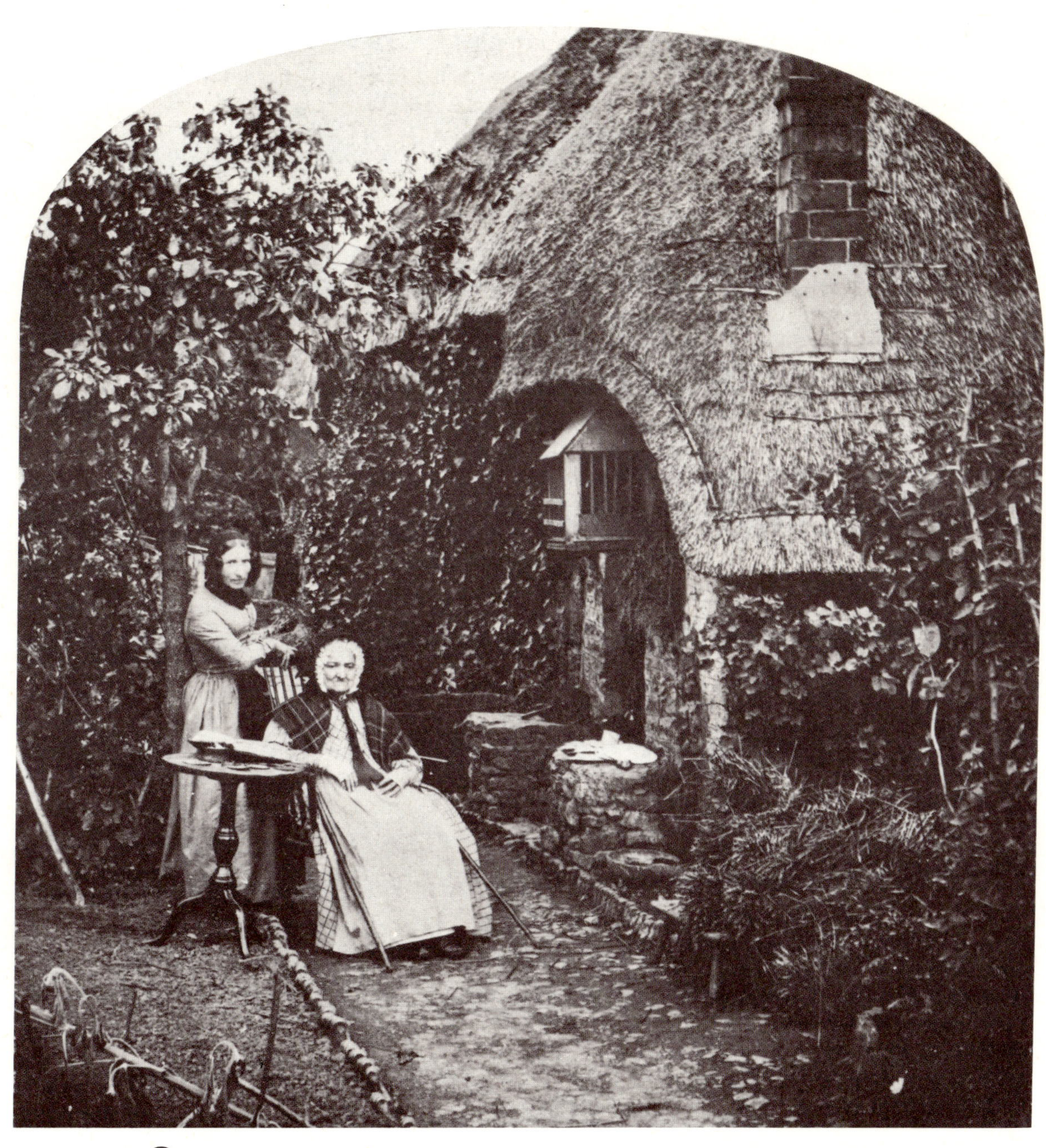

10 *Scenes in Our Village. The Village Schoolmistress.* Photographed by T. R. Williams.

FERRIER'S GLASS STEREOGRAPHS

The glass stereo-views reproduced on pages 42–43 are certainly among the earliest of their kind and about contemporary with those made in the USA by the Langenheims. While Duboscq & Soleil's display at the Great Exhibition of 1851 was attracting so much attention, Claude-Marie Ferrier was busy making glass albumen negatives for the Royal Commissioners; from these, prints were made to illustrate the record of the exhibition, entitled *Reports of the Juries*. Sumptuously prepared presentation copies of the report were given to monarchs, politicians and archives all over the world. In the same year Ferrier made his first glass positive stereographs and later, with his son and his partner, Charles Soulier, published impressive and detailed panoramas of the Alps and Pyrenees, and views of Paris and other European towns and cities. The picture of Malaga, illustrated here, shows the great depth of focus of which the stereo-camera was capable, as does the view of Notre Dame with its delicate detail which includes, in the foreground, a pattern of damp patches left by the street-cleaning wagon. In addition to the glass views, Ferrier also issued similar views on cards, though these lack the extraordinary quality of the former: because light passed through them direct to the eye the glass views are, like modern transparencies, capable of vivid clarity, and the extreme

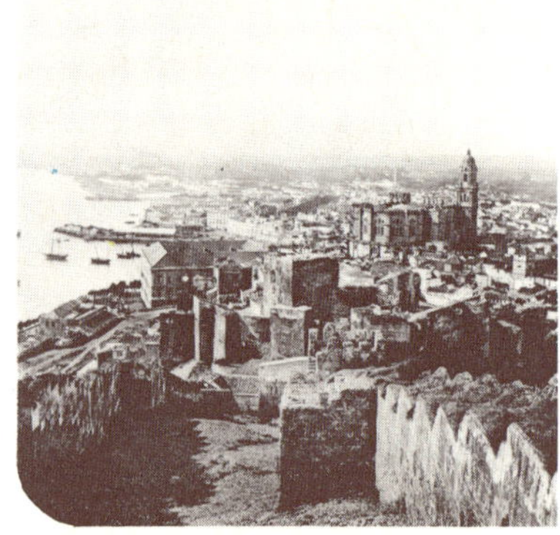

Panorama de Malaga. Glass view by Ferrier, père et fils et Soulier.

detail in stereo was superior to that of any other photographic image. They were expensive, but enormously popular.

Ferrier seems to have been one of the first to recognize the power of the camera to report current events. He made pictures during the flooding of the Loire in 1856, and with Soulier accompanied Napoleon III on his Italian campaign of 1859, during which he did not shirk to photograph the rotting dead and wounded. The terrible objectivity of modern front-line photographers was anticipated by Ferrier's early deglamourizations of war. In contrast is this peaceful view of the Seine, opposite, in which steamships gently ripple the surface of the water and a pillow of smoke is held motionless in the air.

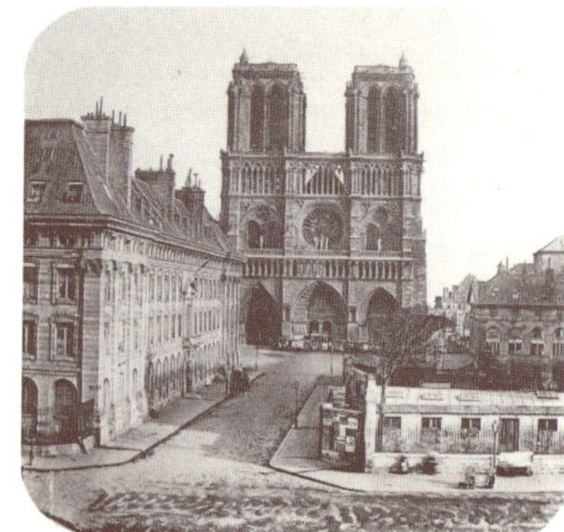

Notre Dame de Paris. Glass view by Ferrier, père et fils et Soulier.

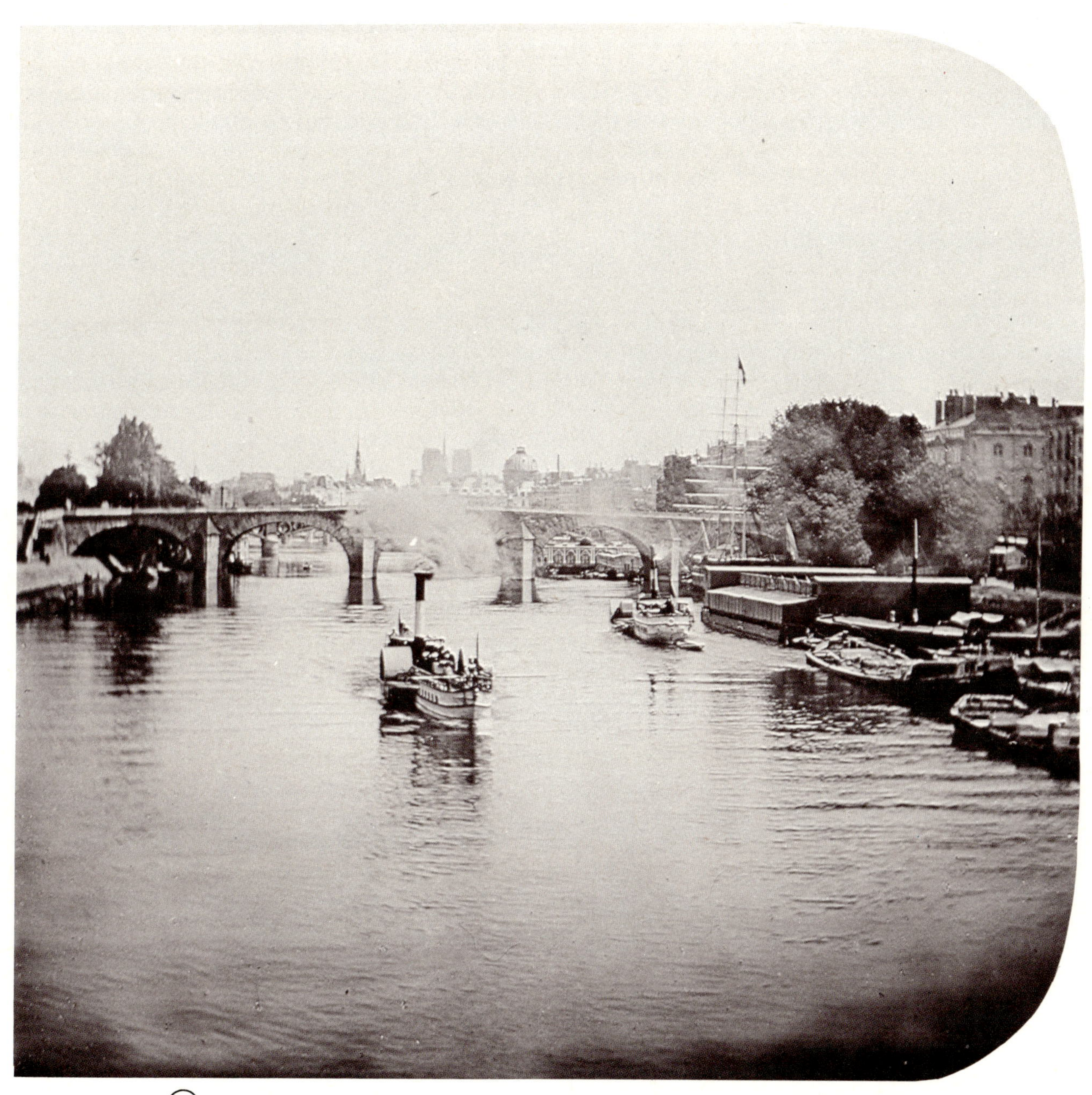

(11) *Départ du Bateau de Saint-Cloud, Paris*. Glass view by Ferrier, père et fils et Soulier.

AN ASTRONOMER'S EXPERIMENT

In the 1850s it was felt that astronomical observations would be improved if the viewing position were raised above the lower part of the earth's atmosphere. To confirm this, a large equatorial telescope was transported on board the yacht *Titania* from England to Teneriffe in the Canary Islands, where it was mounted on the slopes of a volcano at a height of 10,000 feet.

C. Piazzi Smyth, the Royal Astronomer of Scotland and Professor of Practical Astronomy at Edinburgh University, in 1858 published an account of the experiment, illustrating it with stereographs he had taken himself. This was the first book to be illustrated in this way. In addition to dealing with the scientific aspects of the expedition, Smyth's book also relates the minutiae of daily life.

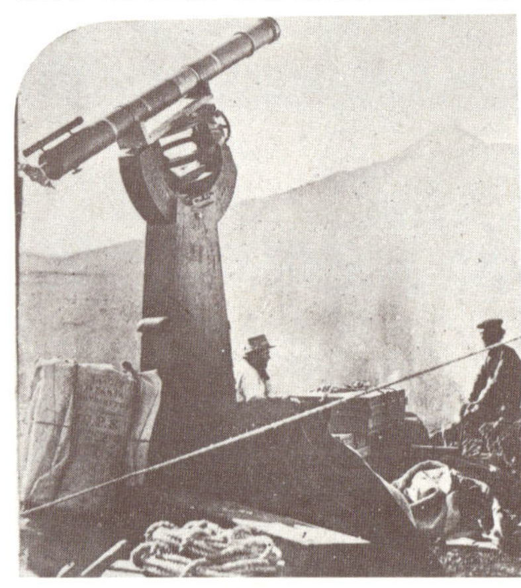

Sheepshanks' Telescope
First Erected on Mount Guajara,
the Peak of Teneriffe in the Distance.
From Piazzi Smyth's book
Teneriffe,
an Astronomer's Experiment.

The telescope had to be set up twice. The first position, although above cloud level, was too low to escape the optical interference of a layer of dust particles. The illustration on this page shows the first site: the guy rope of a tent stretches across the scene in which two exhausted sailors sit among packing cases they have helped to drag 8,903 feet up the mountainside. In the distance is the peak of the volcano near which the telescope was eventually installed. Arduous as the enterprise was, and man-handling so much delicate apparatus to the second site was a notable feat of endurance, Smyth found time to observe and comment on numerous plants and animals and on the geological and climatic characteristics of the island. One feature that much engaged his attention was the 'dragon' tree. He took photographs of trees of different ages including one 'to which most sober naturalists attribute the age of six thousand years. They say it is the oldest tree on the face of the earth; "so old", add the catastrophic geologists of the Gallic school, that "it may have witnessed some of the latest revolutions that our planet underwent prior to the advent of man". "The Great Dragonier of Orotava" has occupied its site so long that it may even contend with the Peak itself, for being that veritable dragon which protected the golden fruit, in the beautiful gardens of the Hesperides.' Smyth blames errors in the available botanical information about the tree on the misleading nature of artists' drawings of it. 'Never,' he writes, 'was the debt that mankind owe to the inventors of photography more apparent.'

Smyth was himself an inventor, designing a camera which solved the problem of dust and sand encountered by Frith in Egypt (see page 40). He used it in February 1865 to take the first photograph of the interior of the Great Pyramid. To do so he used magnesium flash, another photographic 'first'.

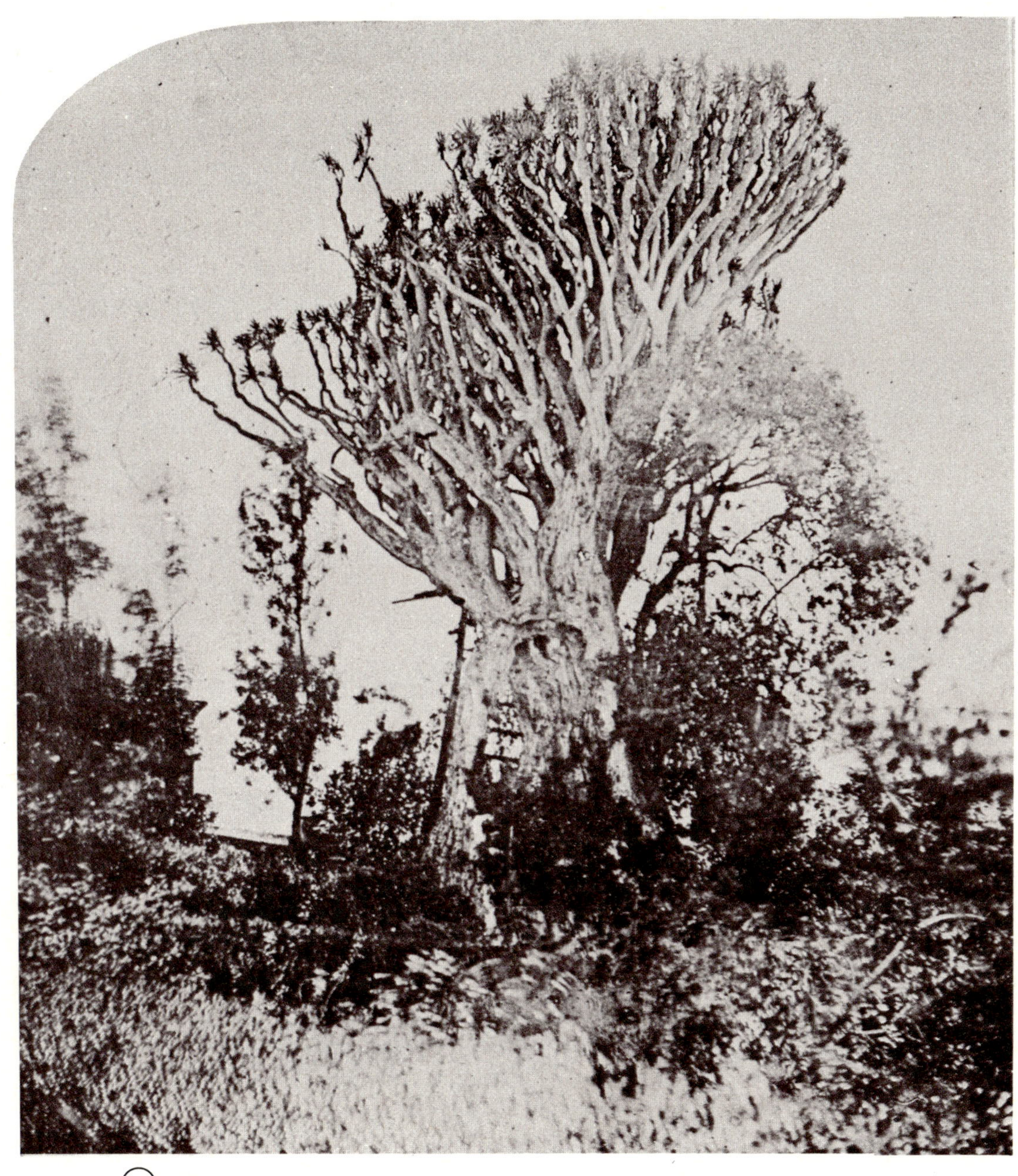

The 'Great Dragon Tree' at the Villa de Ortovara. Trunk of the Great Dragon Tree.
Photographed by Charles Piazzi Smyth. 1856. Illustration to *Teneriffe, an Astronomer's Experiment or Specialities of a Residence above the Clouds,* published by Lovell Reeve, London, 1858.

THE BRITISH LANDSCAPE (1): THOMAS OGLE

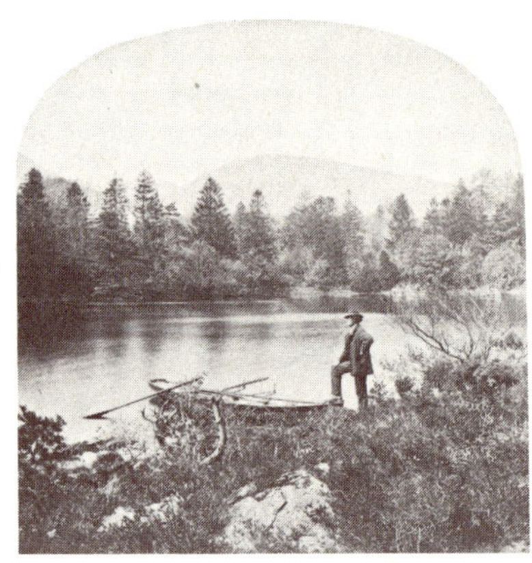

Derwentwater Bay and Causey Pike, by J. Garnett, who had a studio near the Lakes.

The year after the appearance of C. Piazzi Smyth's *Teneriffe* (see previous pages), its publishers issued *The Stereoscope Magazine*. This was a monthly publication, and in each edition three views appeared with descriptive notes; these the *Art Journal* reviewer pronounced long and tedious, and predicted (I report uneasily): 'They will only ensure the views being cut out for the stereoscope while the letterpress is thrown aside unnoticed.'

There are practical difficulties to viewing a stereograph on the page of a book, but as the number of publications illustrated by photographs grew during the 1860s, several books made use of halves of stereo-views. Howitt's two-part *Ruined Abbeys and Castles of Great Britain and Ireland 1862–64* was illustrated in this way. A view of *Tintern Abbey* by Russell Sedgefield, one of the book's illustrators, is shown here. Earlier, in the mid-1850s, Sedgefield had published an eight-part work, *Photographic Delineations of Scenery, Architecture and Antiquities of Great Britain and Ireland*; he also produced a superb series of stereographs entitled *Sedgefield's English Scenery*.

Another illustrator of Howitt's book was Thomas Ogle, of Ogle and Edge, a firm operating from Preston, Lancashire. Ogle was described as a 'patriot' by one *Art Journal* writer who thought his photographs would dissuade the English from holidaying on the Continent, since they made people 'more content with "home", inculcating not only a duty to be fulfilled, but a happiness to be enjoyed by visits to the scene which nature and genius have made "holy".' The 'genius' the reviewer had in mind was that of the Lake Poets, and later in the year (1858) he wrote again about Ogle's 'holy' scenes:

'The views are principally taken in the vicinity of the Northern Lakes . . . which have become deeply interesting, not only for their natural beauties, but as associated with the histories of some of the most distinguished men of mark of the age and country – Wordsworth, Southey, Coleridge, Wilson, and a host of lesser stars. Wordsworth especially has made famous nearly every spot that bears a name in this charming locality; and those who read his works . . . will feel grateful to those photographers for supplying so many delicious accompaniments to his poems . . .' Inspired, perhaps, by this opinion, a book, *Our English Lakes, Mountains and Waterfalls, as seen by William Wordsworth*, photographically illustrated by Thomas Ogle, came out in 1864.

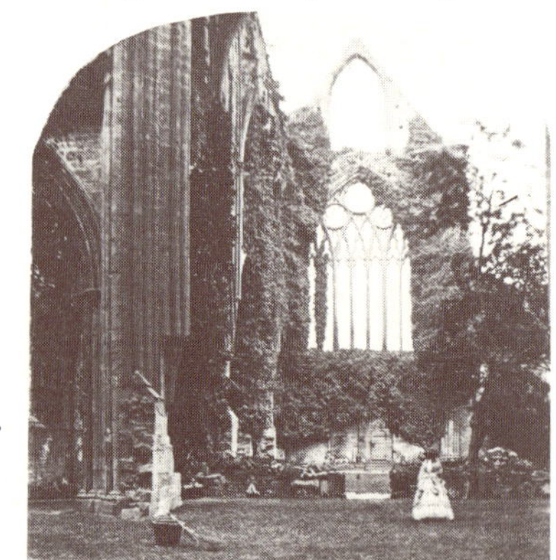

Tintern Abbey, the Nave and West Window, by Russell Sedgefield. A note on the back of the card states, 'Bought at Clevedon. September 23rd. 1859'.

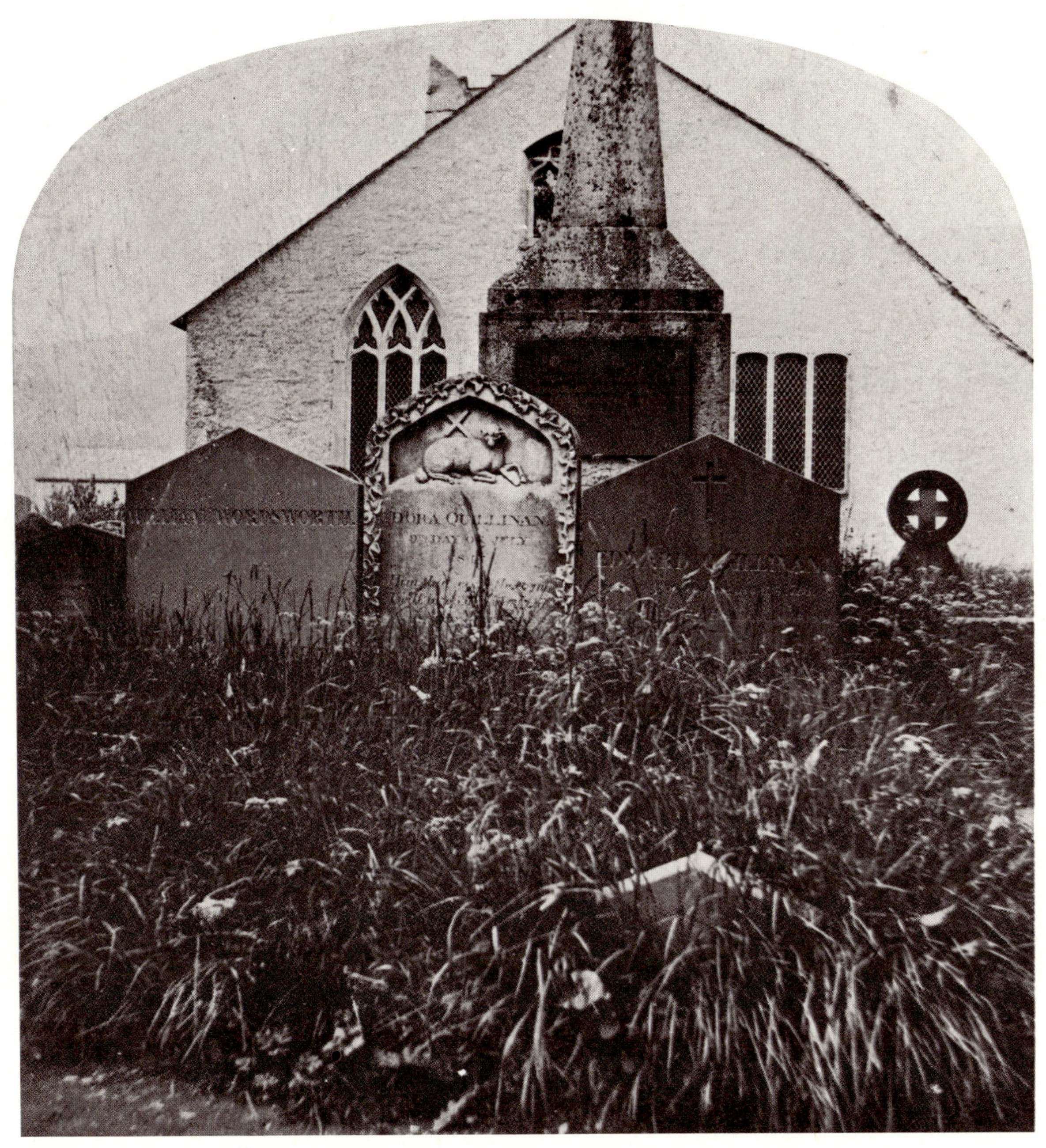

⑬ *Wordsworth's Grave, Grasmere Church-yard,* by Thomas Ogle.

THE BRITISH LANDSCAPE (2): W. M. GRUNDY

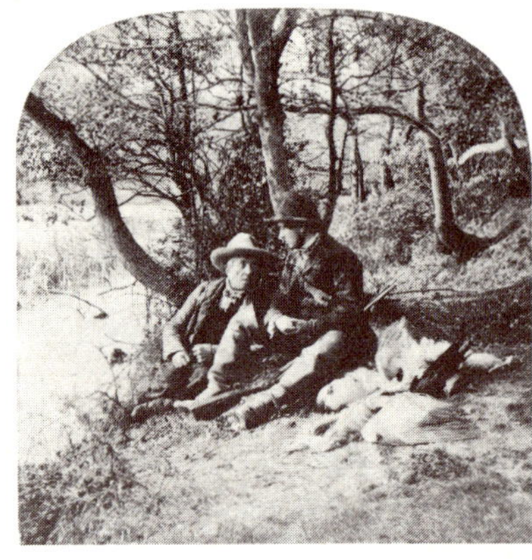 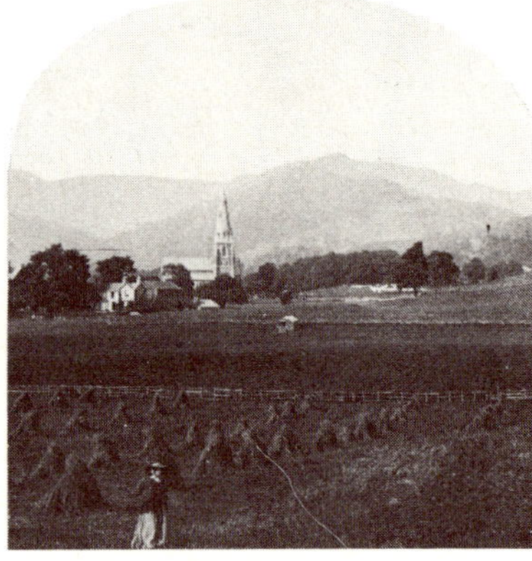

(LEFT) Untitled scene with huntsmen and their game, by W. M. Grundy.
Illustration to *Sunshine in the Country*. 1861.
(RIGHT) *Ambleside, Westmoreland*, possibly by Henry White.

The collodion process and its accessories made landscape photography heavy work and photographers were disinclined to waste their efforts on hit-or-miss snap-shooting. Exposures were made with deliberation and planning; sites to which one hauled 120 pounds of equipment were not hastily selected. This consideration and care may explain why, among the very large number of stereographs of rural scenes, so many have an unforced 'rightness' about them, a restrained intensity which transcends their topographical interest. One collection, called *Sunshine in the Country* and further described as 'a book of rural poetry embellished with Photographs of Nature by the late Mr Grundy of Sutton Coldfield', is one of the most charming of its kind by a photographer about whom next to nothing is known. It was published in 1861, and some of the illustrations to the book, such as the two shown here, were in the form of stereographs.

Henry White, a London solicitor and amateur photographer, may have taken the enchanting view, above, of *Ambleside, Westmoreland*, although the only evidence for this is that the subject, a hayfield, was one of his favourites. A figure in a landscape may only be there to give scale or a focal point, but its inclusion can sometimes go beyond pictorial utility. The lady in the hayfield is not improbable, yet she is unexpected enough to give the scene its singular potency. Her presence brings particularity to the field.

In pictures like that from Hudson's 'Irish Scenery' series of *Colleen Bawn Rock, Torc Mountain*, a human figure in modern dress might be an irritating interruption of its terrible prehistoric stillness; whereas the boy in *Lough-Eske. A Misty Morning* gathers the quiet chilliness of the early-morning scene into himself and personifies it.

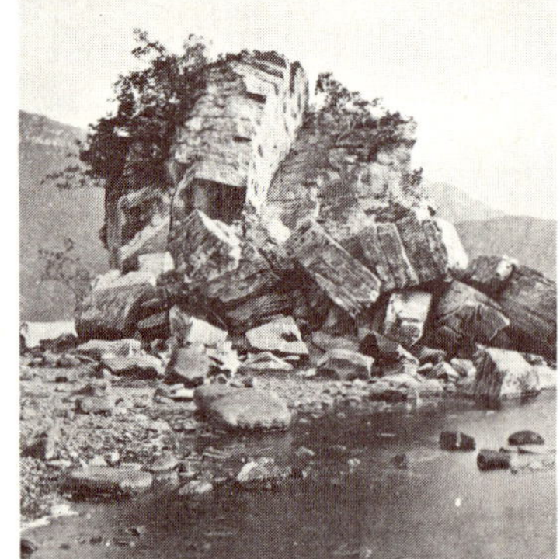 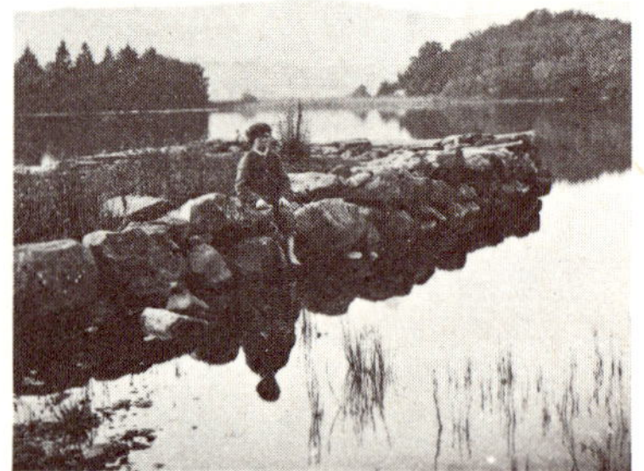

(LEFT) *Scenery of Killarney. Colleen Bawn Rock, Torc Mountain.*
No. 87 in Hudson's 'Irish Scenery' series. (RIGHT) *Lough-Eske.*
A Misty Morning. Co. Donegal. Photographer unknown.

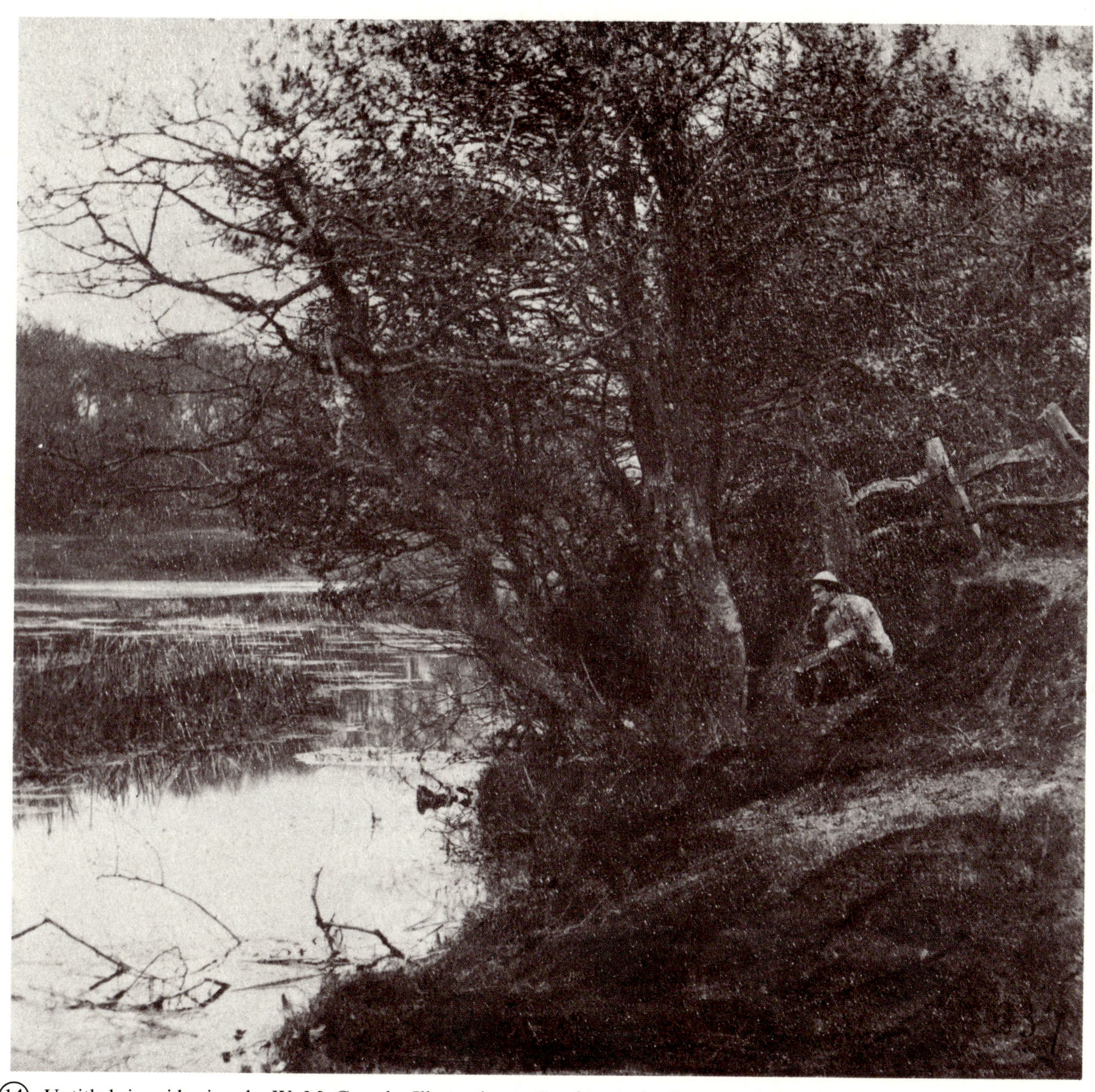 Untitled riverside view, by W. M. Grundy. Illustration to *Sunshine in the Country*, a book of rural poetry published in 1861.

THE BRITISH LANDSCAPE (3): GEORGE WASHINGTON WILSON

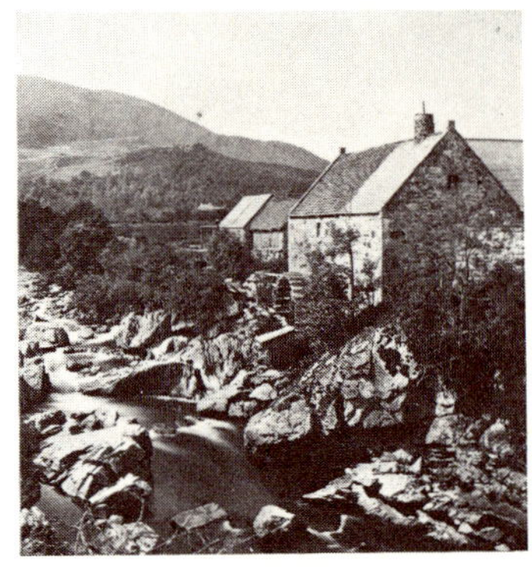

Mill on the Cluny, Braemar, by
G. W. Wilson. Described on the
label as 'No. 1'.

Landscape photographers with an international reputation, men such as Francis Frith, often became directors of large companies publishing their own work and that of their travelling staff. The firm of George Washington Wilson, a painter of miniatures who changed his career to portrait and then landscape photography, became the world's largest publisher of photographs. At his establishment in Aberdeen prints were made from negatives by exposing them to the sun in an elaborate system of frames situated on the roof of the building, as many as two thousand negatives being exposed in one day. Wilson's early stereographs are of a consistently high quality, and he is credited with taking the first successful instantaneous views, in 1856.

The distinctive labels of his stereographs are numbered: the view, illustrated here, of *Mill on the Cluny, Braemar* is 'No. 1', and if this means that it was the first stereograph of the tens of thousands he published, it becomes an item of some historical moment. His stereo picture entitled *Edinburgh – Dugald Stewart's Monument, Calton Hill* (No. 116A) conveys, even in two dimensions, an impressive sense of distance. In the picture opposite, *Fountains Abbey, from the South* (No. 540), the seated figure and the foreground frame of grass and trees enhance the three-dimensional qualities of the view.

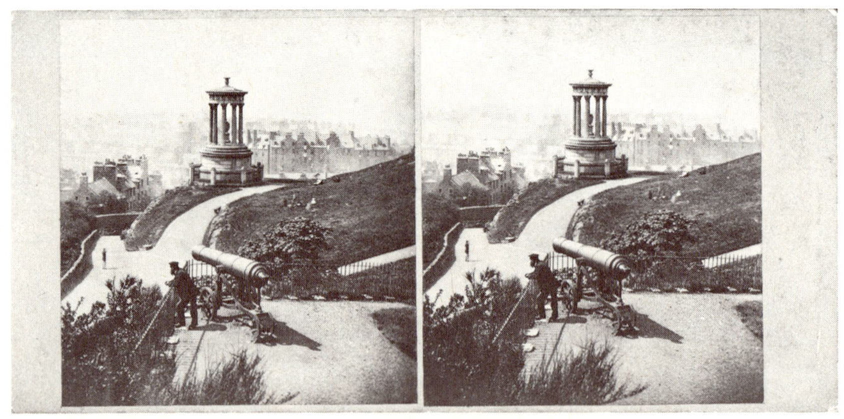

Edinburgh – Dugald Stewart's Monument, Calton Hill, by G. W. Wilson.
Described on the label as 'No. 166A'.

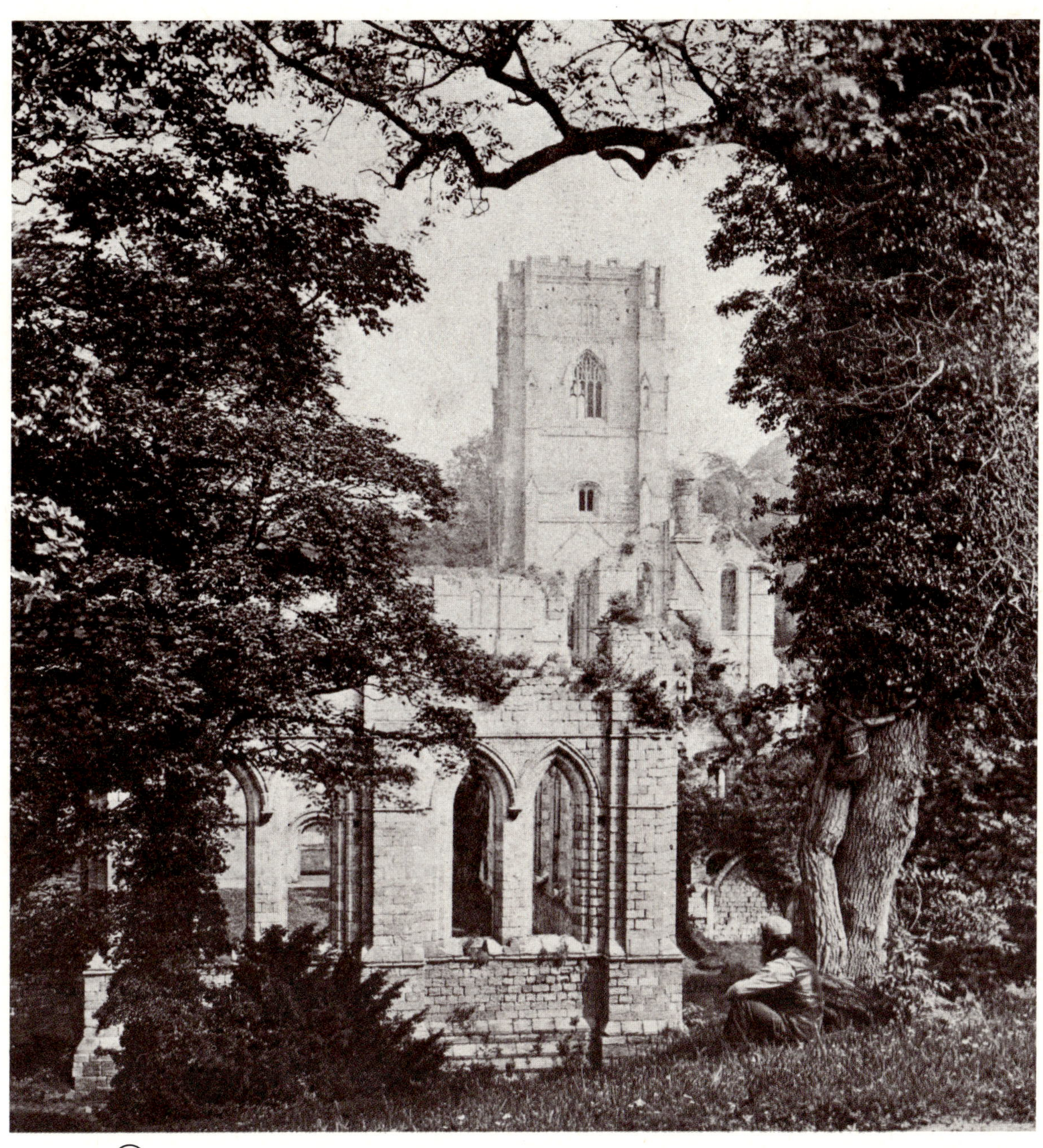

(15) *Fountains Abbey, from the South,* by G. W. Wilson. Described on the label as 'No. 540'.

THE BRITISH LANDSCAPE (4): FRANCIS BEDFORD

Queen Victoria's interest in photography thrust greatness on several photographers, and Francis Bedford was one whose work, with landscape and architecture, came to her attention. In 1862, when her son the Prince of Wales came of an age to benefit from a tour of the Near East, Bedford was requested to accompany him. Though it meant holding up the royal progress from time to time, Bedford took many photographs of points of interest, some including the royal party; the Prince himself attempted one or two views. To protect his apparatus Bedford was given a guard of fifty soldiers. The views were said to be excellent in spite of it all. The results were shown in Bond Street where the admiration of one reviewer knew no bounds. He wrote, 'This is the most interesting series of photographs that has ever been brought before the public . . .' and later, perhaps forgetting himself, declared that it was 'the most interesting ever offered to the Christian and the scholar'.

Bedford is also famous for several thousand stereoscopic views of the British Isles which were published in sets, each covering a different region – 'South Wales Illustrated', 'Malvern Illustrated', etc. Although some are much like anyone else's (there aren't so many different ways to photograph an abbey), many of Bedford's views have a characteristic asymmetry which sometimes gives them a casual look and sometimes an odd kind of drama. The latter is stressed by the placing of tiny figures, obviously posed, like toy actors in a model theatre, as in the view of *Aberyswyth – the Castle*, opposite. The view of *Coes Faen, and Cader Idris* also has this toytown look. Bedford's series, 'Welsh Costumes', to which the group round the spinning wheel belongs, are also clearly posed and self-consciously folksy. They are typical of a kind of tourist 'novelty' still to be found all over the world.

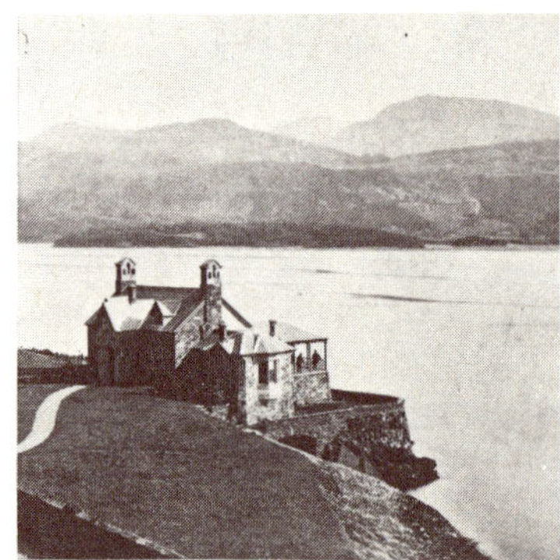
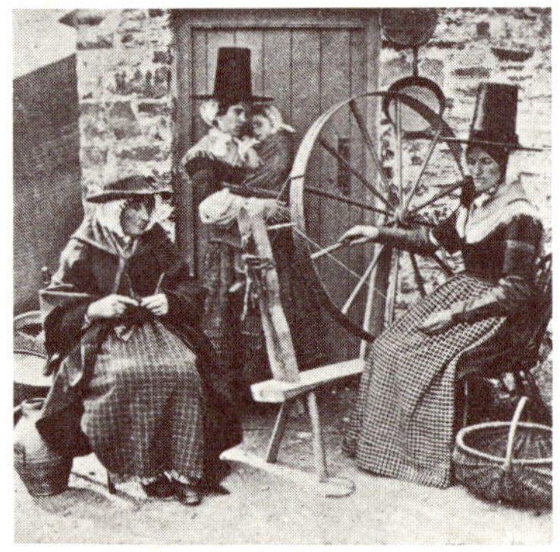

(LEFT) *Coes Faen, and Cader Idris,* by Francis Bedford. From 'North Wales Illustrated'. (RIGHT) *Group – the Spinning Wheel,* by Francis Bedford. From 'Welsh Costumes'.

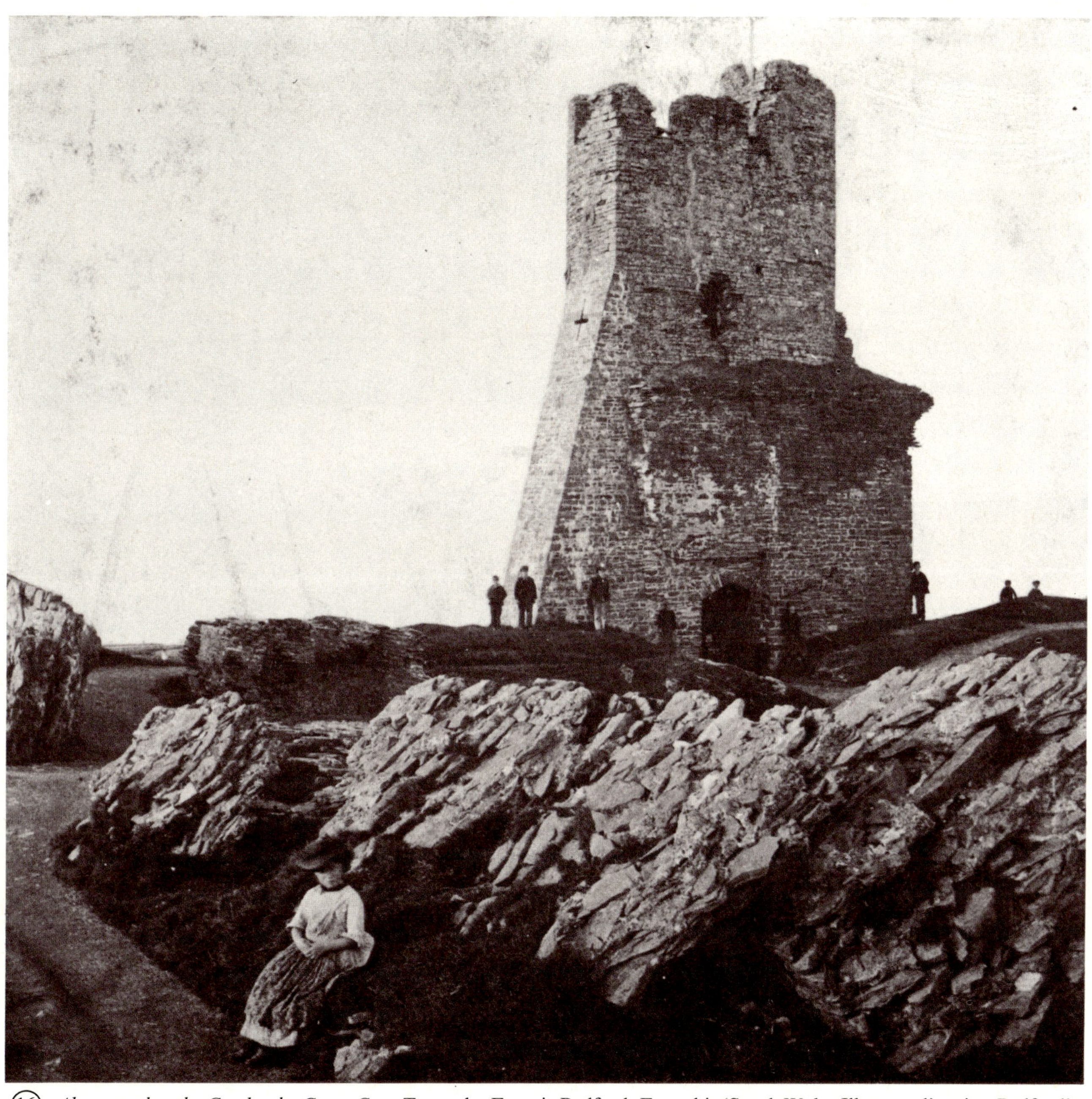

⑯ *Aberyswyth – the Castle, the Great Gate Tower,* by Francis Bedford. From his 'South Wales Illustrated' series. Bedford's printer has evidently misspelt the name of the town, Aberystwyth.

ITALIAN VIEWS

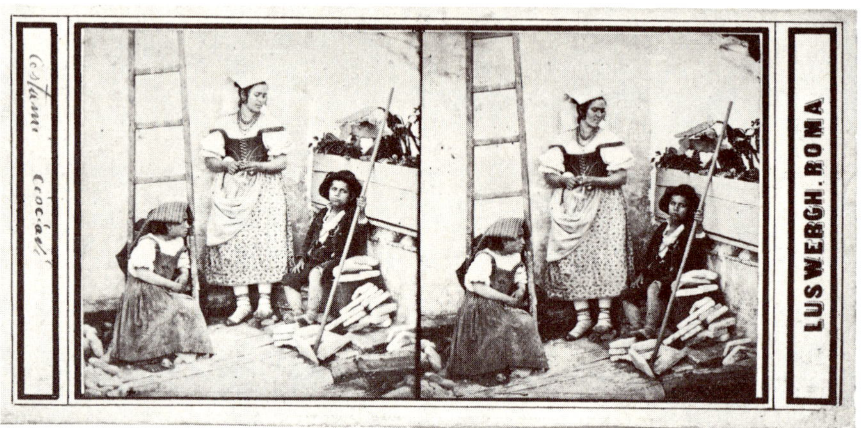

Costumi Ciociari, by Luswergh of Rome.
Peasants of the Roman countryside in local costume.

While catering to the tourist demand for pictures of costumed peasants, like the view above by Luswergh, the early photographers of Italy were mainly inspired by its masterpieces of art and architecture. Robert McPherson, a Scottish surgeon who retired to Rome for his health and took up painting, began in 1851 to take photographs of Rome's ancient monuments; these were of such sensitivity that he was soon regarded as Italy's leading architectural photographer. Another expatriate Briton, James Anderson, a water-colourist, was inspired by McPherson's success and began to photograph architecture and, later, famous paintings. He established a firm which continued to reproduce works of art until the 1960s, when his stock was acquired for a huge archive in Florence. The success of these photographers depended

greatly on the interest of historians, aristocratic art collectors and ordinary tourists, to whom albums of photographs and individual prints of Italy's artistic treasures were sold in large quantities. Local Italian photographers, notably the Alinari brothers and Carlo Ponti (later optician to Victor Emmanuel II) also produced superb work in this field.

During the heyday of the stereoscope the demand for views was met by several photographers of distinction. Giorgio Sommer, based in Naples, produced fine

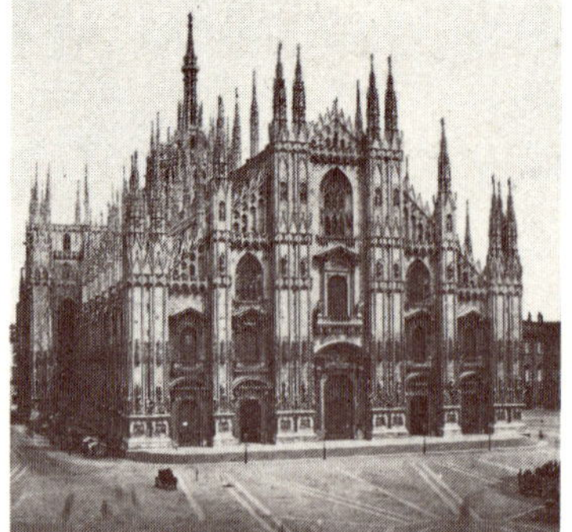 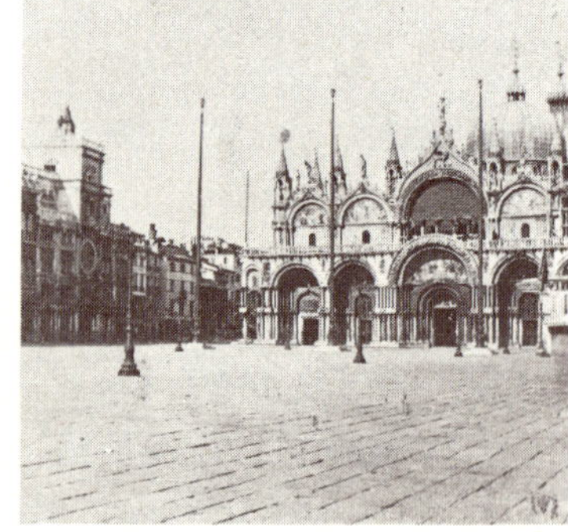

(LEFT) *Il Duomo, Milano* (The Cathedral, Milan), by Giorgio Sommer. From his 'Vedute d'Italia' (Italian Views) series. (RIGHT) *Venezia Piazza di S. Marco* (Venice. St Mark's Square), by C. Naya.

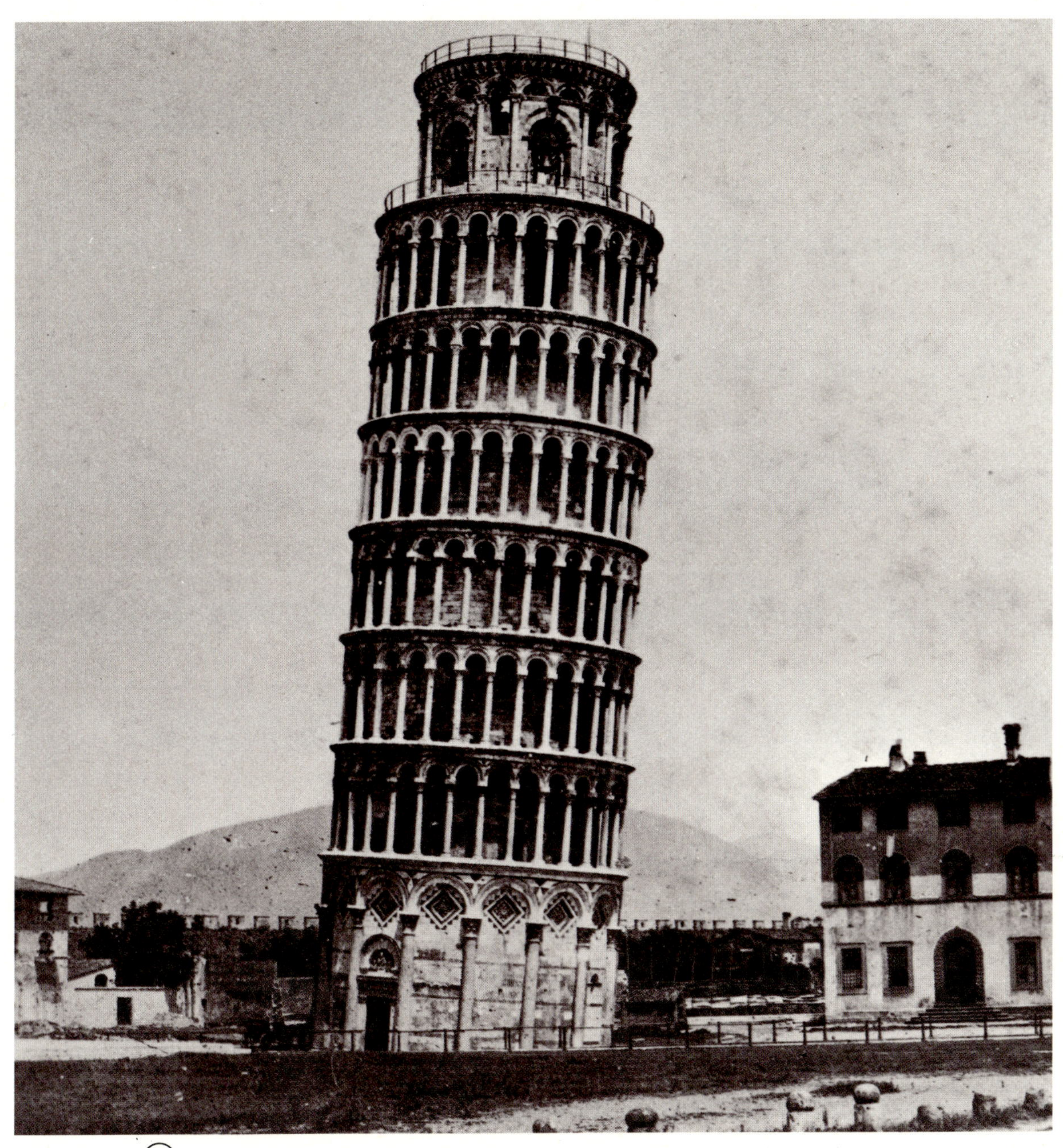

(17) *Il Campanile (Pisa)*, by Giorgio Sommer of Naples. A view of the Leaning Tower.

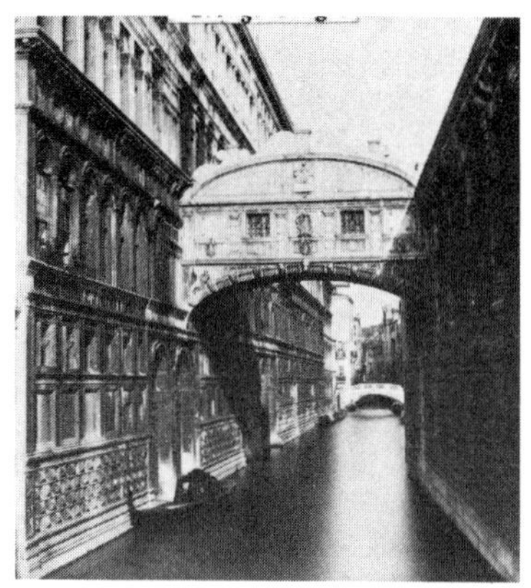

Ponte dei Sospiri, Venezia
(Bridge of Sighs, Venice),
by C. Naya.

examples of all the principal items in the tourist itinerary: the Leaning Tower of Pisa (illustrated), Giotto's Tower in Florence, Milan Cathedral, etc. Later, when fast exposures made it possible to photograph the moving pedestrian, these early efforts, with their smudged and ghostly figures, were referred to as 'cities of the dead'.

In Venice C. Naya photographed the Piazza San Marco and the famous features of the canals, mercilessly. His stereographs are typical of thousands. In Florence in the late 1850s Giacomo Brogi published reproductions of paintings, some of which appeared as stereo-views. This is curious since there is no way of photographing a painting so that it appears three-dimensional. The psychological effect of the stereoscope may, occasionally, have cast its spell over purchasers of such pictures, inducing them to believe that they were seeing a 'solid' painting; but the photographer must to some extent have been exploiting the gullible. Brogi's details of famous buildings are nevertheless excellent, especially useful for the serious student needing more than the stock view of a building. Here is one of a number showing parts of the upper section of Milan Cathedral, and another of an arcade in the Ospedale Maggiore, Milan. Brogi's view, opposite, of the Galleria Vittorio Emanuele in Milan gives an idea of its vastness – something the stereograph does better than any other image.

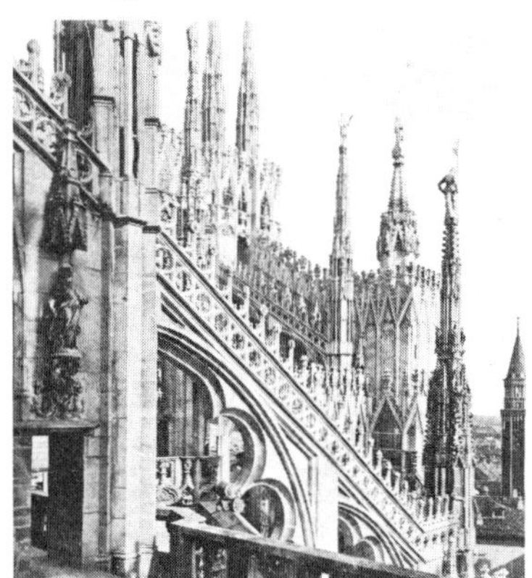
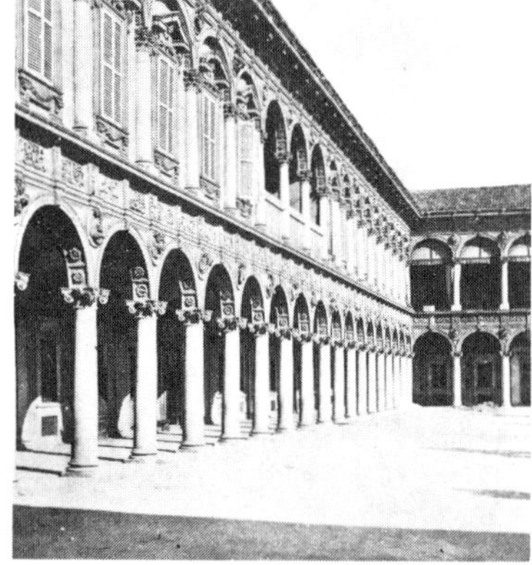

(LEFT) Untitled view of spires and buttresses of Milan Cathedral, by Giacomo Brogi. (RIGHT) *Milano. Interno dell' Ospedale Maggiore* (Milan. Interior of the Ospedale Maggiore), by Giacomo Brogi.

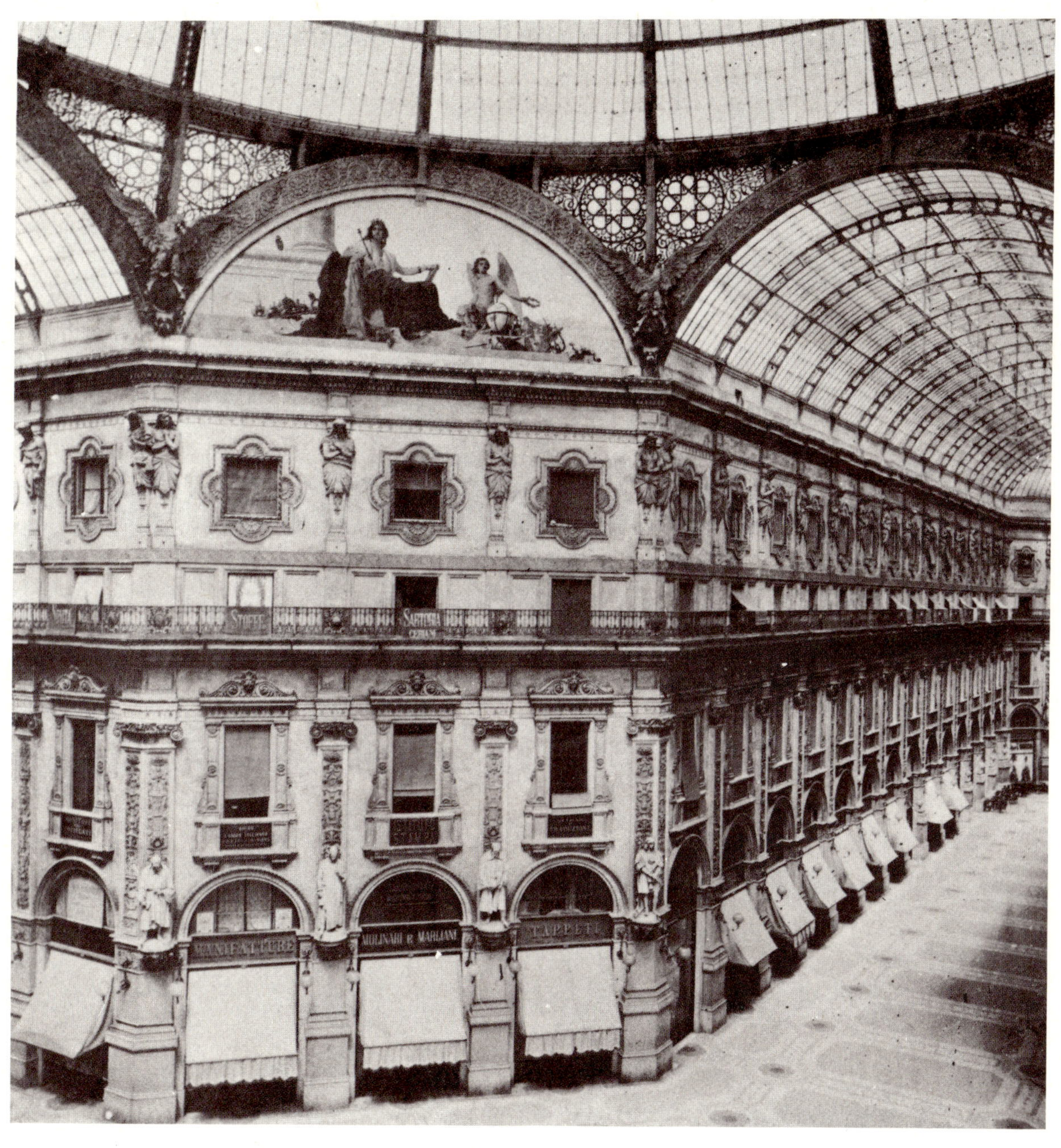

⑱ *La Galleria Vittorio Emanuele, Milano,* by Giacomo Brogi of Florence. A view of the Galleria, the famous arcade in Milan.

STUDIES IN MOVEMENT

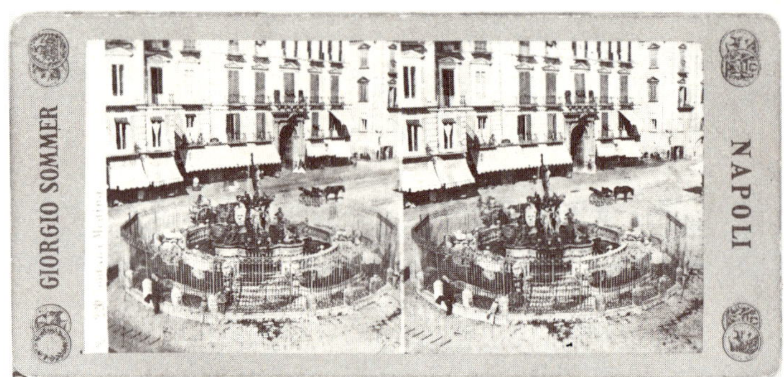

Fontana Medina, by Giorgio Sommer.

The footstool in the foreground of Claudet's Victorian interior (page 32) appears only in the picture on the right. Claudet was evidently using a single-lens camera, and during the time it took to change the position of the camera before the second exposure, the footstool must have been either removed from the field of vision or introduced into it, depending on the sequence. Perhaps Claudet used it to stand on while making an adjustment to the camera and forgot to put it back. This oversight could have been avoided, but in many early stereo-views similar discrepancies were beyond the photographer's control. For example, in Giorgio Sommer's *Fontana Medina*, illustrated here, a horse has failed to hold the pose, some ladies have disobligingly wandered about, and, as they still do, a small boy has rushed in at the last minute to have his picture taken looking through the railings (or, halfway through the proceedings, has remembered a pressing engagement elsewhere).

Such trivial accidents acquire significance in the history of cinematography. In his book *The Stereoscope* (1856) Sir David Brewster reported the achievement of an Admiral Lageol who, having positioned his subject looking straight at the camera for the first picture of a stereo-portrait, for the second picture instructed him to look at an object forty-five degrees to his right. In the result, viewed through a stereoscope by someone opening and closing each eye alternately, the sitter's eyes could be made to appear to swivel to and fro. Brewster's comment, made more than thirty-five years before Lumière's cinematograph, was prophetic:

'This fact must have been noticed in common stereoscopic portraits by everyone who has viewed them alternately with each eye, but it is not merely the eyes which move. The nose, and indeed every feature, changes its place, or, to speak more correctly, the whole figure leaps from one binocular position into the other. As it is unpleasant to open and shut the eyes alternately, the same effect may be more agreeably produced in ordinary portraits by merely intercepting the light which falls upon each picture, or by making an opaque screen pass quickly between the eyes and the lens, or immediately below the lens, so as to give successive vision of the pictures with each eye, and with both.'

The *Epreuve à Mouvement*, opposite, comes from a stereo-view which attempts a primitive form of animation, the dog's coat seeming to be brushed by a moving hand. (Readers can experience this effect by placing the appropriate stereo-card in their viewer, and then opening and closing each eye in turn.)

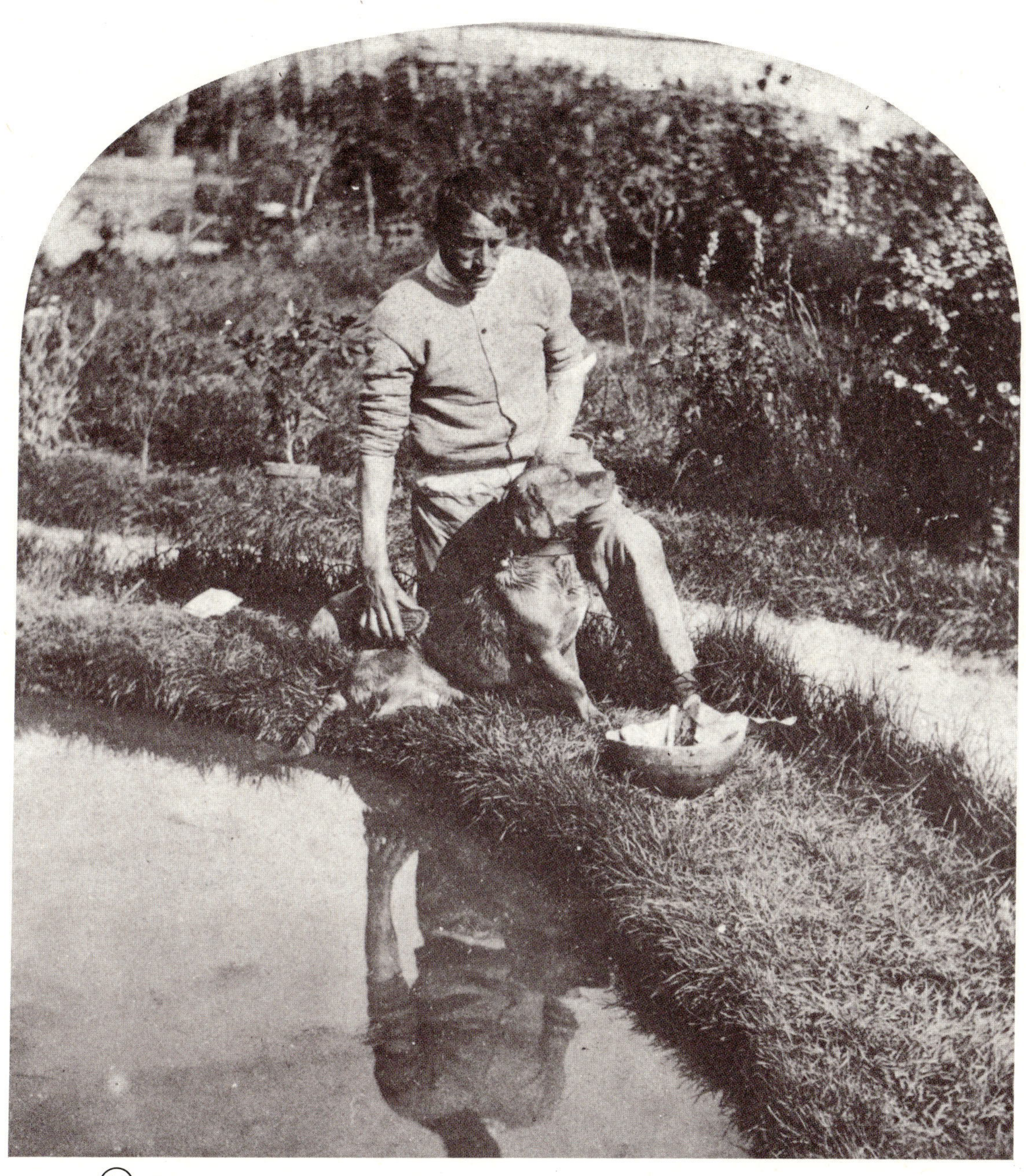

⑲ *Epreuve à Mouvement* (Experiment with Movement). Photographer unknown. 1870s.

MOUNTAIN PEAKS AND SNOWFIELDS

A colossal hindrance to travel, agriculturally ridiculous and unspeakably uncomfortable, the Alps must for centuries have seemed like a divine error of judgment. Until the coming of photography people must have wondered seriously what they were *for*. But with the stereograph the Alps were vindicated: they were made for each other. The English critic John Ruskin seems to have been the matchmaker in this happy union, claiming that his daguerreotype of the Matterhorn, made in 1849, was the 'first sun portrait . . . of any Swiss mountain'.

The reputation of the great French photographer Ferrier (see page 46) was to some extent founded on his glass views of peaks and snowfields. A beautiful example of the many excellent Swiss views that came later is the *Glacier du Viescherkorn et Mer de Glace*, opposite, by C. Lamy, whose firm was one of the largest French publishers of stereo-views.

Another Alpine specialist was Adolphe Braun. He became celebrated as a still-life

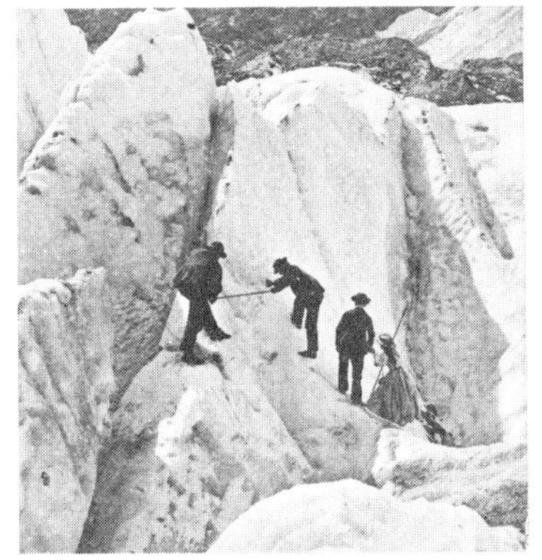

Untitled view near Grindelwald, by Adolphe Braun. Female climbers in crinolines made many appearances in Braun's Alpine studies.

photographer, and also achieved success as a portraitist for the court of Napoleon III and as a recorder of street scenes in Paris. When he turned his attention to the Alps, Braun proved himself a determined man, his attitude to physical discomfort perhaps epitomized by the artist on his perch in the stereograph overleaf, *Station des Grands-Mulets, Mont Blanc*. On another occasion, when he ascended the Stralhorn, fifteen porters were needed to carry the camping and photographic equipment. The journey took three days and Braun returned with only five plates.

As a photographer's adventure playground, the Alps had a rival in America. No subject compelled the early photographers, both commercial and amateur, like the Niagara Falls. According to William Culp Darrah (*Stereo Views*, 1964), the first glass slides of the American pioneer photographers, William and Frederick Langenheim, were of Niagara. Mason, Reilly, Bierstadt, Babbit and McPherson led the hordes of photographers who recognized that the spectacle of the Falls demanded three-dimensional representation. For more than a hundred years visitors to the Falls proved ravenous customers for such views (see also the adventures of Blondin on pages 68–69).

The card overleaf is by George Barker. He, like many others, set up a studio near the Falls and photographed them in all seasons. In this example, a departure from routine commercial shots of the Falls, Barker was clearly captivated by the fantastic shapes created by the ice and snow, which here cluster to form a surreal, ambiguous image. The card is inscribed in pencil, 'Luna Island Scenery/1 March 1868'; while this date may record when the view was taken, it could, as sometimes happens, be a note by the owner recording the date on which the card was bought.

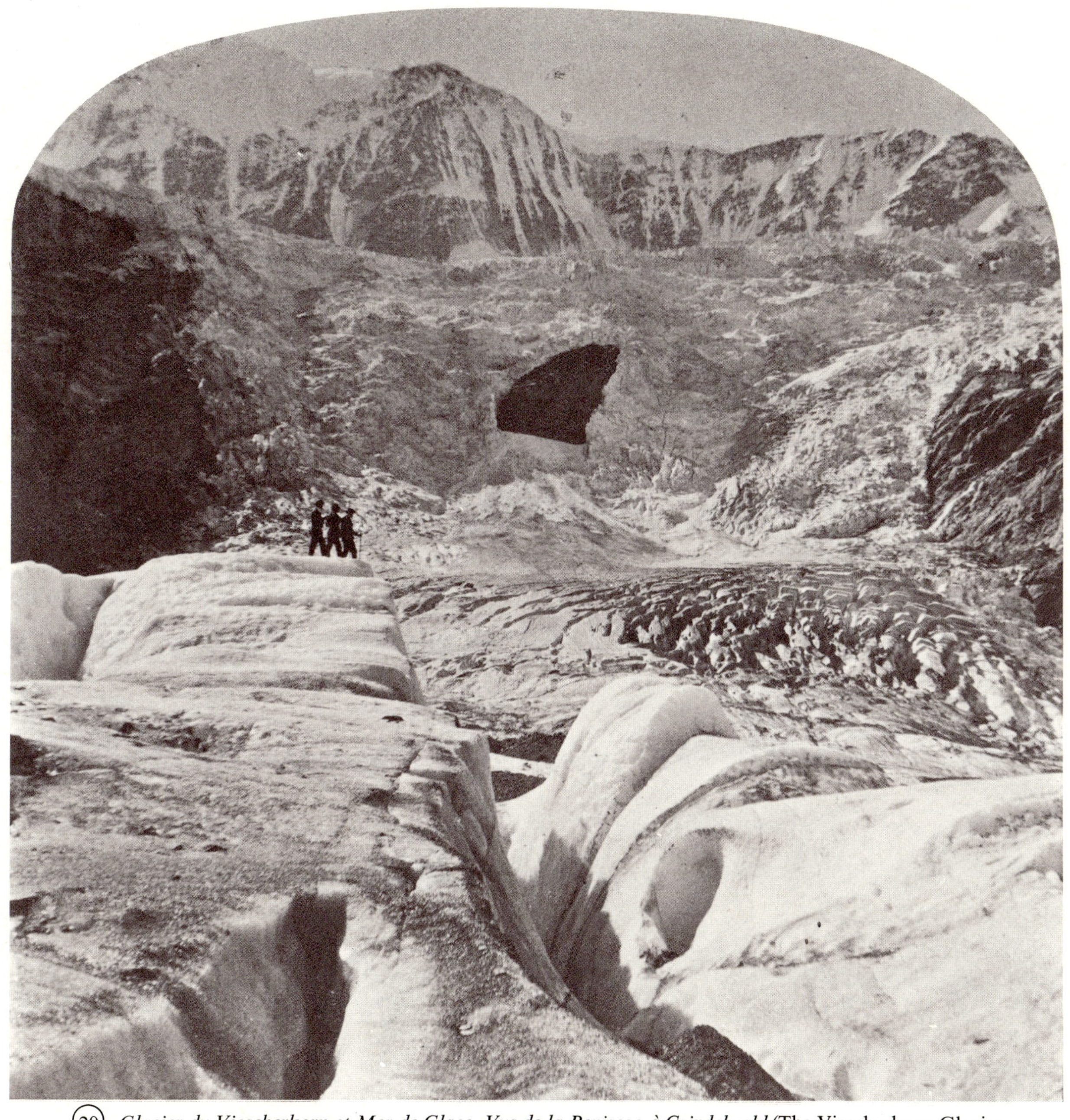

⟨20⟩ *Glacier du Viescherkorn et Mer de Glace, Vus de la Benisegg à Grindelwald* (The Viescherkorn Glacier
and the Mer de Glace. Seen from the Benisegg at Grindelwald). Photographed by C. Lamy.
The Mer de Glace is the name of the glacier of Mont Blanc.

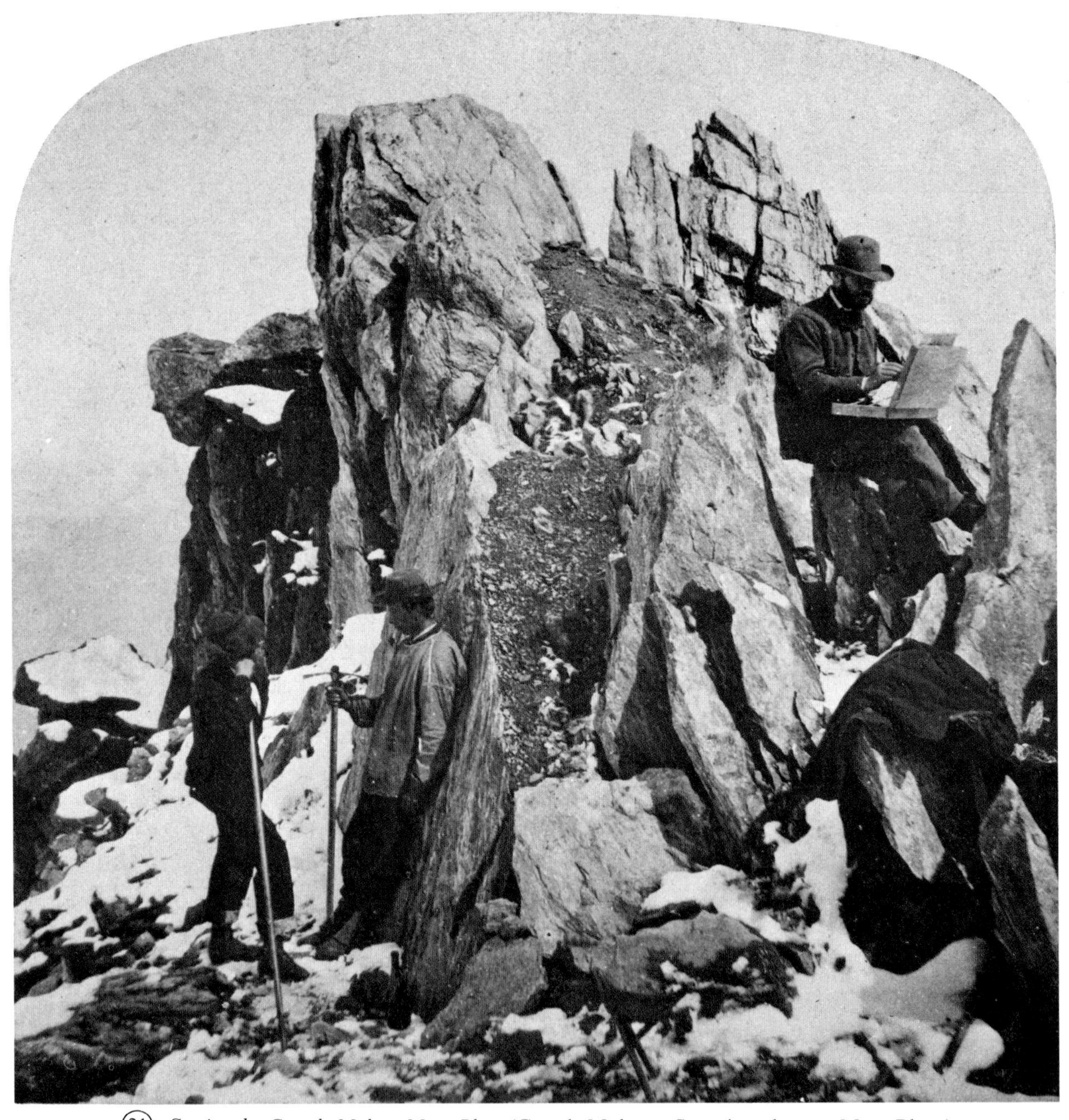

(21) *Station des Grands-Mulets, Mont Blanc* (Grands-Mulets, a Stopping-place on Mont Blanc).
Photographed by Adolphe Braun.

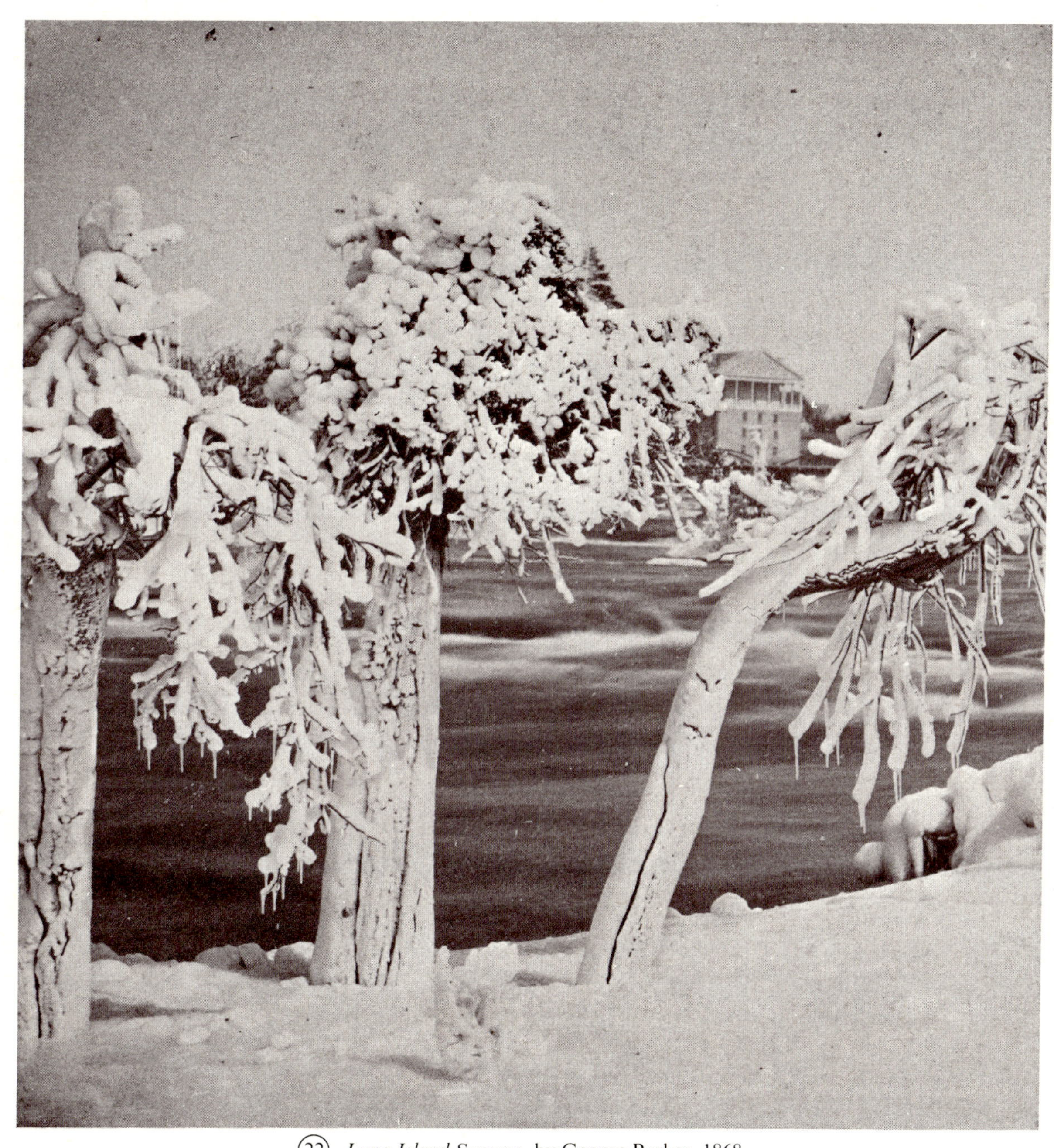

(22) *Luna Island Scenery*, by George Barker. 1868.

BLONDIN AT NIAGARA FALLS

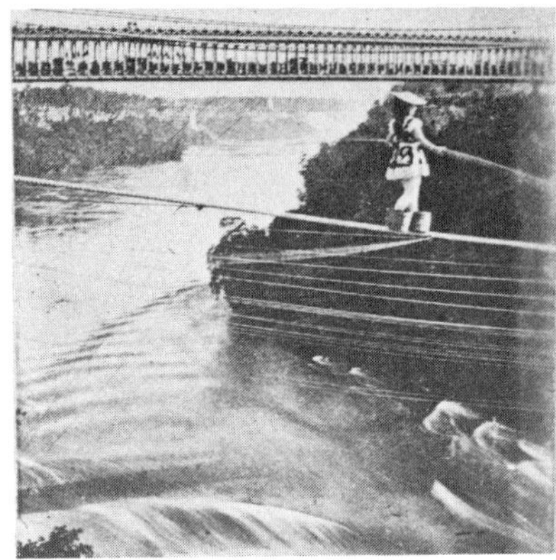

*Signorina Maria Spelterini
Crossing Niagara Rapids, N.Y.*
Photographer unknown.
From an
'American Views' series.

Like the Falls themselves, the essence of Blondin's tight-rope walk above the Niagara rapids is the grandeur of the scheme. Without the stereo effect the vertigo-inducing nub of the thing would never have been preserved for us. Blondin's first walk was in 1859; he repeated the performance many times and stereo-views of it were published by several photographers. In this view his stork-like moment of repose may have been, in part, for the benefit of the photo-journalists, their film-speed not being up to shooting him at full throttle. In any event, Curtis's camera failed to arrest the wobble of Blondin's balancing pole, here seen ominously blurred. Less well known, perhaps unrecorded save for the view illustrated here, is the audacious act of Signorina Maria Spelterini, who upstaged Blondin by crossing the Falls with her feet in buckets.

Below them foam Niagara rapids, also recorded in stereo by Curtis; on the reverse of this card is a notice whose function is evidently to remind the Travelling Public that nature *in extremis*, however diverting, is but a prelude to commerce in the shape of souvenirs and 'Fancy Goods'.

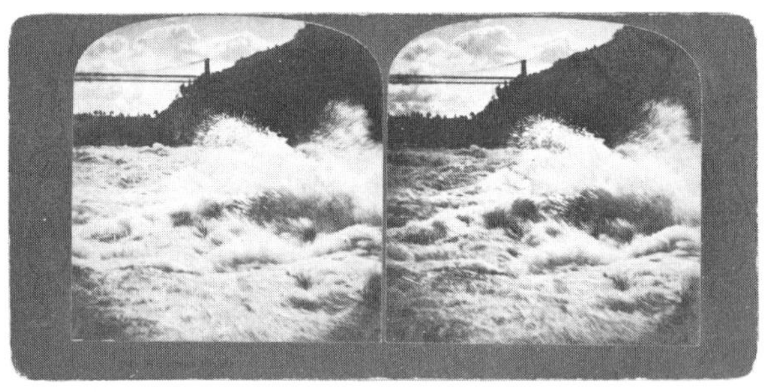

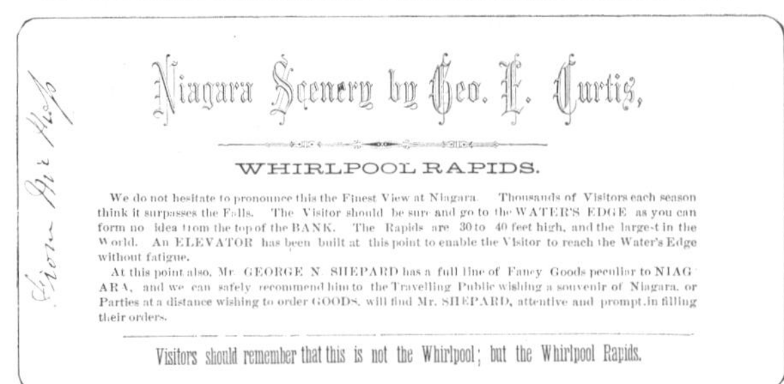

(ABOVE) *Whirlpool Rapids,* by George Curtis. (BELOW) The flamboyant advertising on the back of Curtis's card.

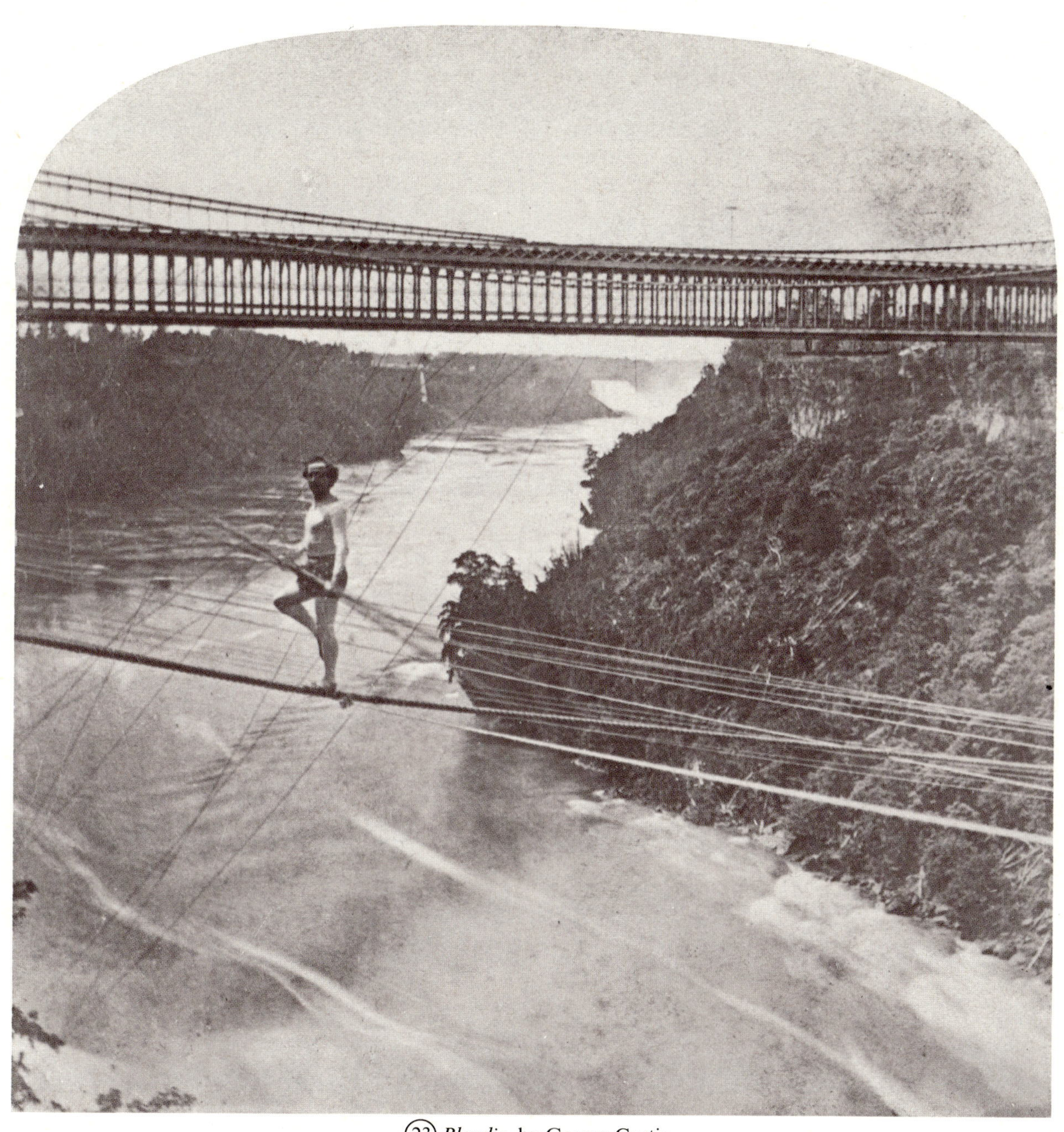

(23) *Blondin,* by George Curtis.

69

WILLIAM ENGLAND, OFFICIAL PHOTOGRAPHER

The memory of the throng of photographers that attended the Great Exhibition of 1851 may have influenced the Royal Commissioners in their arrangements for the International Exhibition held in London in 1862. They sold the exclusive photographic rights to the London Stereoscopic Company for an exorbitant sum, with additional charges for facilities essential to the photographer's work. Consequently the cost to the public of the finished stereographs was high. William England took the photographs, setting a testing standard for all future stereoscopic records of exhibitions (of which there were many). The *Art Journal* exclaimed: 'Never have more admirable stereographs been produced. Among the *Notabilia* of this exhibition none can rival the stereographs, which render the exhibition itself at once indestructible and ubiquitous.'

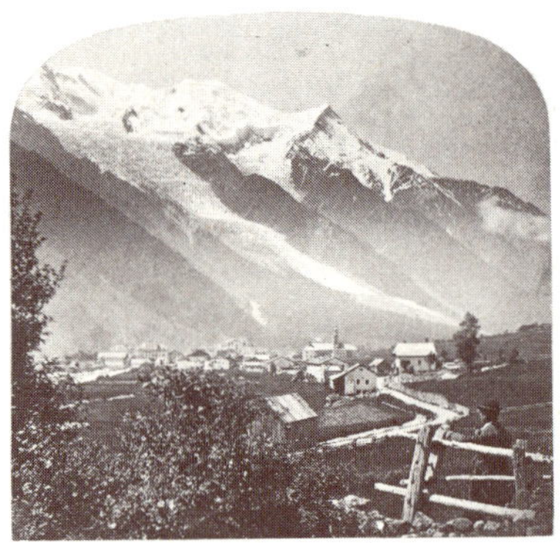 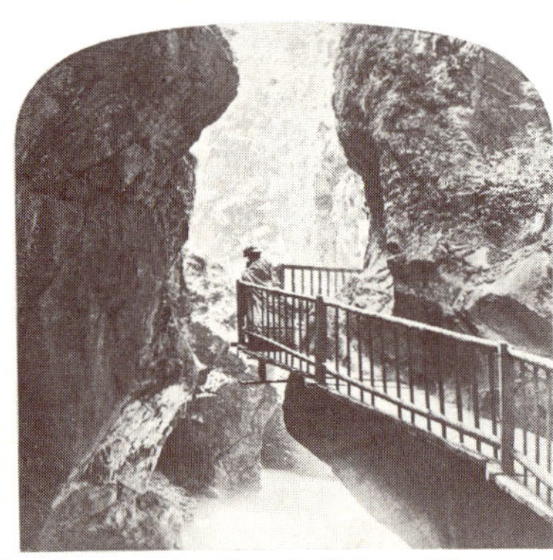

(LEFT) *Mont Blanc et le Panorama de Chamounix. Savoie* (Mont Blanc and Panorama of Chamonix. Savoy). Photographed by William England. (RIGHT) *Gorge du Trient à Martigny. Suisse* (Trient Gorge at Martigny. Switzerland). Photographed by William England.

Earlier in his career William England had been one of the photographers to make a stereograph of Blondin's first crossing of the Niagara Falls. He travelled widely for the London Stereoscopic Company (he was one of their original staff) and in 1859 brought back the first stereo-views of American scenery to be seen in Europe.

In 1851, at the Great Exhibition, the response to stereo-photographs had been to marvel at their detail and clarity, as if they were a superior kind of skilled miniature drawing. By 1862 all the emphasis was on their educational value: 'They are the most impressive of teachers – or rather, through their agency the exhibition, in the most impressive manner conveys its most eminently valuable lessons. . . . We can enjoy this year's exhibition again and again in the stereoscope . . . and thoroughly learn all it has to teach. . . . We are particularly anxious to press upon our readers this teaching quality' (*Art Journal*). England's pictures record the opening and official ceremonies of the exhibition, general views of its vast layout, the sculptures, collections, particular groups of exhibits and individual objects on display. The study of engraved glass, opposite, a classic photographic essay with lighting, is particularly delicate in three dimensions.

For those who had seen the Exhibition, its splendours could be repeatedly recalled with the stereoscope. One reviewer with ambivalent memories of his visit was moved to write: 'The galleries again rise up in their true images; and all the diversified reminiscences of the struggles for refreshments revive in the full force of their original annoyance.'

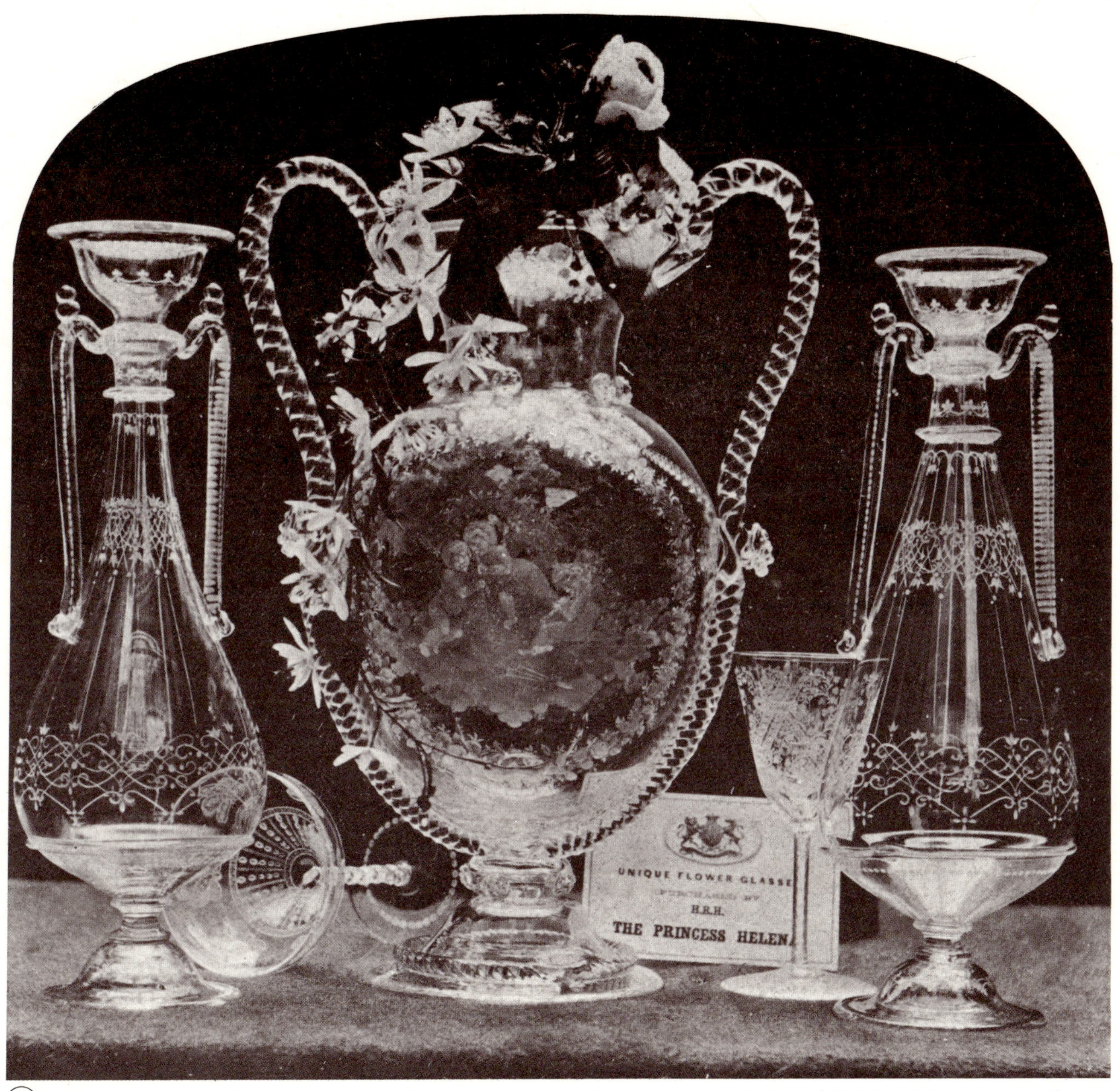

(24) *Engraved Glass, by Messrs Naylor & Co.* Photographed at the International Exhibition of 1862 by William England for the London Stereoscopic Company.

DISTINGUISHED AMATEURS

The bulk of photography is by amateurs; no other hobby has such a following. Appropriately, the 'professional' standing of a photograph often comes with the passing of time to seem less important than its historical interest; the work of Box Brownie amateurs may in fact contain more valuable sociological information and a less affected kind of 'human interest' than the professional has the innocence to record.

The amateur, even today, has little opportunity to show or discuss his work outside the family circle unless he belongs to a club. This was certainly the reason for the creation in 1861 of the Amateur Photographic Exchange Society in the USA. It had a distinguished membership of learned men, who agreed to exchange photographs with each other every two months or so. However, the most exclusive club of all, the Amateur Photographic Association, was set up in England in the following year. The Prince of Wales agreed to be its president, and the roll-call included many noble lords and the Archbishop of York. At their first meeting there was an exhibition of prizes for which members were to compete, consisting of two richly ornamented claret jugs, three silver goblets and two silver inkstands. It would be a nice irony if one of those costly items had been won with a stereograph like that, opposite, featuring a plebeian group in a tanyard in Bermondsey, which was submitted by one of the Society's non-titled members, T. Revington.

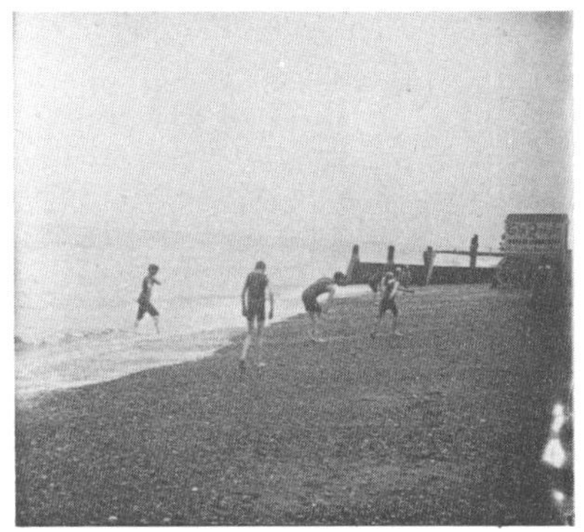
Untitled English beach scene.
Glass view.
Photographer unknown. *c.* 1913.

To the modern eye some large amateur collections from earlier days hold out the promise of a mystery tour in a time-machine. One such collection, by an anonymous Edwardian traveller who seems to have carried his Richard's Verascope round half the world, comprises about a thousand slides. I have passed over his camel cavalcades and Riviera fishermen in favour of a moment from what may have been his last holiday before the Great War (its likely date is 1913). This grey spectacle of English pleasures, which could have been taken by any inexperienced seaside snap-shooter, chills the cockles of the heart.

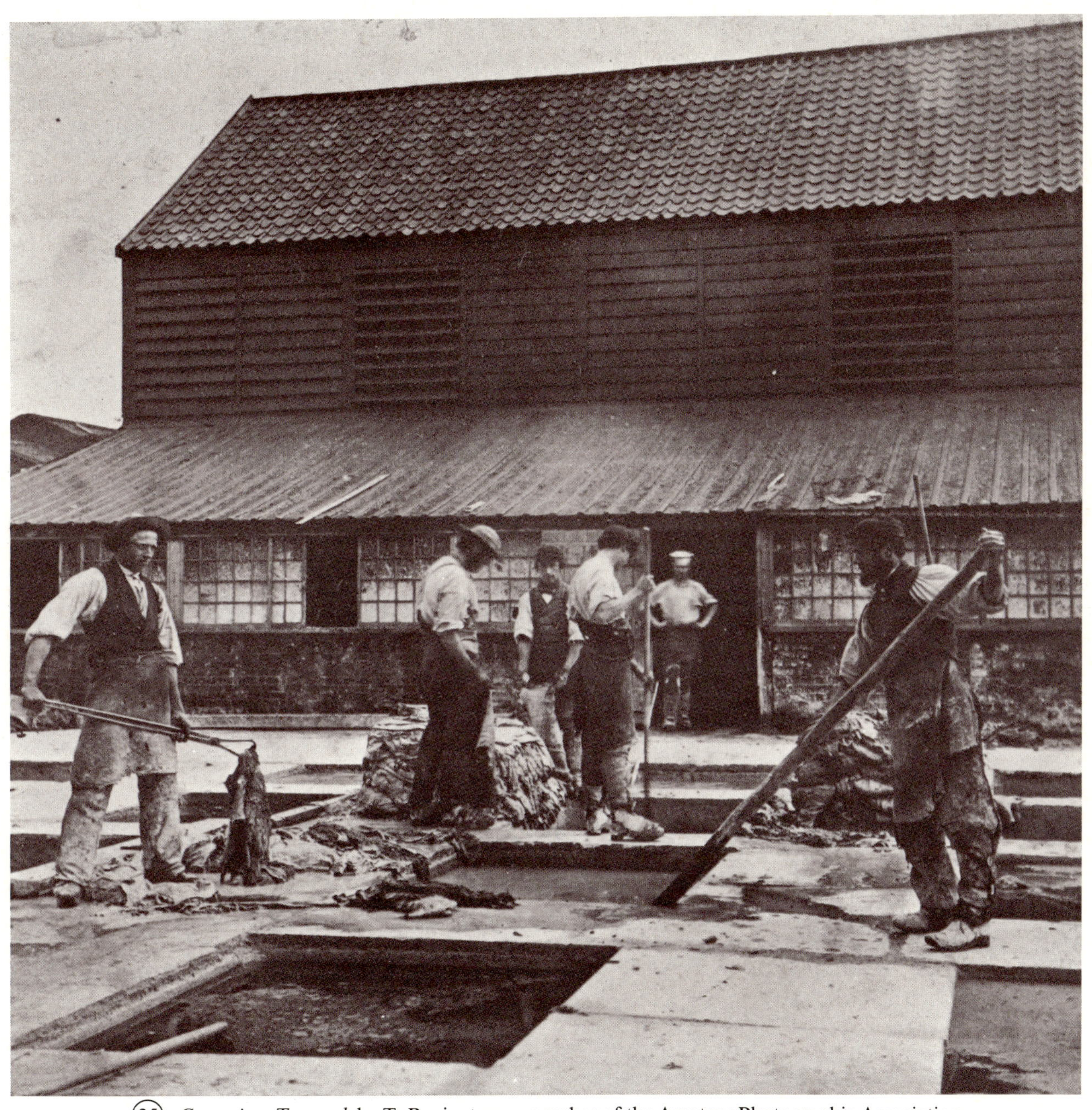

㉕ *Group in a Tanyard,* by T. Revington, a member of the Amateur Photographic Association.

RAILROADS

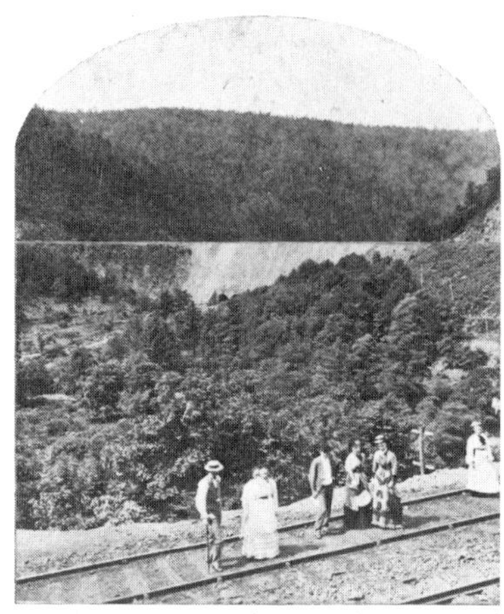

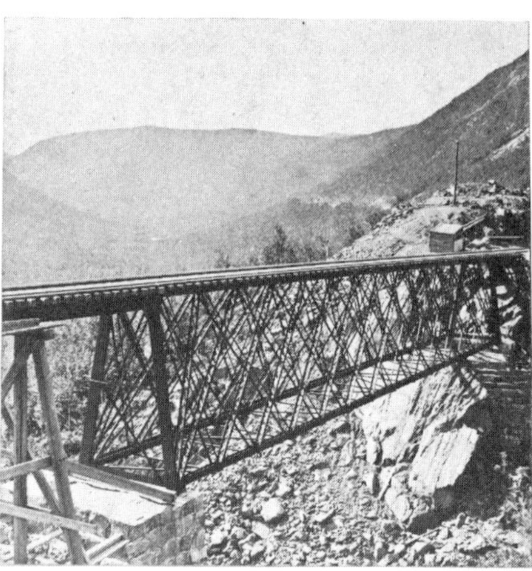

The glamour of machines is not widely acknowledged but most men are susceptible to it. Trains are especially infatuating; and railway stations, in the range of human feeling they witness and engender, can rival the theatre. Old photographs of such things are full of pitfalls for the sentimental. The view, opposite, of the south tip of Manhattan Island in the mid-1870s, which combines port, railroad depot and the emotive word 'emigrant', is oddly uninhabited. As the imagination gives in to the

(LEFT) *Horse Shoe on the Pennsylvania Railroad*, by F. Gutekunst. (RIGHT) *Saco Valley, from Willey Brook Bridge, P. & O.R.R. White Mountain, N.H.* Photographed by N. W. Pease of Conway, New Hampshire.

impulse to populate the scene, its compassionate appeal can be unexpectedly striking.

Notably rich in stirring associations are the great trans-continental railroads which played such an important role in the history of America. Photographers recorded their construction by gangs of immigrants who built them, virtually by hand, against the most daunting physical obstacles. Each mile of track became a souvenir of achievement, and stereo-views like Gutekunst's *Horse Shoe, on the Pennsylvania Railroad* were sold at every station. In this little group, dwarfed by the wilderness behind the figures, the lady in white has moved. This must have been particularly irritating for Gutekunst, a photographer with an international reputation, whose portrait of President Grant was, according to Robert Taft, author of *Photography and the American Scene* (1938), the most satisfactory ever taken.

Bridges for the railroad were other favourite photographic targets. Memorable as engineering feats, their euphonious names are equally unforgettable: the Secrettown Trestle, the Kinzua Steel, and the Willey Brook Bridge over Saco Valley, here illustrated.

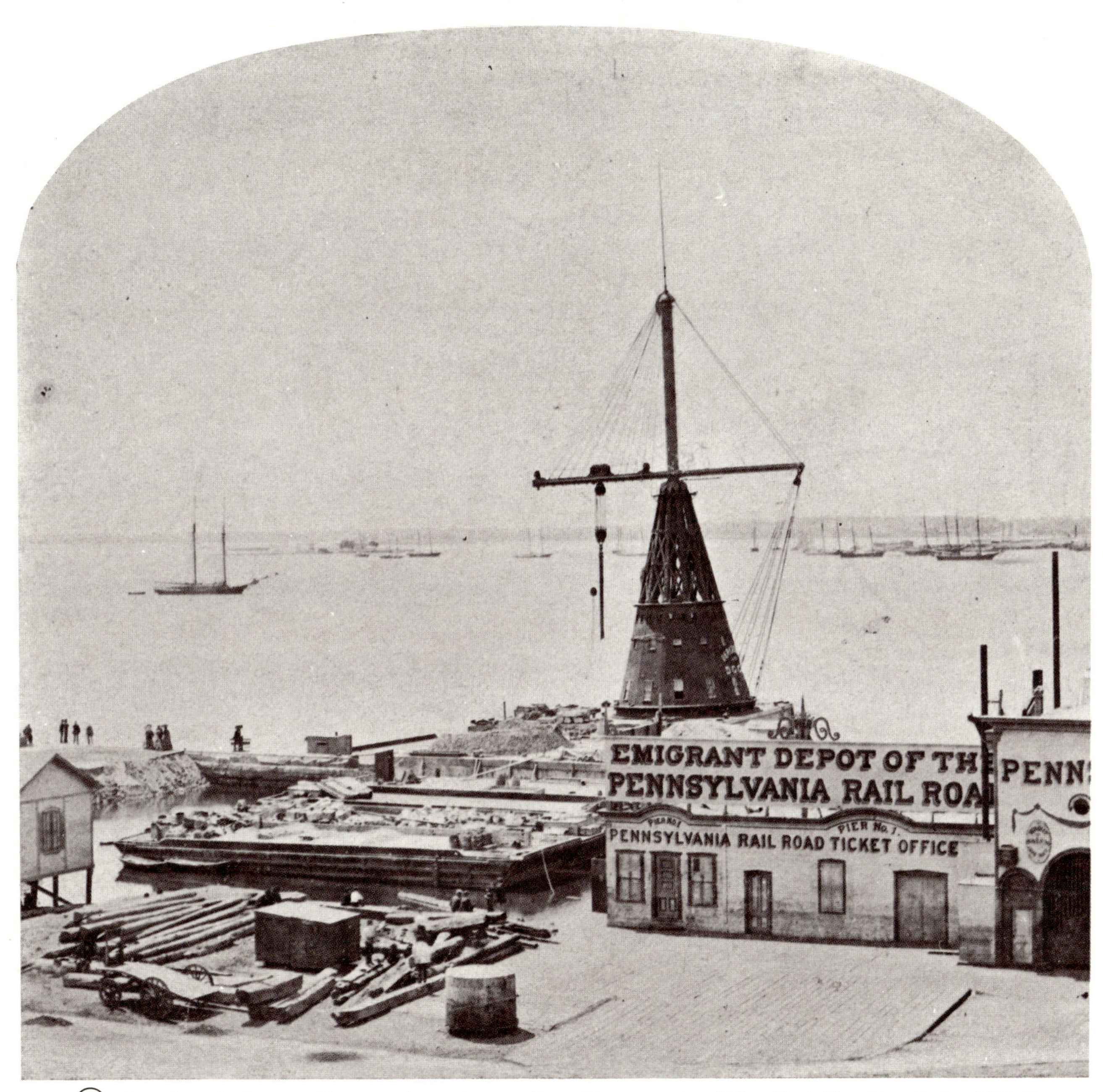

26 *View from the Battery.* Photographer unknown. From 'Stereographs of New York City, New Series, 1874–5'.

IRON HORSES

Not only were American railroads and stations thoroughly documented by stereographers, William Culp Darrah in *Stereo Views* (1964) records how 'for five decades the changing iron horse was photographed in magnificent detail'. One of the rarest tinted glass views produced by the brothers Langenheim is of the *First Locomotive in America*; taken in 1857, it shows the Baltimore and Ohio engine at the end of its days.

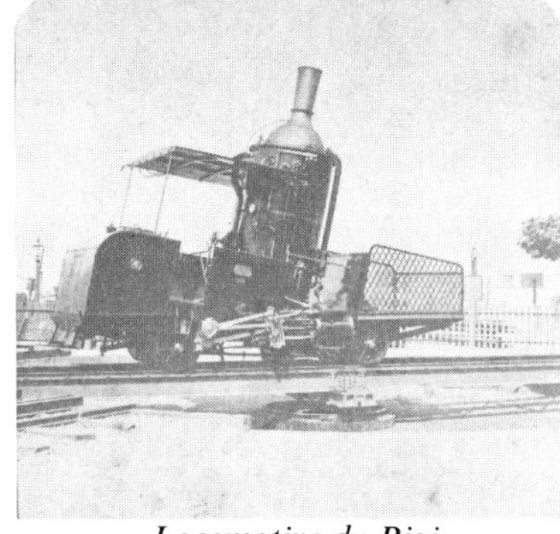

Locomotive du Rigi,
by F. Charneaux, Geneva.

The view opposite is the English equivalent, a paper stereograph of about the same date portraying a George Stephenson locomotive described on the label as: 'No. 1 ENGINE, "THE ACTIVE". The first Locomotive Engine that travelled upon the first public Railway, viz – from Shildon to Stockton, which was opened in September, 1825. *Its Weight, 8 Tons – Its Maker GEORGE STEPHENSON.*' Originally these early locomotives were not named, that in the stereograph being referred to as the 'company's locomotive engine'. Later it was given a name: this was not *The Active*, however, but *Locomotion*, the name by which it is known today. The label on the stereograph in fact perpetuates an error that seems to have begun with Samuel Smiles, who refers to *The Active* in his *Lives of George and Robert Stephenson* (1857).

All kinds of locomotives appeared in European views taken in the latter part of the century. One of the more unusual appears several times in a series of pictures of Switzerland and the Savoy by F. Charneaux of Geneva; issued in the early 1870s, these are for the most part views of Alpine scenery. The engine is the Locomotive of Rigi, built by the Swiss Central Railway in 1870 for the steep gradients of the Vitznau–Rigi Railway, oldest of the Alpine rack-and-pinion mountain railways. In its original version, shown here, it had a vertical boiler to keep the top of the firebox covered with water when on the mountainside; hence its tilted appearance on the flat.

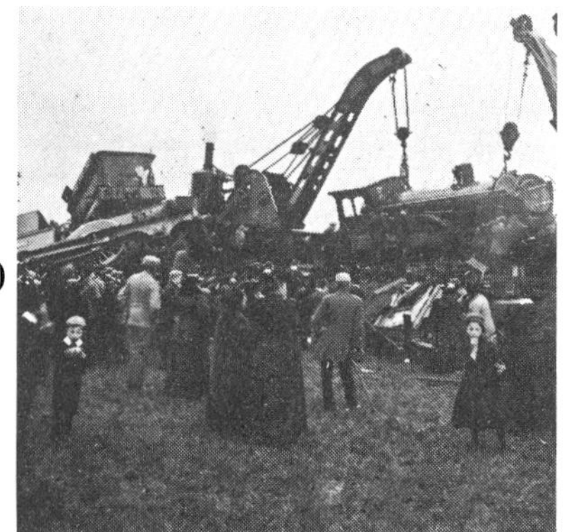

The Accident to the Flying Scotsman, nr Northallerton, Oct/94. Photographer unknown.

The English love affair with trains has meant a proliferation of amateur photographs of engines, of which *The Flying Scotsman* was perhaps the most beloved of all. This view of it is certainly rare: it was taken in October 1894 by a local photographer after an accident near Northallerton in Yorkshire.

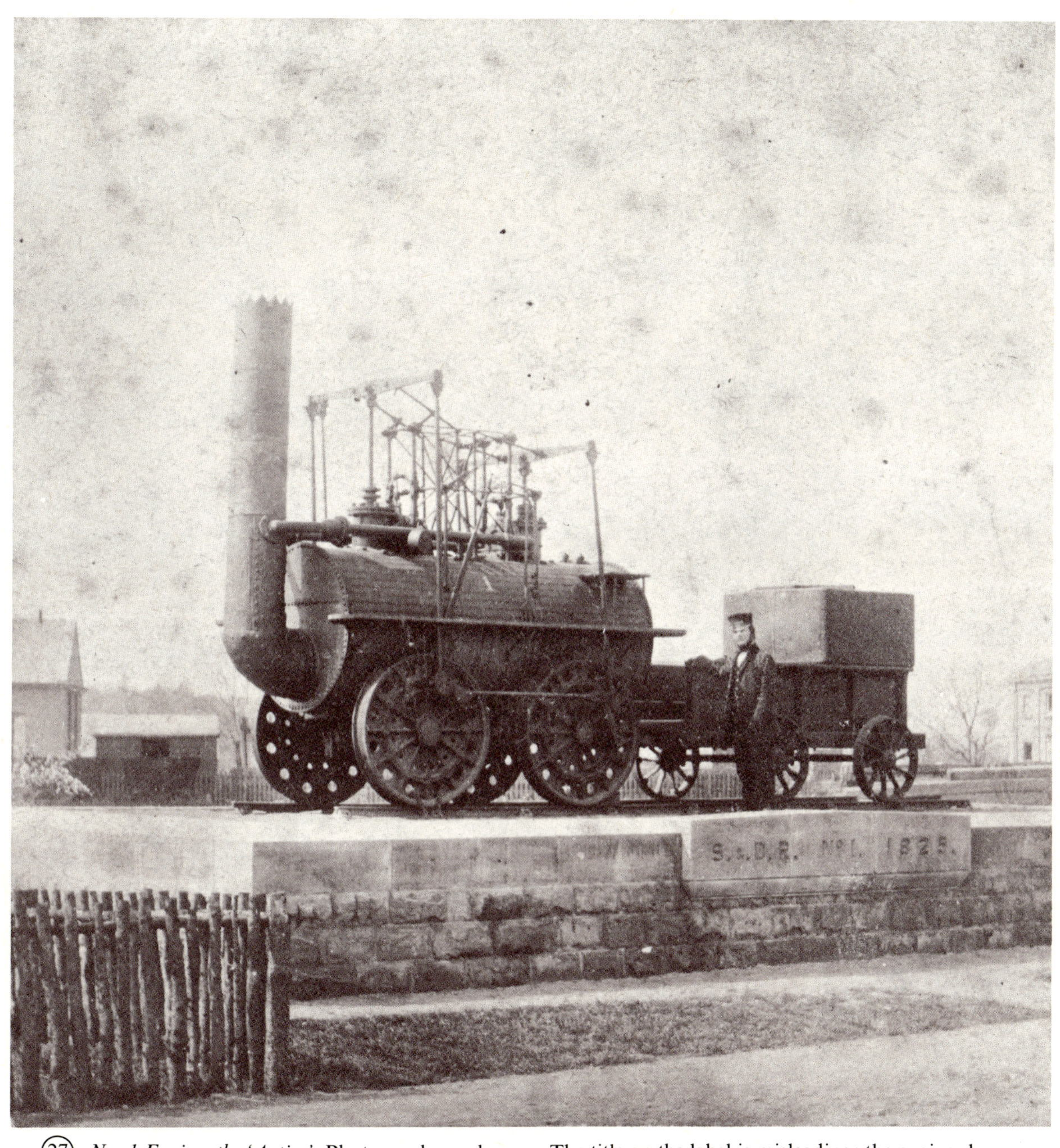

(27) *No. 1 Engine, the 'Active'*. Photographer unknown. The title on the label is misleading: the engine shown is in fact George Stephenson's *Locomotion*.

77

THE OTHER AMERICANS

Described in F. S. Dellenbaugh's *A Canyon Passage* as 'one of the greatest feats of exploration executed on this continent', a party led by J. W. Powell in 1869 followed the course of the then unknown Colorado River. Throughout the 1870s the region was surveyed by Powell for the United States Government. According to Dellenbaugh, Jack Hillers was employed as general handyman on the second expedition;* although ignorant of photography, he assisted the official photographers, E. O. Beamann and Clement Powell, and evidently learned a great deal from them. The following year he was in the Grand Canyon, assisting James Fennemore on another stage of the survey. Fennemore fell sick, and Hillers took over his photographic work. The small group of seven suffered considerable hardship, not lessened by the bulk of the photographic apparatus, but Hillers managed to bring back some excellent photographs. This work and the material collected on several other pioneering expeditions established him as a first-class photographer, and he later became the chief photographer of the United States Geological Survey. The view opposite, *Ku-Ra-Tu at Rest*, is one of 140 collected on the survey which show Indians.

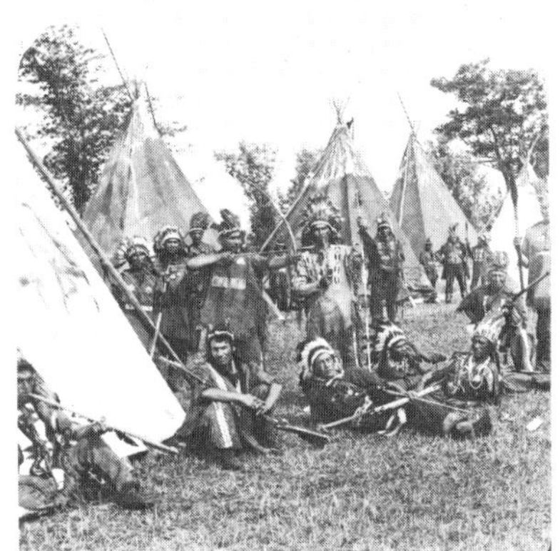 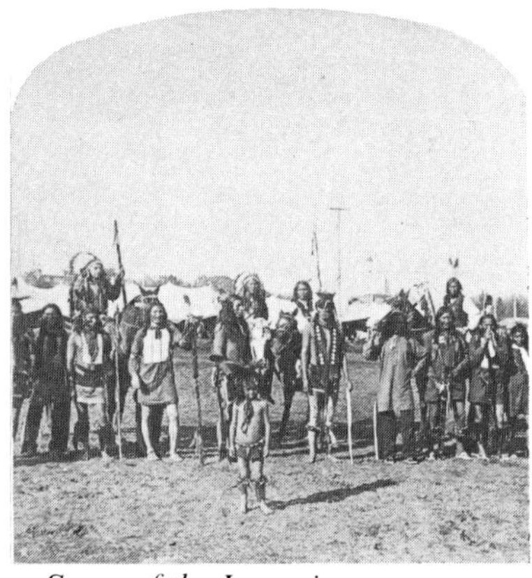

(LEFT) *Picturesque Village Scene of the Iroquois.*
Published by Underwood & Underwood. (RIGHT)
Little 'War Eagle', the Pride of the Tribe.
Published by Underwood & Underwood. 1889.

There are not many early stereographs of American Indians. Later pictures of groups, such as the two by Underwood & Underwood illustrated on this page, have the posed look of anthropological specimens on display, or side-show performers. This theatricality must reflect the Indians' tragic dilemma, whereby racial identity is retained at the risk of becoming a freakish spectacle on the tourist programme.

* Both Dellenbaugh references are taken from Robert Taft's *Photography and the American Scene* (1938).

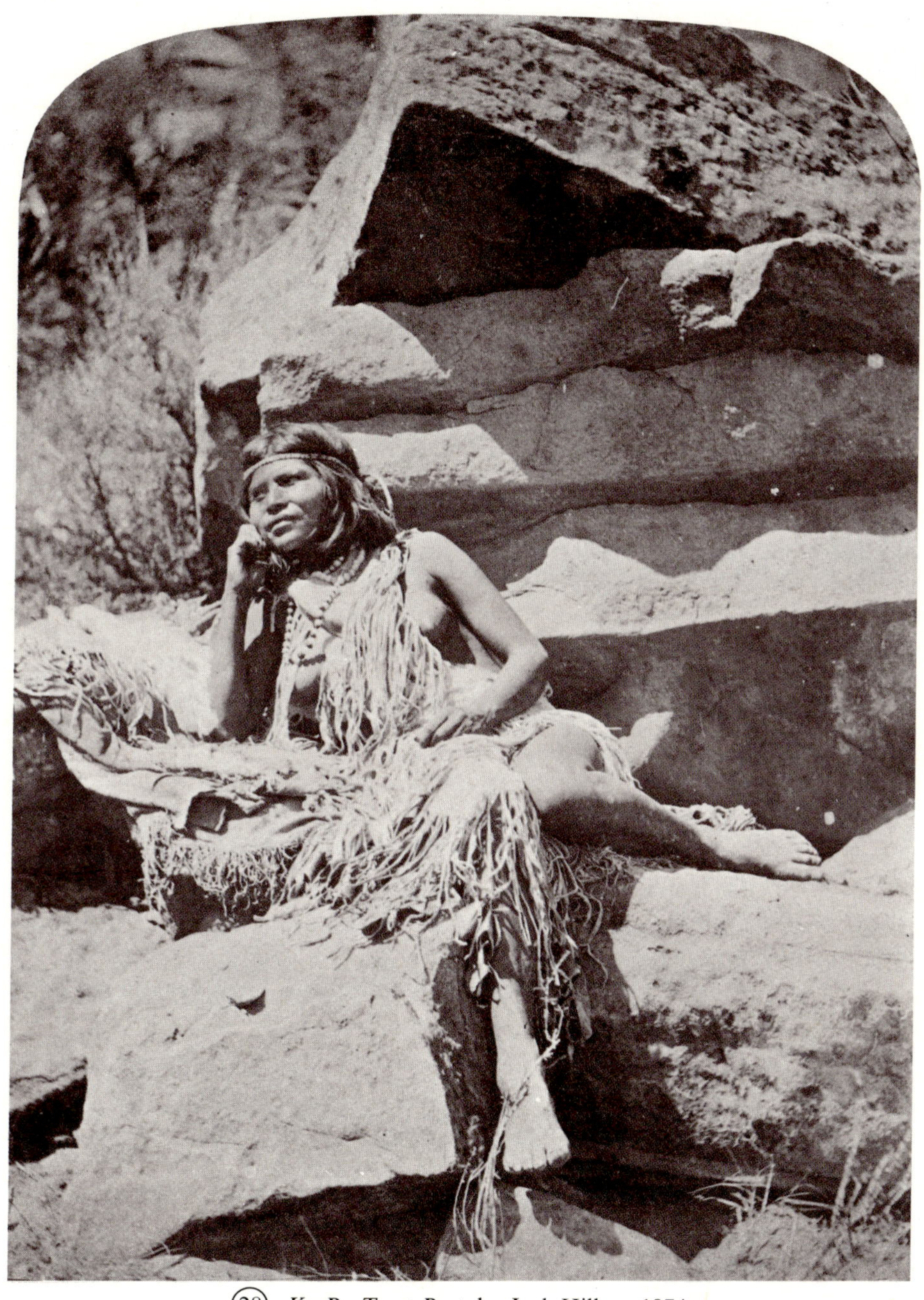

(28) *Ku-Ra-Tu at Rest*, by Jack Hillers. 1874.

SPIRIT PHOTOGRAPHS

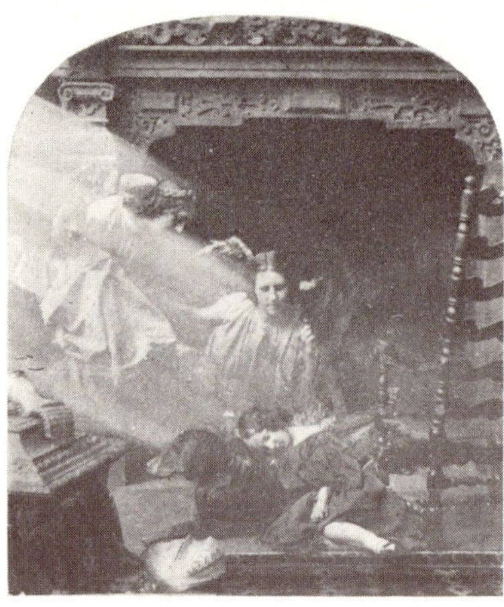

The Orphan's Dream, by James Elliot. Hand-coloured card. Published by the London Stereoscopic Company. 1850s.

Viewed through a stereoscope, Claudet's footstool in the Victorian interior on page 32 appears to be transparent and two-dimensional, because it is seen by one eye only. It looks like the ghost of a footstool. In *The Stereoscope* (1856) Brewster described a way of making 'spirit' photographs of three-dimensional, see-through people:

'While a party is engaged with their whist or their gossip, a female figure appears in the midst of them with all the attributes of the supernatural. . . . In order to produce such a scene, the parties which are to compose the group must have their portraits nearly finished in the binocular camera, in the attitude which they may be supposed to take, and with the expression which they may be supposed to assume, if the vision were real. When the party have nearly sat the proper length of time, the female figure, suitably attired, walks quickly into the place assigned her, and after standing a few seconds in the proper attitude, retires quickly.'

Elliot's picture, opposite, entitled *A Ghostly Warning*, is the horror-comic result. Or is it? There is an important difference between Brewster's written prescription and the way Elliot has realized it. Brewster places the ghost in innocent domestic circumstances, presumably the more to dramatize its dreadful presence and to make a simple joke about a 'party' being given a fright. But in Elliot's picture, as the ominous title suggests, the card game is less innocuous than whist, and the presence of decanter and tilted top hat indicate an occasion of mild depravity. No longer a random hair-raiser, the apparition has been endowed with moral purpose – to reprove or chastise, even, perhaps, to demonstrate the 'reckoning' that lies in wait for gamblers and tipplers. The scene is still a joke, but an *improving* one.

There are many other examples of such 'ghosts'. As well as spooky jokes there were tear-jerkers: the wounded soldier's vision of his dear ones at home, the bereaved recalling their departed, and *The Orphan's Dream*, illustrated here.

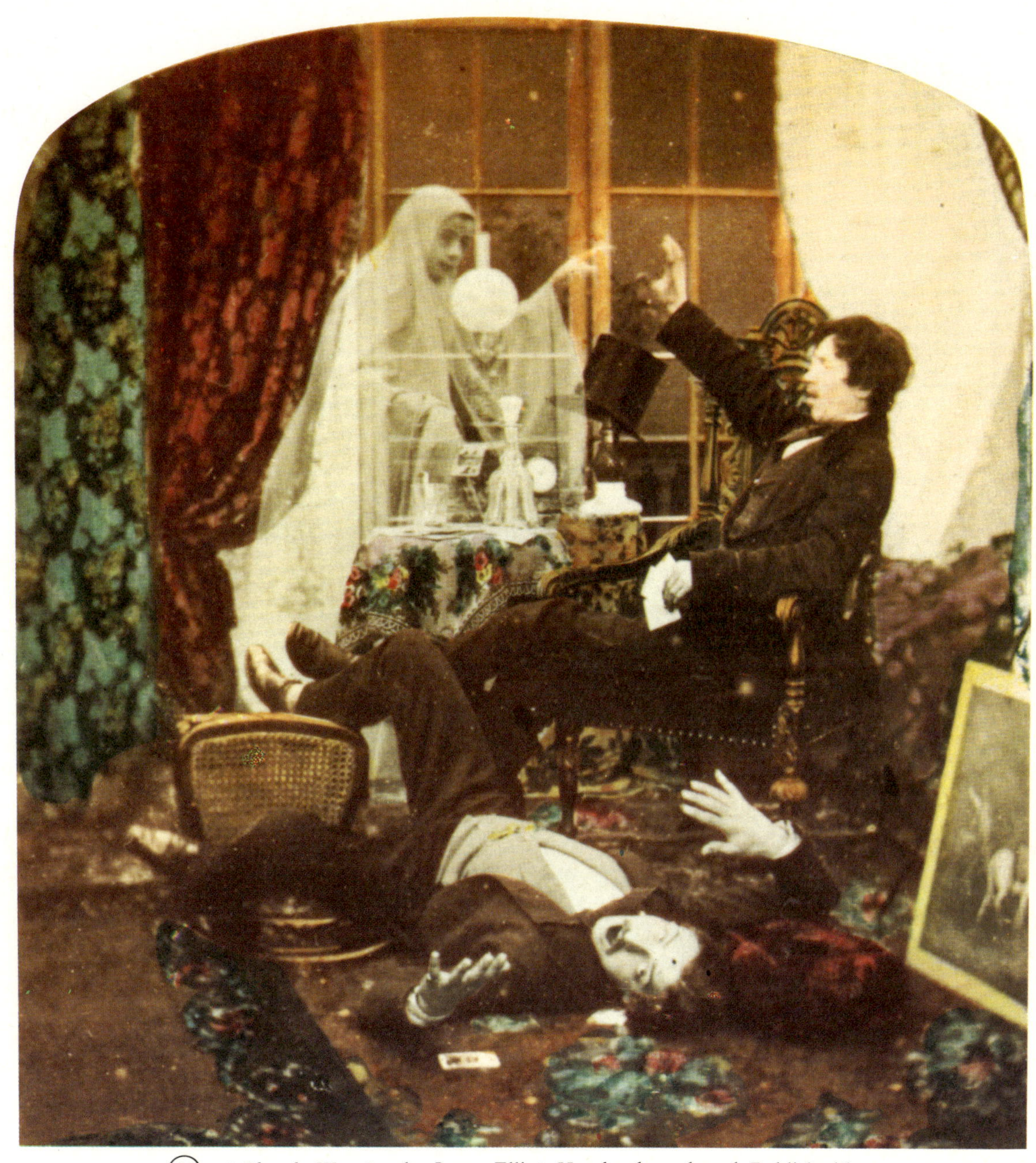

㉙ *A Ghostly Warning*, by James Elliot. Hand-coloured card. Published by
the London Stereoscopic Company. 1850s.

'HISTORY' VERSUS NATURE

Sir David Brewster, in a long discourse on the proper way to make stereoscopic portraits, railed against photographers who used large lenses which distorted for effect, his contention being that they were 'untruthful'. 'No question of science can be a matter of taste,' he wrote, 'and no illusion can be artistic which is a misrepresentation of nature' (*The Stereoscope*, 1856). This may appear inconsistent with his proposal (see previous pages) to stage jokes about ghosts. By 'nature', moreover, he must have meant 'appearances'. In short, fiction should have the semblance of nature.

In 1858 James Elliot photographed a series, *The Sacking of the Jew's House*, which, when looked at consecutively, told a story. It was the first of its kind. A contemporary review stressed its 'authenticity': '. . . the grouping must have presented many difficulties, for there is *a considerable amount of reality* in all the compositions; and the several objects, which are in admirable keeping, could not have been obtained without much trouble and care. The result is highly satisfactory; they are truly pictures, and have all the value and interest of *pictures on which the mind has been engaged.*' My italics underline two aspects which the Victorians repeatedly demanded of pictures, that they should be both real and thought-provoking.

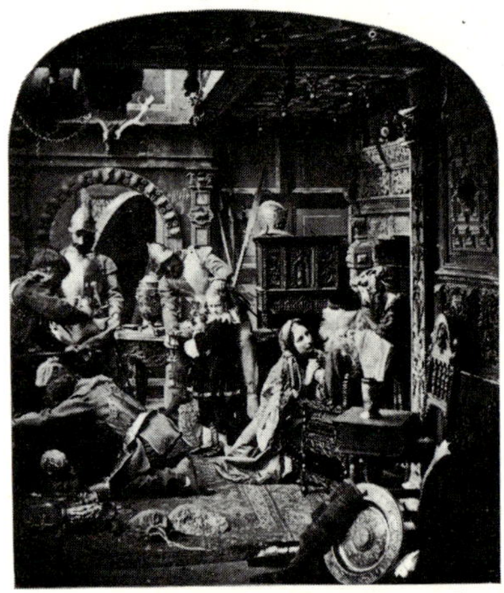

The Sacking of the Jew's House, by James Elliot. One of a sequence-set published by the London Stereoscopic Company. 1858.

In spite of the care taken over props and costumes the scene does not appear very convincing today. Our uneasiness may derive from the knowledge that it is a photograph, which forces us to look at it, not as an historical fact but as a contrived charade. Elliot's concern with verisimilitude is again reflected in his stereograph, opposite, the *Death of Thomas a' Becket,* on the reverse of which is printed a list of 'Authorities for Armour, &c.', much in the same way that Cecil B. De Mille later credited his 'historical advisers'. No one is really convinced by such testimonials. Baudelaire, no less, is responsible for the definitive tirade against mock-bygones:

'Strange abominations. . . . By bringing together a group of male and female clowns, got up like butchers and laundry maids at a carnival, and begging these *heroes* to be so kind as to hold their grimaces for the time necessary for the performance, the operator flattered himself that he was reproducing tragic or elegant scenes from ancient history . . . a double sacrilege . . . insulting at one and the same time the divine art of painting and the noble art of the actor.' Baudelaire's essay, from which this fragment is taken, was occasioned by the introduction of a section of 'artistic' photographs into an art exhibition, the Paris Salon of 1859.

The existence of this type of photograph, and the vexation it caused, both arose from a conflict in nineteenth-century thinking which measured art by its fidelity to nature while at the same time valuing 'history painting' above all other genres.

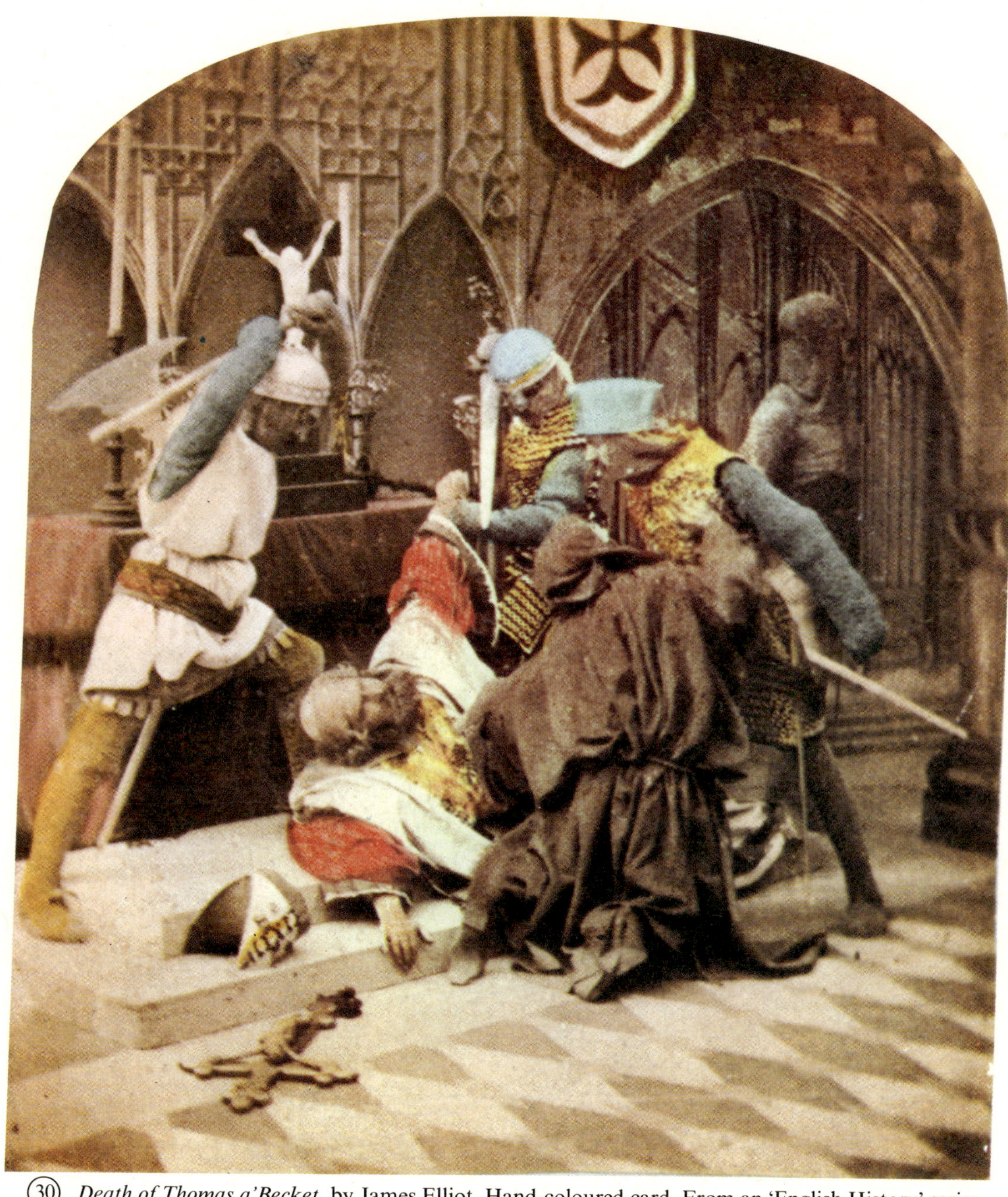

(30) *Death of Thomas a'Becket*, by James Elliot. Hand-coloured card. From an 'English History' series published by the London Stereoscopic Company.

HIGH ART PHOTOGRAPHY

Photography's unrivalled 'truth to nature' can only have alarmed most Victorian artists. To compete with the camera seemed both inevitable and impossible. Robert Hunt wrote: 'Few men could paint as the sun paints; it is not to be desired that they should do so, since the expenditure of time in producing all this wonderful detail would swallow up too much of a man's life, and it would I fear, as a final result, produce marvellous mechanism, to the sacrifice of mind.' But what, one wonders, should the mind be doing? Baudelaire recommended imagination and 'not what the painter sees, but what he dreams!' To some artists, however, the only course open at the time seemed to be to devise still more complex, story-telling history pictures and to paint illustrations to poetry and romantic fiction; but already photographers, too, were doing these very things.

Hunt's observation comes from a review of an exhibition which included photographs by Lake Price, a painter-turned-photographer. In a most practical book, *Photographic Manipulations*, Price often advises the reader to acquaint himself with the masterpieces of painting as an essential part of an apprenticeship in photography. His own celebrity depended on his presentation of historical and literary subjects: his photographs, for example, of Robinson Crusoe, Don Quixote, and the Princes in the Tower. One genre, irreproachable as subject matter for painting and authorized for photography by Daguerre himself, was still life. In his book, Price recommends the opportunities it offers to contrast textures, clearly a strong feature of his *Retour de Chasse*, opposite.

Another photographer who led the invasion into High Art territory was Oscar Gustave Rejlander. Also a painter, usually of moralizing allegories, Rejlander produced – as an aid to composition – large photographs in which more than thirty negatives were employed. He combined the photographs in different ways to a point where it seemed superfluous to paint the picture.

It is not impossible to make stereographs from more than one negative but only for very simple effects. Rejlander's technique was too complicated for stereoscopic application. For Charles Darwin's *The Expression of Emotions in Man and Animals* he provided photographs of himself and others miming grief, rage, surprise, etc., and it is conceivable that the unidentified stereographs, left, are by him.

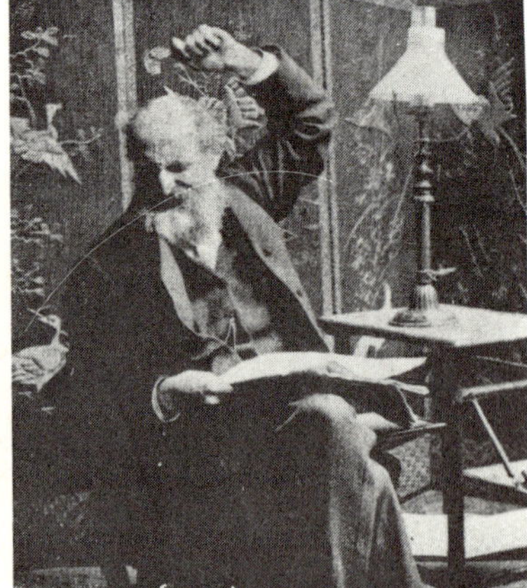

Jolly, I've Won and *Hang It, I've Lost*. Joy and chagrin are registered by the subject, who is possibly the photographer O. G. Rejlander.

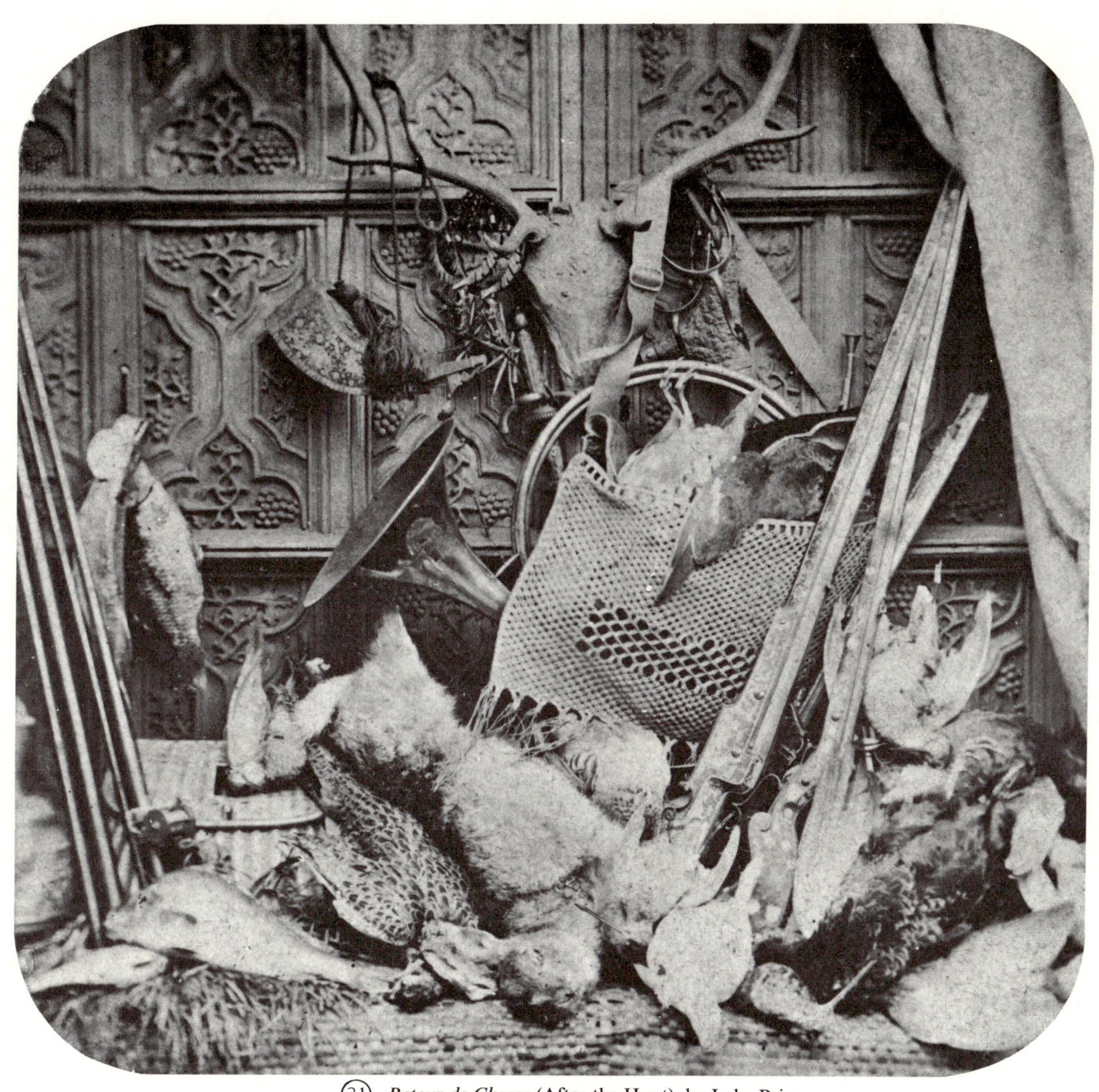

(31) *Retour de Chasse* (After the Hunt), by Lake Price.

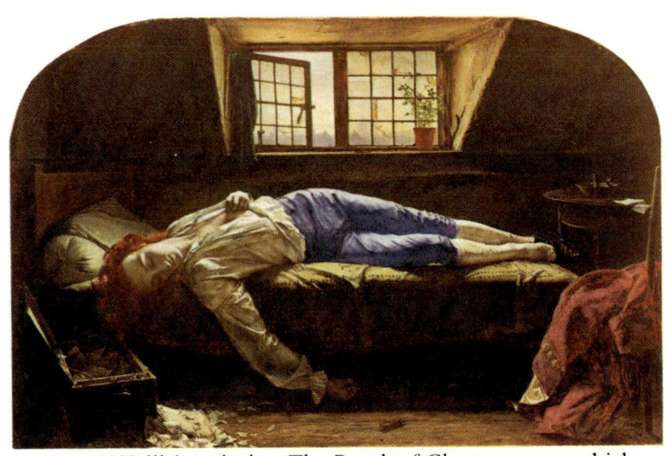

Henry Wallis's painting *The Death of Chatterton*, on which
Robinson modelled his stereoscopic view
using his assistant in the role of the poet.

The inconstancy of taste has sentenced Lake Price and Rejlander to half a century of derision for morbidity, mawkishness and moralizing. What tends to be forgotten is that more often than not the painters who deplored this use of photography when it first appeared were themselves exponents of the same precepts. The threat of artistic redundancy was real.

It was real in a more practical sense, too. The artist had two available sources of income besides easel painting: miniature portraits and engraving. Photography disposed of the former almost overnight, and profoundly influenced the latter. The use of photographs for book illustration took some time to establish itself, but eventually sophisticated printing processes made hand-engraving virtually obsolete. In the meantime the engraver, who had previously relied on artists' drawings, came more to depend on photographs as source material. There was also a large industry in engraved copies of paintings, the only form in which most people knew the old masters; photography offered an alternative to this as well.

What has all this to do with stereoscopy? Around the stereograph of *The Death of Chatterton*, opposite, all these issues cluster. Chatterton, a poet, committed suicide at seventeen. His tragedy provided just the right ingredients for the romantic image-maker, his death becoming the subject for a famous painting by Henry Wallis, described by Ruskin as 'faultless and wonderful'. Wallis's painting was bought by a fellow-artist, Augustus Egg, who sold the engraving rights to a print-seller named Turner. Before Turner had published an engraving of it, however, he found that a Mr Robinson had been at work. As the *Art Journal* reported: 'Mr. Robinson, a photographist of Dublin, having planned a series of illustrations to the life of Chatterton, desired to make this scene its finale, and dressed up his apprentice, and arranged a room as nearly as he could to represent the sad incident as Mr. Wallis had represented it; this photograph he published, but only as a stereoscopic view. Mr. Turner considered this an infringement of his copyright and applied for an injunction . . .' When first reporting the affair, the *Art Journal* believed that Turner's injunction had been refused, and used the occasion to demand legislation to protect the artist from those who profit from his work without giving him his due. But when they later discovered that the decision had gone the other way they added: 'We confess we cannot see what injury could have been sustained by the publisher of the intended print; we believe, on the contrary, the photograph might have been its best advertisement.' The ambivalence of their opinion characterizes the responses at the time to photography, not only in its relation to engraving but also to its subject matter.

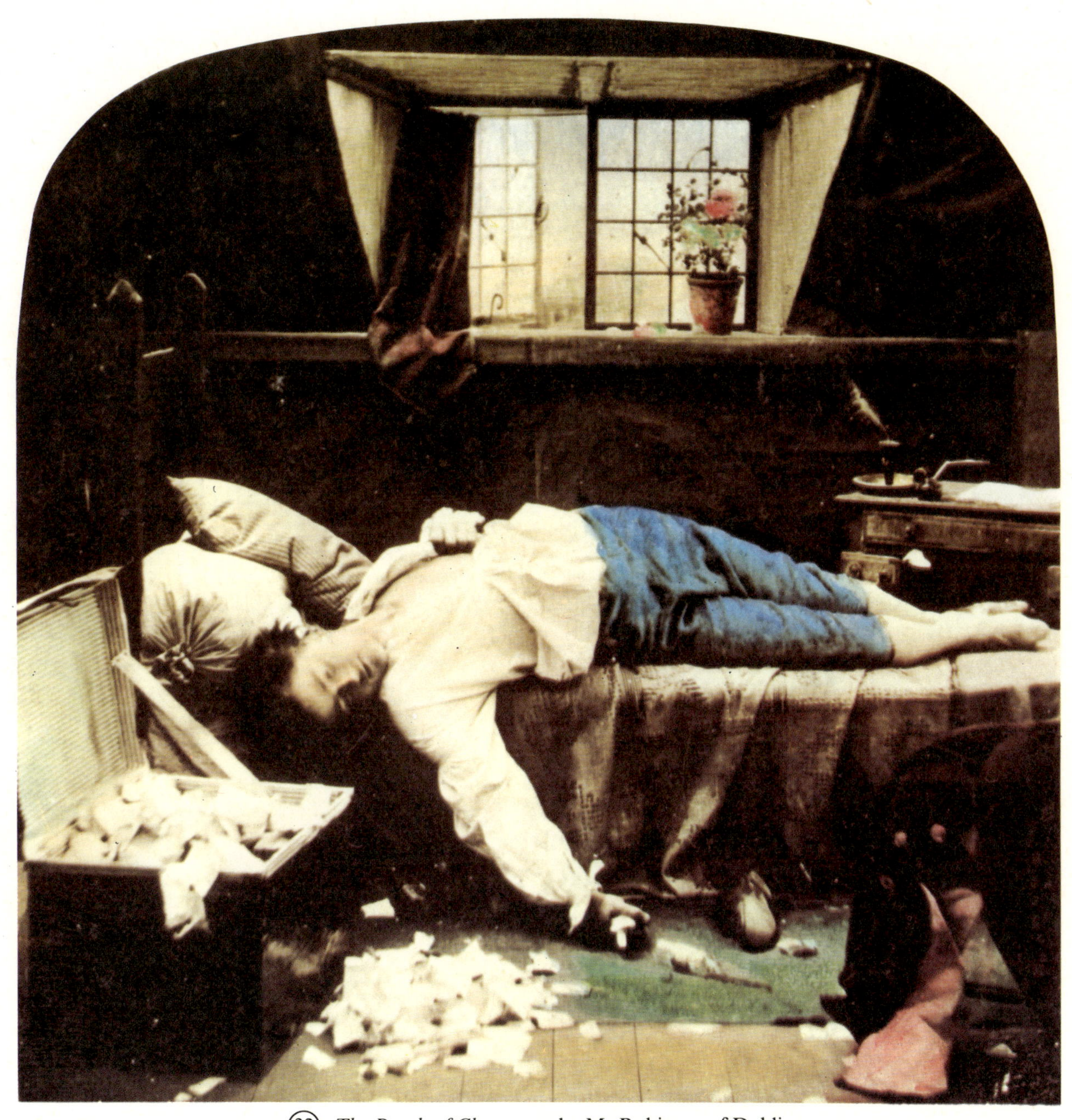 (32) *The Death of Chatterton*, by Mr Robinson of Dublin.

THE RACE COURSE

Anyone who knows the painting *The Derby Day* (1856–58) by William Powell Frith, which was so immensely popular in the nineteenth century, will be reminded of it by Alfred Silvester's stereograph, opposite. Frith's extraordinarily detailed style of painting has been thought to owe a great deal to photography, but he always spoke deprecatingly of painting from photographs. Nevertheless a photograph of the grandstand at Epsom was taken, at Frith's request it is said, and appears to have been used, albeit for a subsidiary part, in the background of the painting. J. B. Priestley, writing about *The Derby Day* in *Victoria's Heyday* (1972), reproduces the painting beside a variant of Silvester's stereograph with a caption claiming that it was 'thought to be used by Frith when painting *The Derby Day*'. It is possible: although the date of the stereograph is not known, it could have been made at the time Frith was painting his picture. Certainly, the elaborately contrived painting is much more like the posed stereograph in feeling than the documentary photograph of the grandstand (by Howlett) in which the crowd is nondescript, dull and anonymous. The real racegoers at Epsom are much less animated than the posed ones: as Priestley comments: '. . . *Derby Day* never suggests to me a real afternoon at Epsom; it is like a huge dream tableau, a giant Still Life, and not our life.' This unreal quality carried over into many 'reconstructions' of reality published by the London Stereoscopic Company.

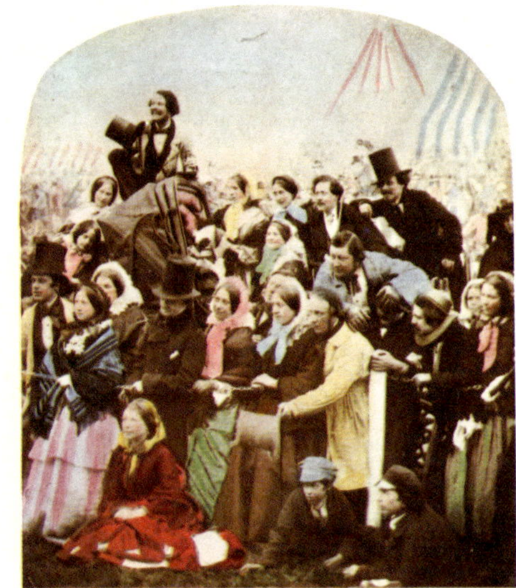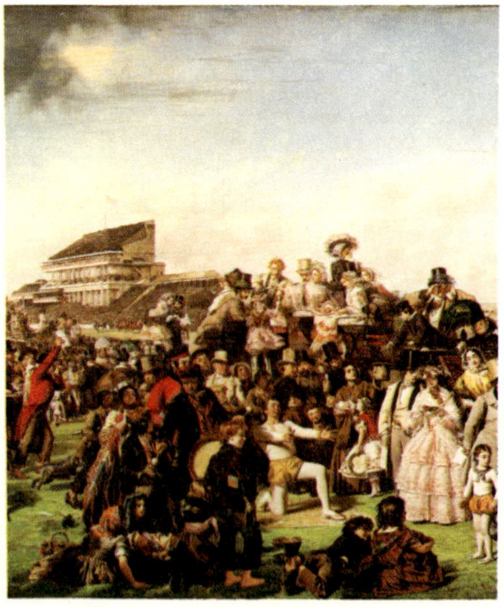

(LEFT) *The Race-Course*, by Alfred Silvester. Hand-coloured card. From 'National Sports',
a series published by the London Stereoscopic Company.
(RIGHT) *Derby Day*. Painting by William Powell Frith.

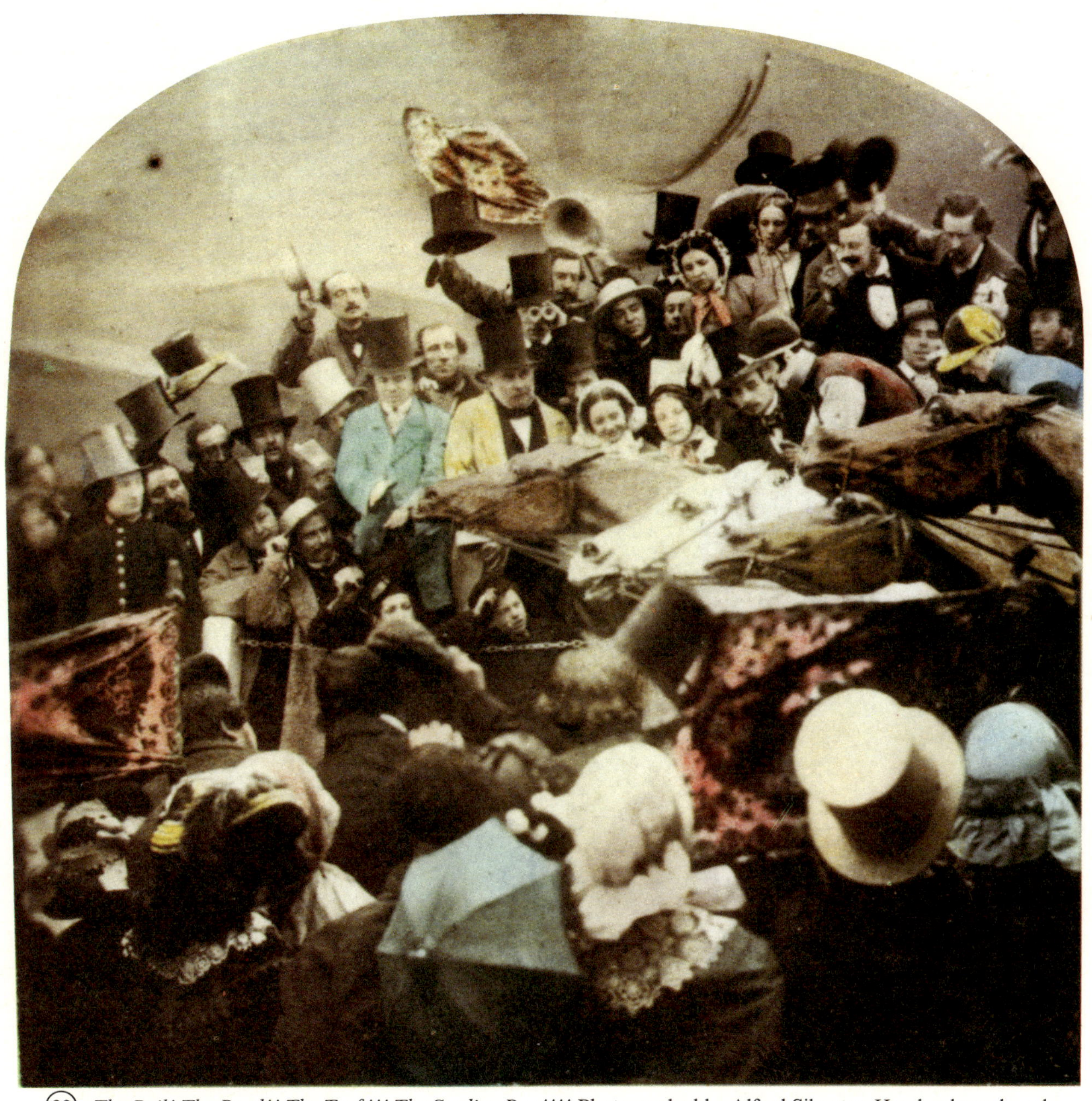

③ *The Rail! The Road!! The Turf!!! The Settling Day!!!!* Photographed by Alfred Silvester. Hand-coloured card.
From 'National Sports', a series published by the London Stereoscopic Company. Cardboard horses and
jockeys stream past a suspiciously over-exultant crowd.

'SENTIMENTALS'

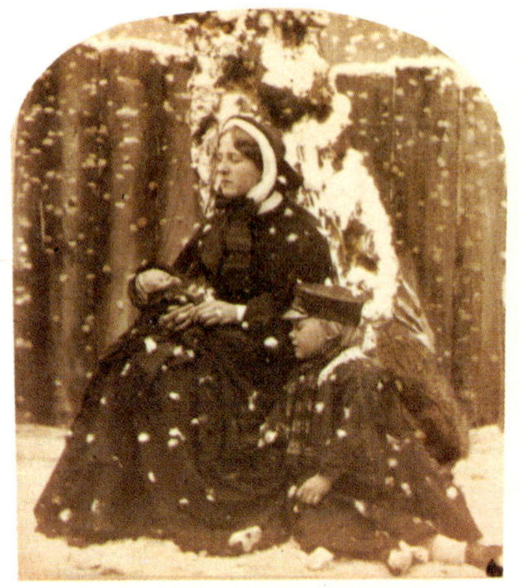 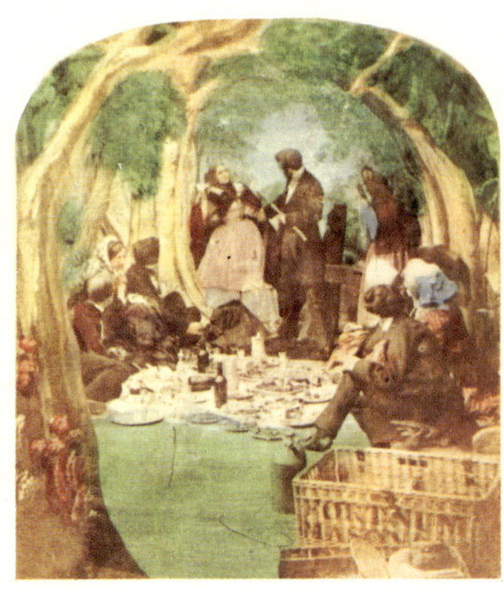

The London Stereoscopic Company produced stereographs sometimes called 'sentimentals', which were related to and sometimes overlapped the 'comic' category. Loaded with emotion, the titles convey the tone: *Broken Vows* – a girl at the church door watches her betrayer's marriage; *In the Bitter Cold* – a homeless widow and orphan in the snow. Another set, just as obviously posed, offers uneventful, bland glimpses of everyday life which, despite their lack of histrionics, never seem quite real.

(LEFT) *In the Bitter Cold*, by Alfred Silvester. Hand-coloured card. Published by the London Stereoscopic Company.
(RIGHT) *The Picnic*, by James Elliot. Hand-coloured card, a variant of the scene opposite. Published by the London Stereoscopic Company.

The Picnic, opposite, is an example. It brings to mind the elaborate studio set-ups of the present-day advertising photographer. From behind a sort-of tree peeps a figure temporarily separated from the in-group. What magic commodity will draw her back into the privileged circle? The answer is probably contained in the Fortnum's basket in the foreground. Such elaborate staging warrants more than one photograph, and several versions of this scene exist. In one, above, a man with what, improbably, may be a flute, has flushed out the eavesdropper. She resists, brandishing a bottle. In contrast, the Victorian laundry view takes us below-stairs where, if these girls are typical of the nineteenth-century laundress, it is clear why she featured so romantically in French realist novels. Like advertisers, the stereoscopic photographers strove to induce Wishful Thought. This, whenever it can, forsakes the drawing room for spicier visions such as that of *Luxury*, shown here.

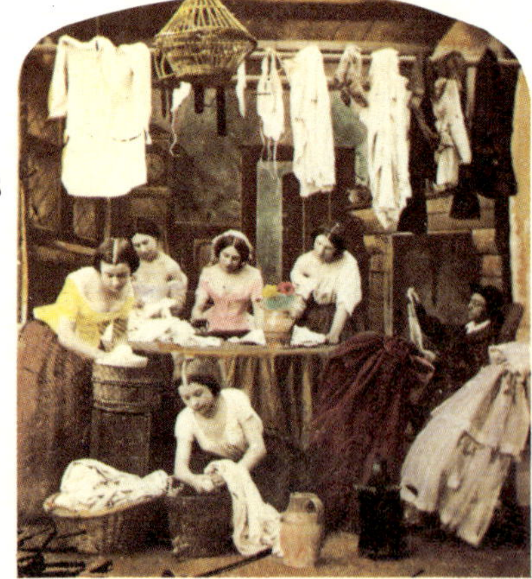 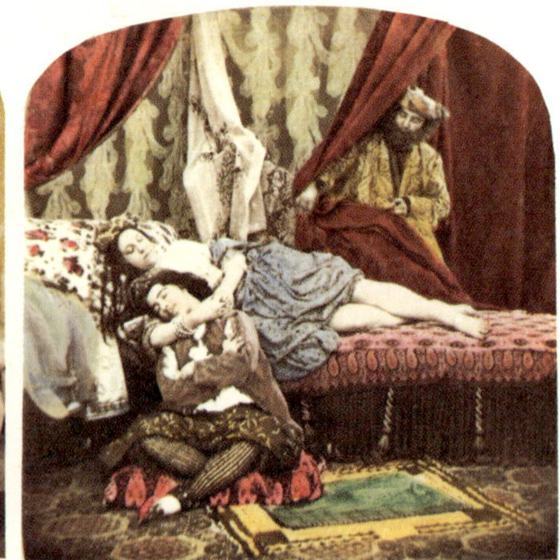

(LEFT) Untitled laundry scene, by James Elliot. Hand-coloured card. Published by the London Stereoscopic Company.
(RIGHT) *Luxury*. Photographer unknown. Hand-coloured card. Published by the London Stereoscopic Company.

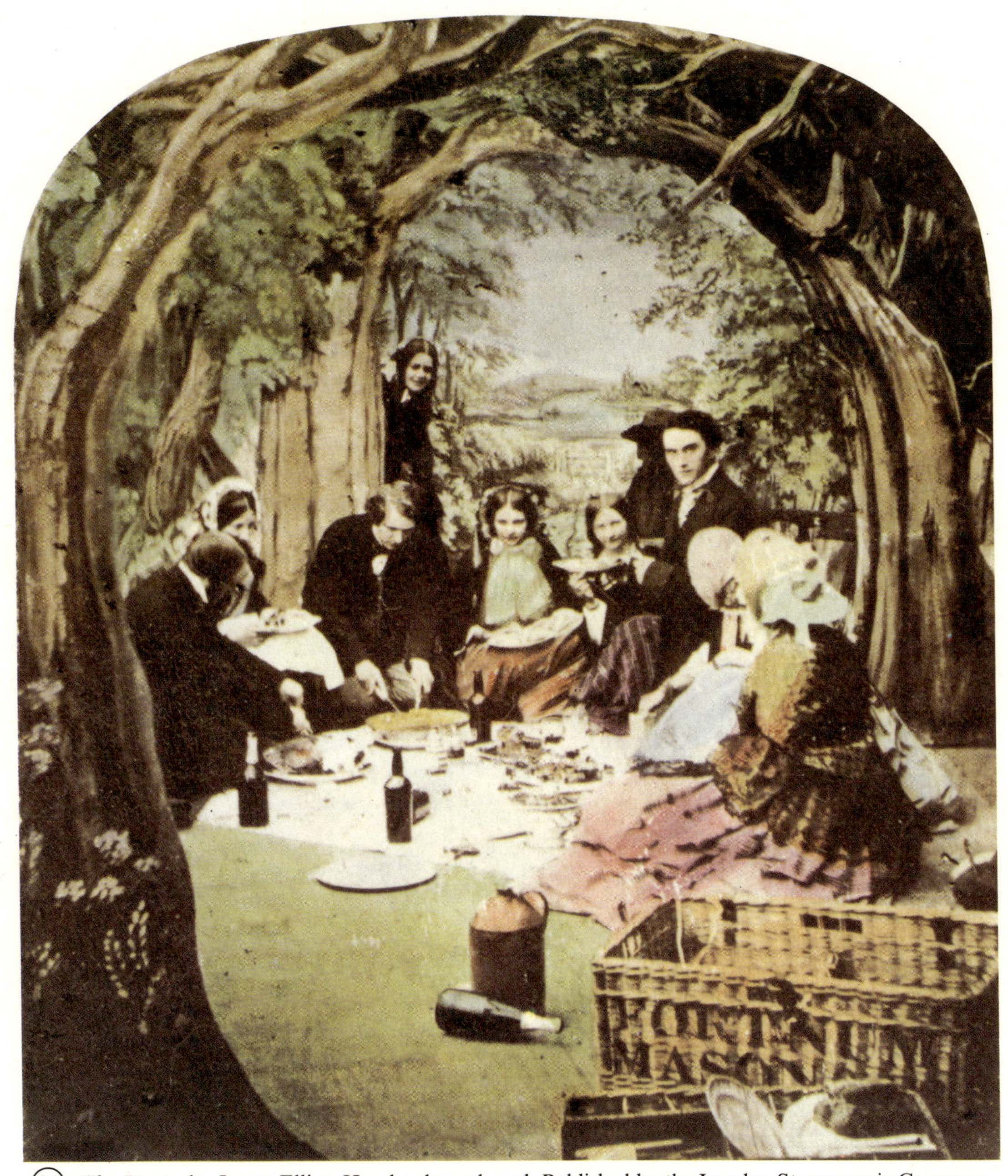

(34) *The Picnic*, by James Elliot. Hand-coloured card. Published by the London Stereoscopic Company.

HAMLET IN STEREOSCOPE

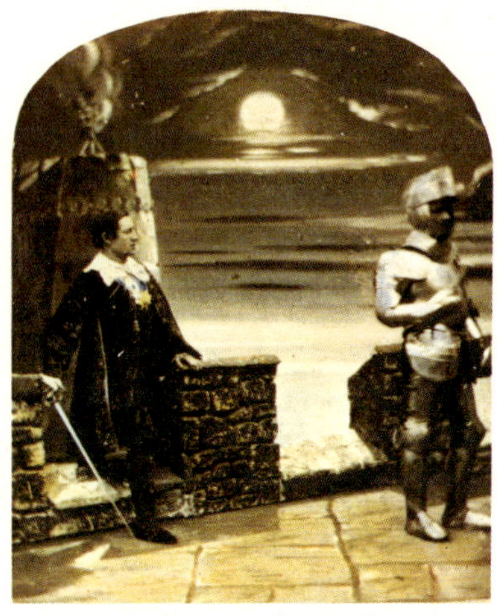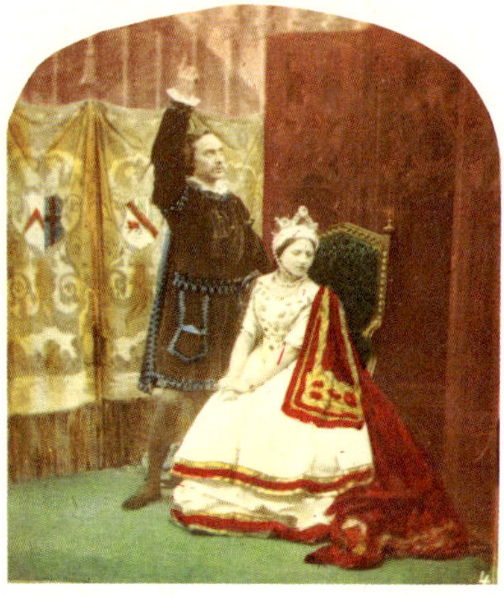

(LEFT) *Hamlet's Father's Ghost*, by Phiz. Hand-coloured card. Published by
the London Stereoscopic Company. (RIGHT) *Hamlet, Act III, Scene 5. 'Confess
yourself to heaven'*, by Phiz. Hand-coloured card. Published by the
London Stereoscopic Company.

Once a photographer had begun to organize his sitters and settings into story-telling groups,
he would become aware of his affinity to the theatre producer. It might occur to him, as it did
in 1856 to someone in the London Stereoscopic Company, that a picture of professional
actors, arranged by a theatre producer in key moments from plays that had rolled them in the
aisles for a couple of centuries, was just what the stereoscope needed. In any event, if photography were to take its cue from art, there were excellent precedents in contemporary
romantic painting, which was life-like but took its themes from dramatic literature.

The first scenes from famous dramas published by the London Stereoscopic Company
were from Shakespeare's *The Winter's Tale*, and they were posed by actors working at the
Princess's Theatre, London under the direction of their leading player, Charles Kean. These
scenes from *Hamlet* are almost certainly by actors from the same company, with Kean himself, his wife Ellen Tree, and perhaps John Ryder, though it is also possible that one of the
Hamlets is Charles Fechter, who played the melancholy Dane at the Princess's in 1861.

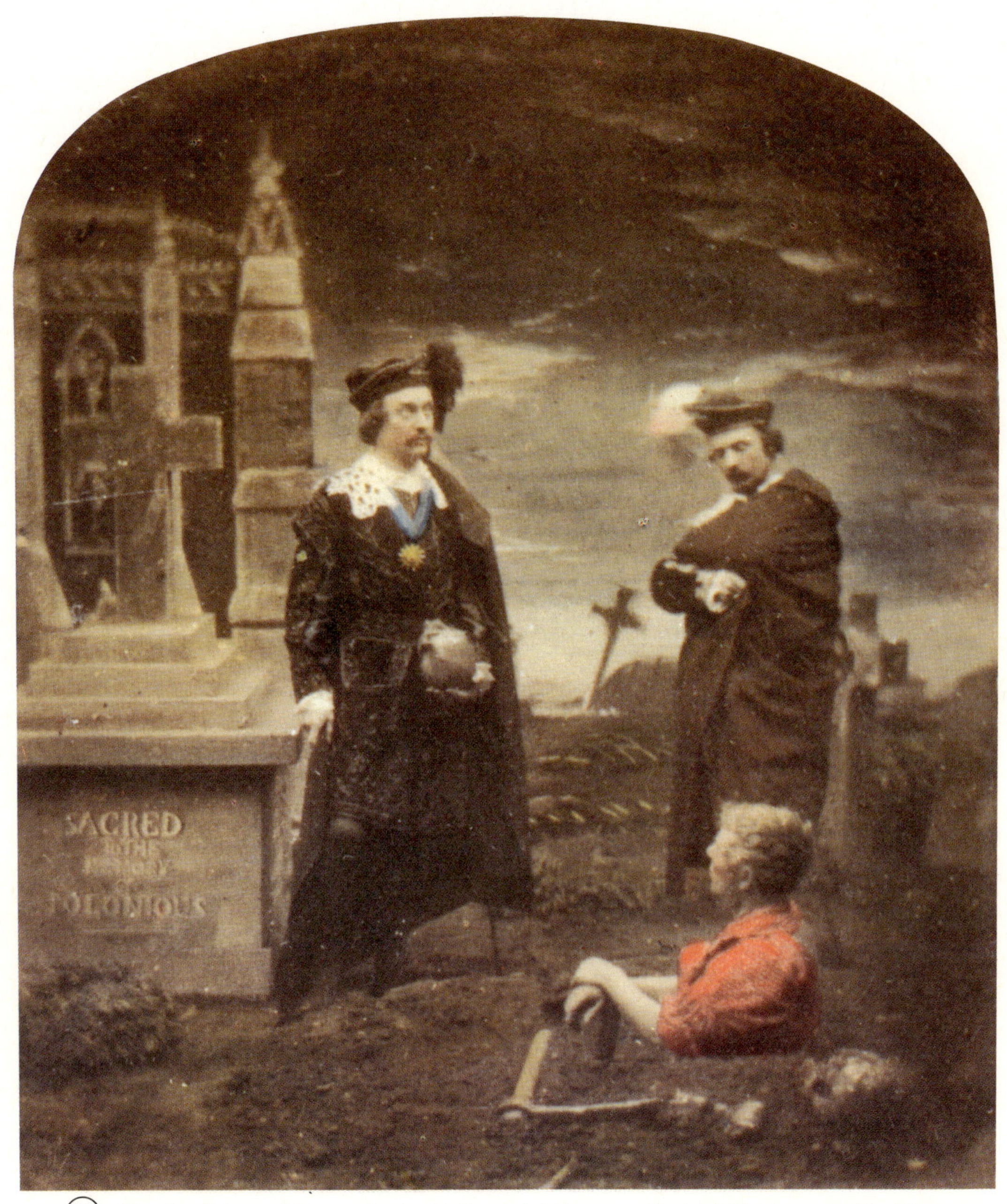

㉟ *Hamlet, Prince of Denmark, Act V, Scene I. 'Alas, poor Yorick!'* Photographed by Phiz.
Hand-coloured card. Published by the London Stereoscopic Company. 1856.

JOKES

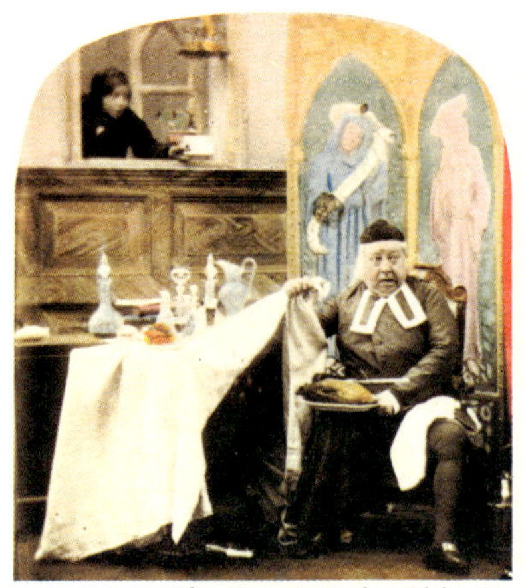 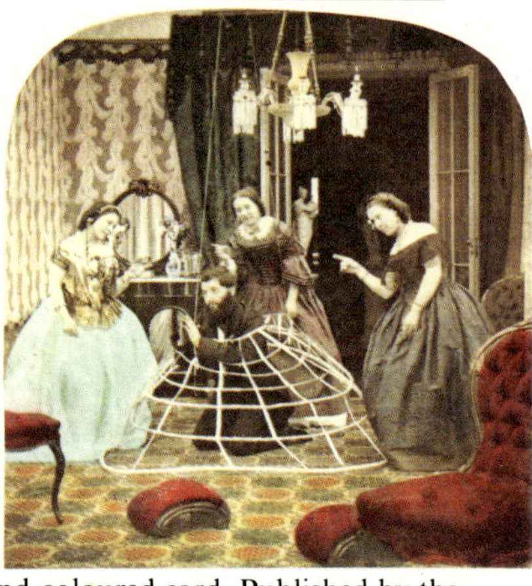

(LEFT) *The Fast Day*, by Phiz. Hand-coloured card. Published by the London Stereoscopic Company. (RIGHT) *The Ladies Revenging the Insults on Crinoline*. Photographer unknown. Hand-coloured card. Published by the London Stereoscopic Company.

Like contemporary picture post-cards, stereographs published by the London Stereoscopic Company covered every kind of subject that the camera could deal with, the comic ones in particular having great popularity. Humour has its fashions, and jokes over a hundred years old can lose their savour; but even when they have become quite incomprehensible, they offer glimpses of the preoccupations and social attitudes of the era in which they first appeared. A mass of material awaits the social anthro-pologist. What with the girl holding the candle, etc., it is tempting for example to read too much into the *Awful Discovery*, opposite, of giant cockroaches in a dark Victorian cupboard. This raw material for the Freudian is by 'Phiz', better known for his illustrations to Dickens.

Two favourite themes of the Victorian humorist can be clearly distinguished: the duplicity or naivety of the clergy, and the ridiculousness of women's clothes. Alfred Silvester and Phiz are both responsible for examples of the former; our example of monkish gluttony is by Phiz. This type of joke is with us less today, perhaps because the authority of the church has receded, whereas the second theme, women's clothes, dies hard. In Victorian times the crinoline was the main target; the problem of getting off a bus, demonstrated here, is typical.

Women fought back in *The Ladies Revenging the Insults on Crinoline*, and in 1897 battle was joined in *The New Woman. – Wash Day*. Bloomers and the bicycle with the cross-bar, seen in the background, deserve to become heraldic signs on the banner of Women's Lib.

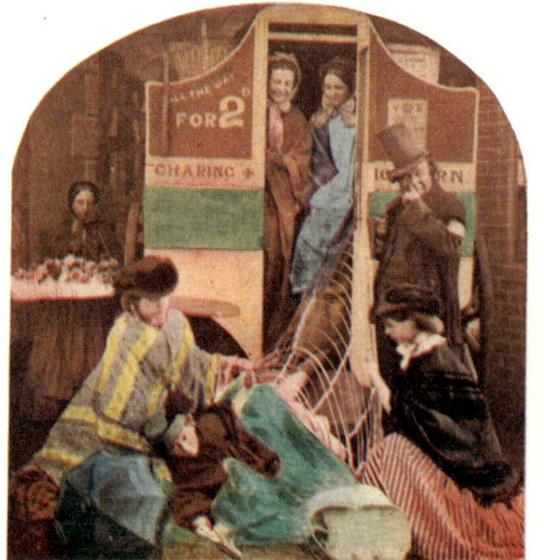 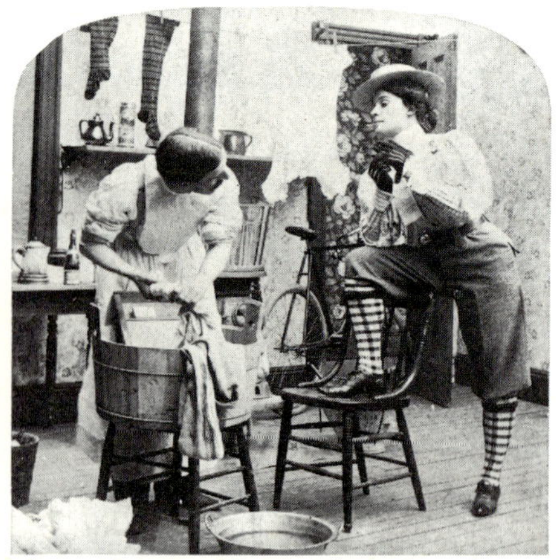

(LEFT) *Crinoline Difficulties*. Photographer unknown. Hand-coloured card. Published by the London Stereoscopic Company. (RIGHT) *The New Woman. – Wash Day*. Photographed and published by Strohmeyer & Wyman.

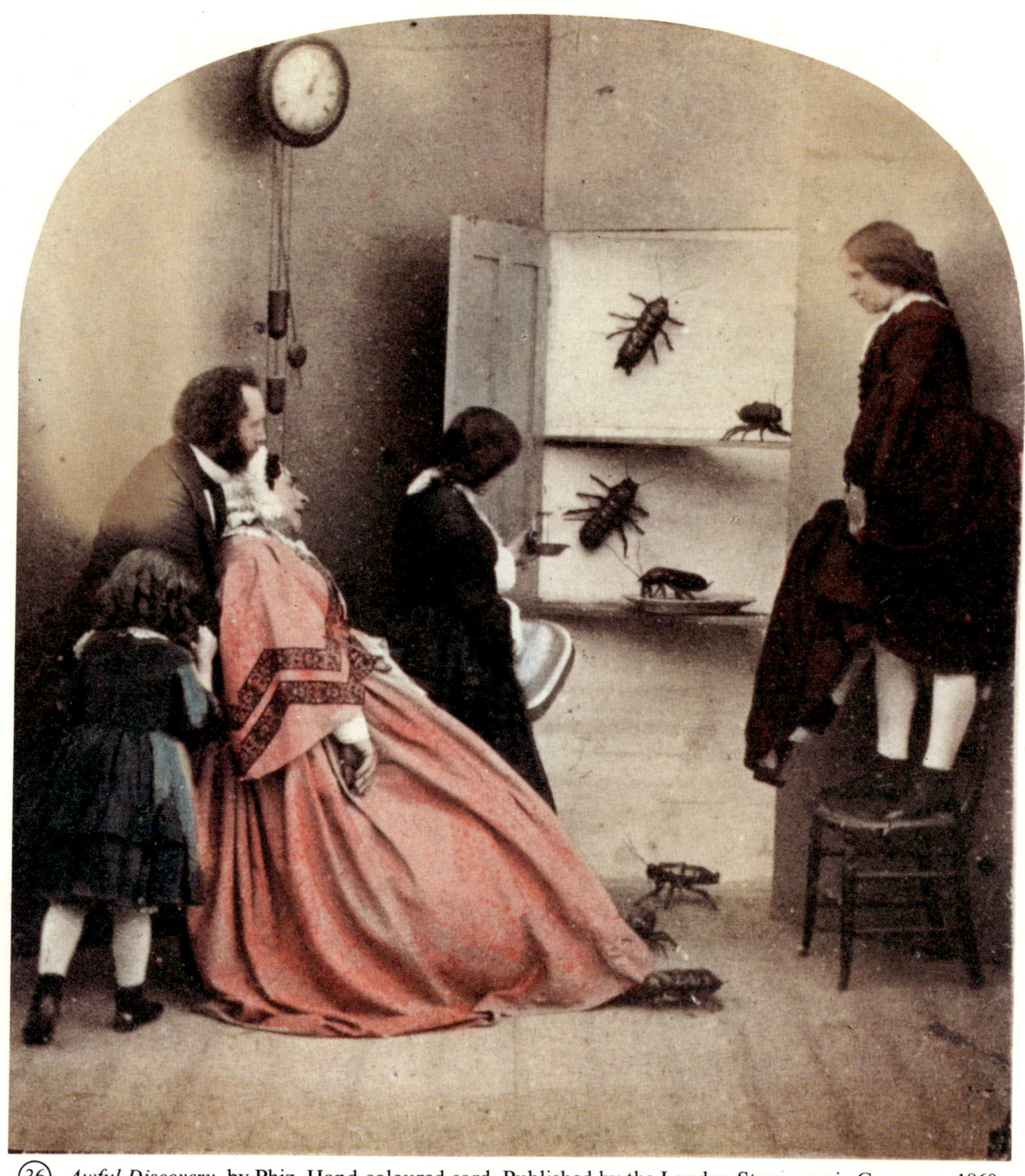

(36) *Awful Discovery*, by Phiz. Hand-coloured card. Published by the London Stereoscopic Company. 1860.

TISSUES

The 'dissolve', a film editing device for moving the action quickly from one place or time to another, in which one shot melts into the next, has a forerunner in nineteenth-century magic-lantern shows. Two or more lanterns were aimed at the same screen in such a way that, as the image projected from one was cut off, it could be replaced by introducing the image from

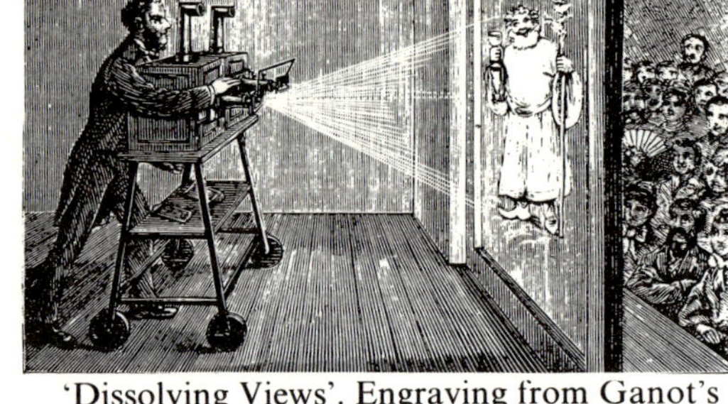
'Dissolving Views'. Engraving from Ganot's *Popular Natural Philosophy* (1887).

another. These 'dissolving views' changed night to day, razed cities and resurrected the dead.

The principle was also applied to engravings: the 'protean view', which was in fact two prints, one concealed behind the other, changed when held against the light, the two prints combining. In dioramas, transparent gauze with dissimilar pictures painted on both sides and lit alternately from the back and the front produced the same kind of metamorphosis.

'Tissues' are stereographs which work on the same principle. Monochrome pictures viewed away from bright light can be flooded with colour by turning the stereoscope to the light. The tissues were photographs printed on thin paper, the backs of which were painted with translucent colours and then covered with another thin layer of paper. To make sharp points of light appear in the picture, to represent candle flames or the glitter of jewels, the tissue was pricked with a pin. The best tissues were produced in France, where they are thought to have been invented in the 1860s. Lavishly decorated interiors like the Galerie des Fêtes in the Hôtel de Ville, Paris, made suitable subjects; our illustration shows one half of the stereograph before, the other after, back lighting.

One series, 'Les Théâtres de Paris', features a model stage on which the actors are extremely life-like dolls grouped in each view to represent a scene from a play. By the same hand ('B.K.') are some curious sets known as *diables*, showing the inhabitants of Hell. For the most part Hell is represented as no more jolly than one has been led to expect: red-eyed, bat-like things with pronged tridents and boiling cauldrons figure prominently (as in *The Valley of the Goblins*, opposite). But some of the cards show a brighter side to damnation: there are feasts and concerts and in one instance the condemned take part in a bicycle race.

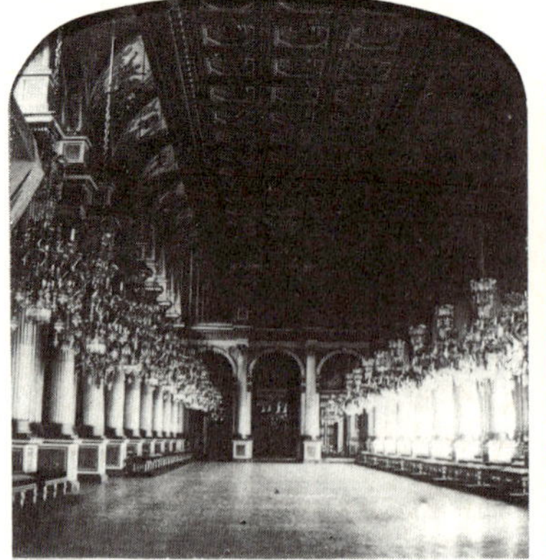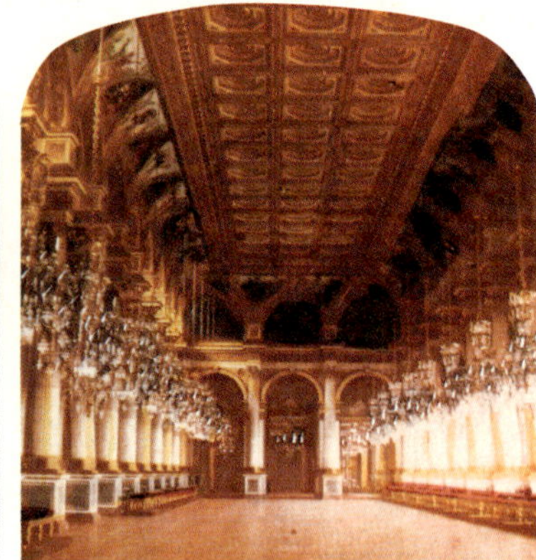
Galerie des Fêtes, Hôtel de Ville. Tissue. Photographed by A. Hautecoeur.

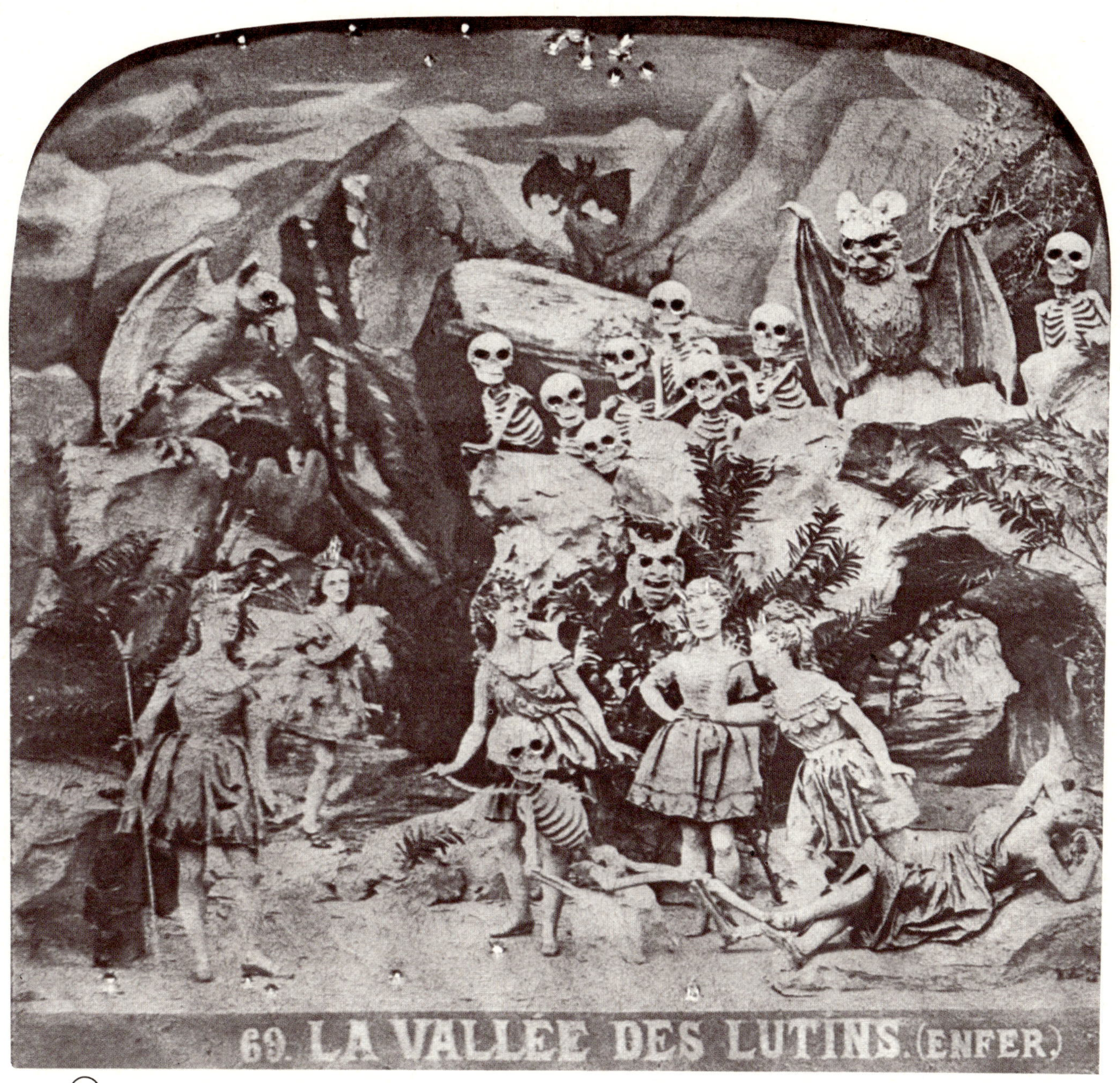

(37) *La Vallée des Lutins, Enfer* (The Valley of the Goblins, Hell). Tissue. Photographer unknown. 'Collection S.L.'

97

COME AWAY DO

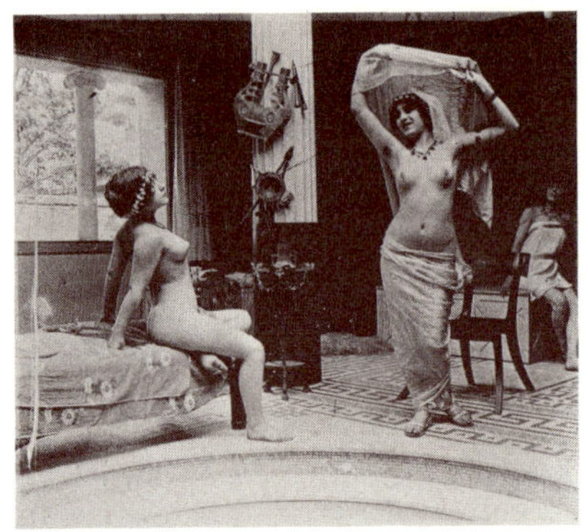

Untitled nude tableau. Glass slide. Photographer unknown. From 'Academie' series. Early 20th century.

Smaller than the Victorian standard card, the glass stereograph on the left measures 6cms × 13cms and fits into a viewer designed to hold a cassette of twenty slides. This is the Stéréoscope Classeur by L. Gaumont & Cie (illustrated on pages 22–23). Untitled and modestly anonymous, the view bears only a small typewritten tag, 'ACADEMIE', identifying it, with others similarly labelled, as part of a set. It is probably a stereo cousin of that ubiquitous family of mail-order nude pictures still euphemistically offered as 'Art Studies'. The illustration opposite, from the same series, is more aggressive: it bears the hand-written title *L'Oeil en Coulisse* (The Glad Eye) and is typical of views found in 'What the Butler Saw' stereo machines on fairgrounds during the early part of this century.

Artists have used photographs for reference since the 1850s. This practice provided the pornographer with a way of rationalizing his publications (and 'in the interests of art' – or science, or religion – is still a legal loophole for obscenity). Many of the early stereo-daguerreotypes were unequivocally bawdy – and refreshing in a period when Salon artists, like pornographers, were presenting their most titillating fantasies under the protection of a po-faced title or 'improving' theme. Baudelaire commented on the hypocrisy of the classical history picture posed for the camera from 'the life': '. . . a thousand hungry eyes were bending over peepholes of the stereoscope, as though they were the attic windows of the infinite. The love of pornography, which is no less deep-rooted in the natural heart of man that the love of himself, was not to let slip so fine an opportunity of self-satisfaction.'*

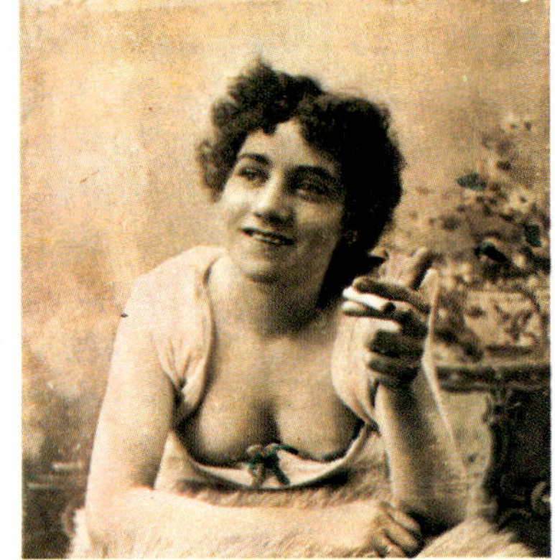

Untitled pin-up girl. Photographer unknown. Hand-coloured card. Published by the Fine-Art Photographers' Publishing Co., London.

Whilst surrounding themselves with erotic imagery, the Victorians habitually frowned on any hint of undisguised lust. The card *Come Away Do* is a late nineteenth-century admission of Victorian double-think, while the great-grandmother of the topless waitress, also portrayed, is a fair sample of the output of a company calling itself the Fine-Art Photographers' Publishing Co. ('varieties sent, by post, to select from').

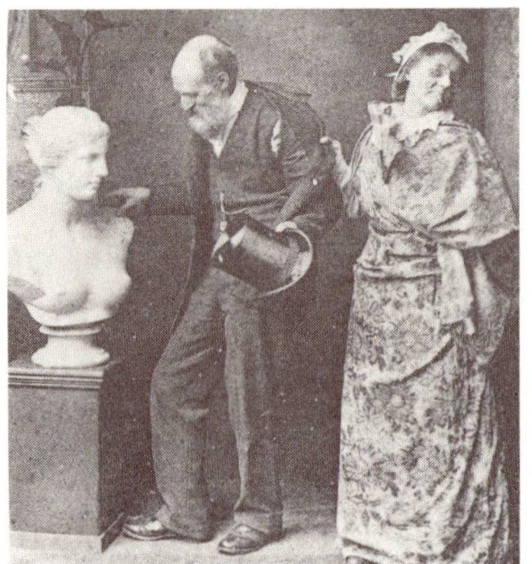

Come Away Do. Photographer unknown, but possibly O. G. Rejlander.

*Baudelaire's review of the Salon of 1859, which included a collection of photographs.

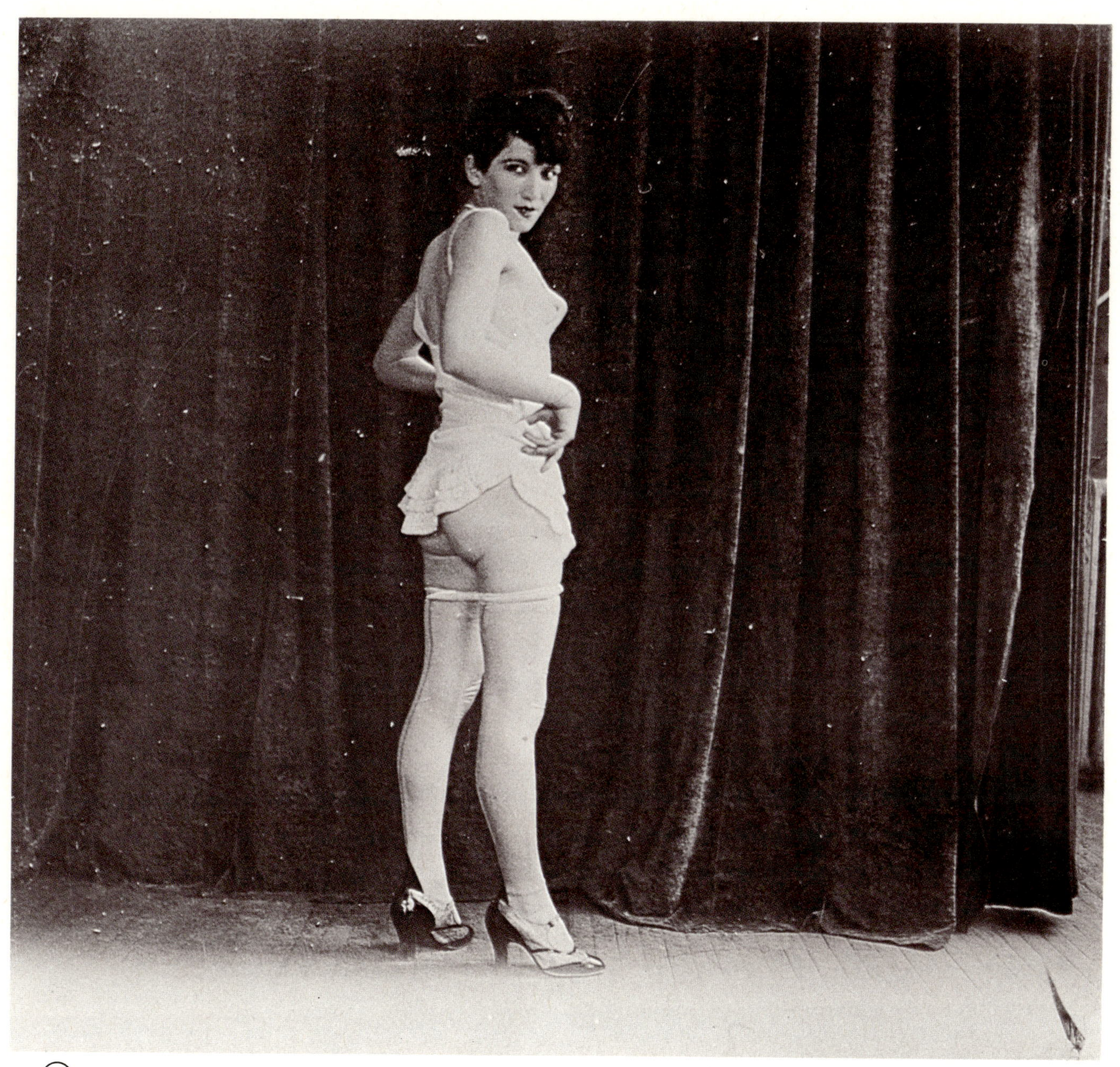

(38) *L'Oeil en Coulisse* (The Glad Eye). Glass slide. Photographer unknown. From 'Academie' series. Early 20th century.

AMERICAN VIEWS BY E. & H. T. ANTHONY

The firm of E. & H. T. Anthony was the principal photographic supply company in America during the second half of the nineteenth century. Daguerreotypists in the United States at first relied on silvered copper plates imported from France, until the Scovill Manufacturing Company found an economic means to produce them. The Anthonys, who supplied other photographic apparatus, got their metal plates from Scovill who began to manufacture cameras and accessories themselves, and eventually created a separate division, Scovill and Adams, solely for photographic items. In 1901 E. & H. T. Anthony combined with Scovill and Adams, forming, in 1907, the famous Ansco Co., which in 1928 joined with Agfa to form the Agfa Ansco Corporation.

The reputation of the Anthonys rests on views from their own negatives, but they also published the work of others, acquiring at one time, in lieu of unpaid debts, the stereographs of the Civil War by the great American photographer Matthew Brady, who had failed to find a market for these moving scenes photographed on the battlefield. The Anthonys had no better success with a public saturated with reminders of war, and the valuable Brady negatives were largely neglected until this century, when their documentary worth was recognized.

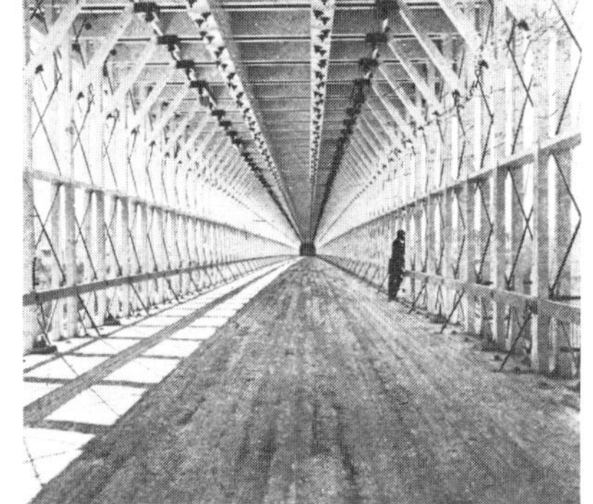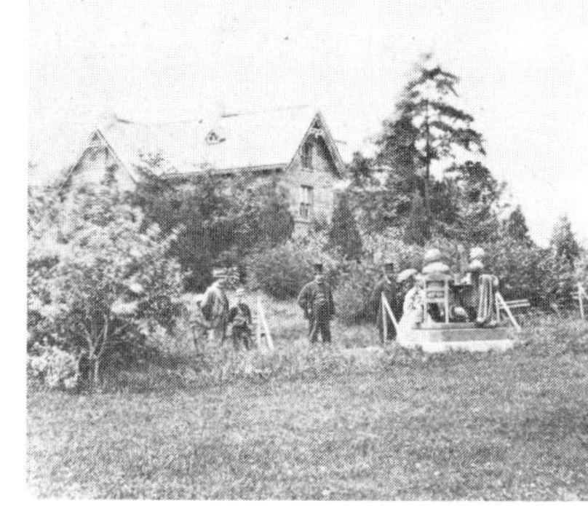

(LEFT) *The Scenery of Niagara*, by E. & H. T. Anthony. A view of the suspension bridge. (RIGHT) *Central Park (New York). The Casino and the Statue of 'Auld Lang Syne'*, by E. & H. T. Anthony.

The Anthony firm specialized in stereo-views of American scenery: their series included the railroads, Niagara, the Catskills, New York, California, the Hudson and many others. The two great themes of the American continent – nature and civilization, the wilderness and man's achievements in his struggle to survive in it – are reflected in these views of the Catskills, opposite, and the Niagara Suspension Bridge. On the one hand is a spectacle of organic profusion, rich and unconfined, and on the other, the severe geometry of the great bridge. Somewhere between the two is the view of New York's Central Park, with its statue of Auld Lang Syne and the Casino, in surroundings just rustic enough to belie its location in the heart of a great modern city.

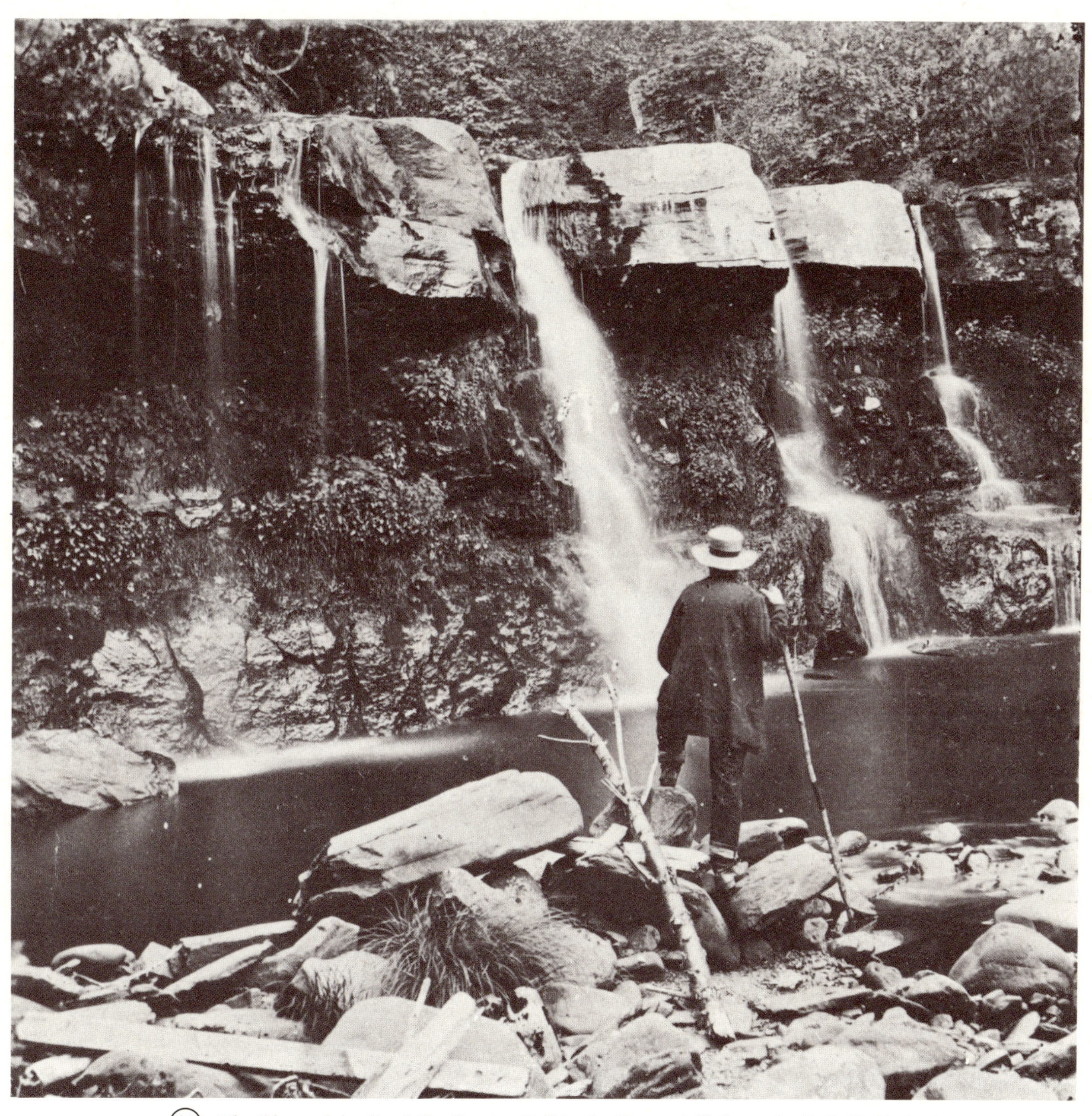

(39) *The Glens of the Catskills. Bastion Fall in the Kauterskill Gorge,* by E. & H. T. Anthony.

THE UNDERWOOD TRAVEL LIBRARY

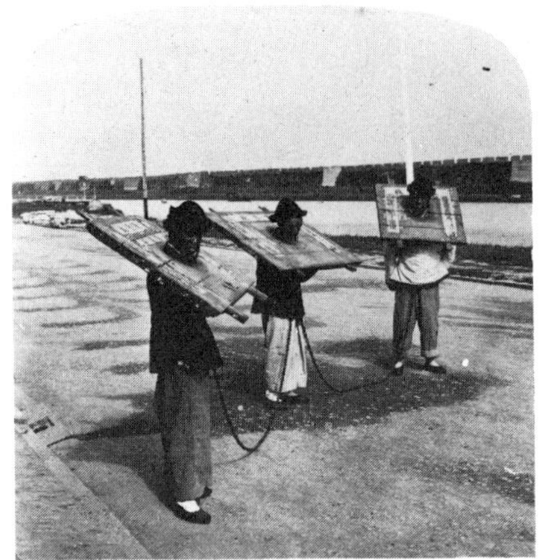

A Chain Gang in China – in the Thoroughfare Wearing 'Cangues' which Record their Crime – Soo-chow. Published by Underwood & Underwood.

An idea that originated with B. W. Kilburn, that of selling stereographs from door to door, was taken up by the Underwood brothers and developed into one of the most successful businesses in the history of stereography. Their salesmen, polite and sober, were trained to conduct themselves with extreme decorum, even to attending church and prayer meetings in the community in which they wished to sell their wares, and to begin their campaign by approaching eminent locals whom the rest of the community was likely to emulate. School and library supervisors were approached next and then every door in every street was systematically visited. At first the Underwoods were distributors of other people's views, but after 1891 they began to publish their own material. What their salesmen had to offer, which could not be obtained except through them, was a selection of views of unprecedented variety. These were packaged in boxes which looked like books, and which contained, in addition to the cards, a real book by an expert on the subject of the set with a map showing the exact position from which the views were taken. Sometimes the reverse of the card carried a short informative essay.

The sets were mostly geographical studies, and featured landscapes and buildings, local people, their industries and pastimes. Some sets were designed for use in schools, with special religious sets (views of the Holy Land) for Sunday schools. It is impossible to give any idea of the richness of these photographs and what their ultimate documentary value will be; already many aspects of the world they record are beyond the reach of the camera. Shown here is a chain gang in China: the men are free to walk the streets but are shackled together and made to wear heavy incapacitating sandwich boards. Any armchair viewer, on the other hand, who wanted to get away from it all might wish to contemplate the *Kyaitteyo Pagoda*, right. The back of the stereograph, opposite, of the musician on the banks of the Jhelum River is packed with information about the buildings in the background, how to hire houseboats and servants, the sitar and how to play it, and general observations on Hindu music. In short, anyone with a library of Underwood sets soon became, as an enthusiastic testimonial to them proclaimed, 'truly a citizen of the world'.

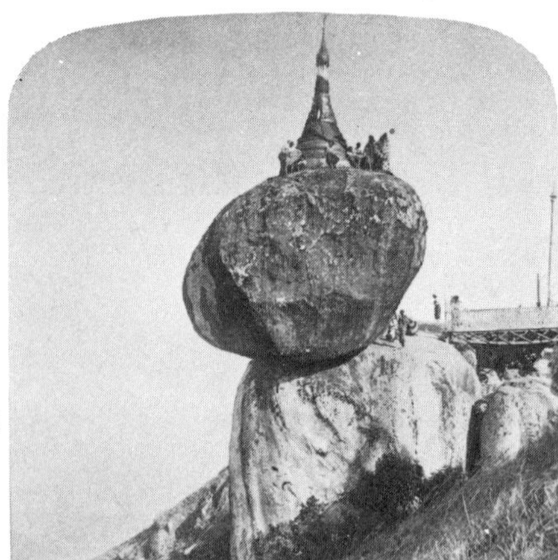

Kyaitteyo Pagoda, Miraculously Balanced by a Hair of Buddha, on Kelasa Hills, Burma. Published by Underwood & Underwood. 1907.

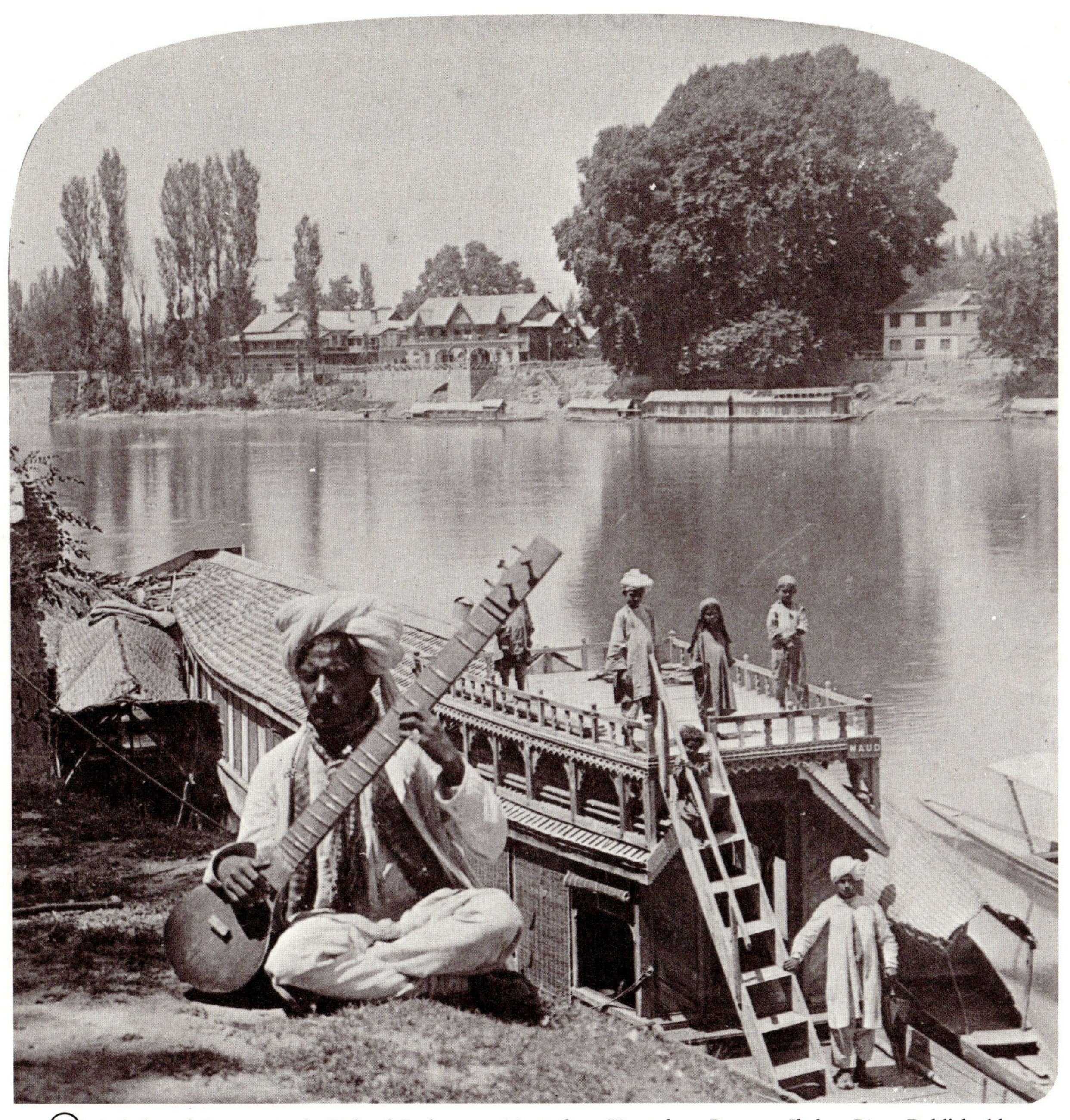

40 *Delights of Summer in the Vale of Cashmere – Music for a House-boat Party on Jhelum River*. Published by
Underwood & Underwood. 1903.

THE STEREOSCOPE IN SCIENCE

Sir David Brewster devotes part of his book (*The Stereoscope*, 1856) to listing ways in which the stereoscope might serve science and the arts. In practice ordinary photographs are adequate for many of the purposes he envisaged, but the clarity which the third dimension adds, though something of a luxury, can be an advantage. Astronomical stereographs are a good example in that, firstly, the relative three-dimensional movement of bodies in space is more easily grasped by the mind if two photographs taken from the same place, but at slightly different times, are viewed in the stereoscope side by side. The three-inch distance between our eyes which allows us to perceive volume on earth is quite inadequate when we look across the vast distances between us and even our nearest neighbours in space; but by waiting a relatively long time between taking the two halves of a stereographic image of, for example, the Moon, the necessary two viewpoints are provided by its changed position relative to the Earth. Using this method stereo-views of the Moon were taken as early as 1864.

In surgery the photograph does not convey the important spatial relationships between parts of the body as clearly as the three-dimensional view. In 1900 the *Edinburgh Stereoscopic Atlas of Anatomy* was issued for medical students: this consisted of five boxes of cards printed with anatomical notes. As our example shows, on each card was a stereo-view of that part of the corpse, dissected and labelled, to which the notes referred.

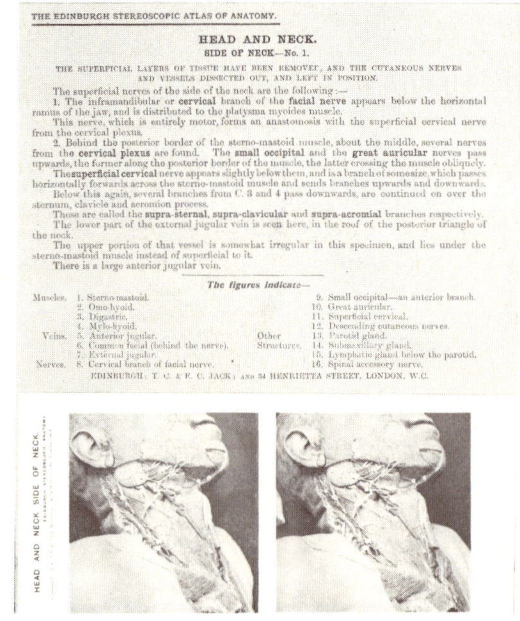

THE EDINBURGH STEREOSCOPIC ATLAS OF ANATOMY.

HEAD AND NECK.
SIDE OF NECK—No. 1.

THE SUPERFICIAL LAYERS OF TISSUE HAVE BEEN REMOVED, AND THE CUTANEOUS NERVES AND VESSELS DISSECTED OUT, AND LEFT IN POSITION.

The superficial nerves of the side of the neck are the following:—

1. The inframandibular or **cervical** branch of the **facial nerve** appears below the horizontal ramus of the jaw, and is distributed to the platysma myoides muscle.

This nerve, which is entirely motor, forms an anastomosis with the superficial cervical nerve from the cervical plexus.

2. Behind the posterior border of the sterno-mastoid muscle, about the middle, several nerves from the **cervical plexus** are found. The **small occipital** and the **great auricular** nerves pass upwards, the former along the posterior border of the muscle, the latter crossing the muscle obliquely.

The **superficial cervical** nerve appears slightly below them, and is a branch of some size, which passes horizontally forwards across the sterno-mastoid muscle and sends branches upwards and downwards.

Below this again, several branches from C. 3 and 4 pass downwards, are continued on over the sternum, clavicle and acromion process.

These are called the **supra-sternal**, **supra-clavicular** and **supra-acromial** branches respectively.

The lower part of the external jugular vein is seen here, in the roof of the posterior triangle of the neck.

The upper portion of that vessel is somewhat irregular in this specimen, and lies under the sterno-mastoid muscle instead of superficial to it.

There is a large anterior jugular vein.

The figures indicate—

Muscles.	1. Sterno-mastoid.		9. Small occipital—an anterior branch.
	2. Omo-hyoid.		10. Great auricular.
	3. Digastric.		11. Superficial cervical.
	4. Mylo-hyoid.		12. Descending cutaneous nerves.
Veins.	5. Anterior jugular.	Other	13. Parotid gland.
	6. Common facial (behind the nerve).	Structures.	14. Submaxillary gland.
	7. External jugular.		15. Lymphatic gland below the parotid.
Nerves.	8. Cervical branch of facial nerve.		16. Spinal accessory nerve.

EDINBURGH: T. C. & E. C. JACK; AND 34 HENRIETTA STREET, LONDON, W.C.

Head and Neck. Side of Neck – No. 1. Card from *The Edinburgh Stereoscopic Atlas of Anatomy,* published in 1900.

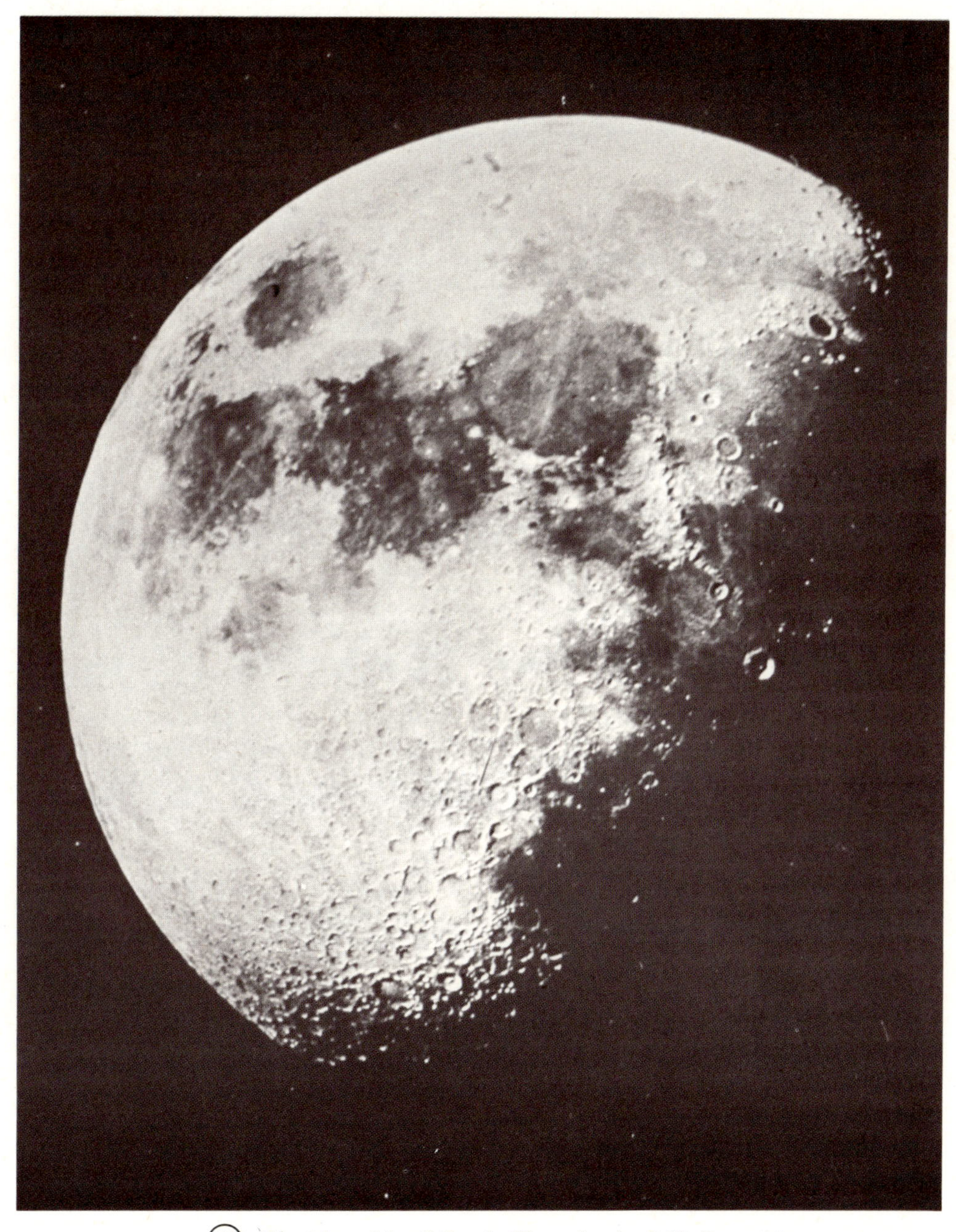

41 *The Moon (Age 9 Days)*. Glass view by J. H. Reynolds.

TYPES AND STEREOTYPES

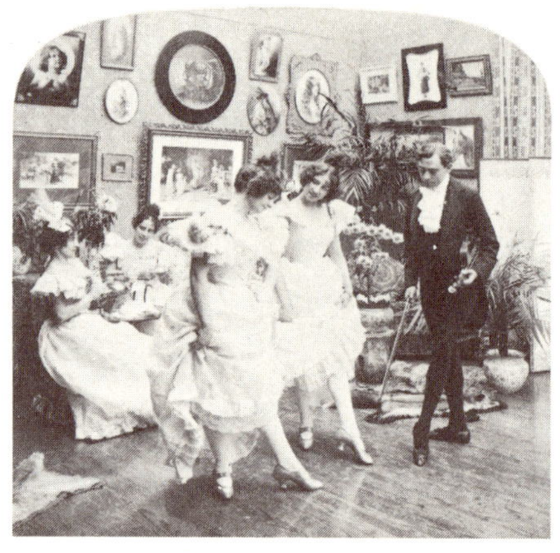 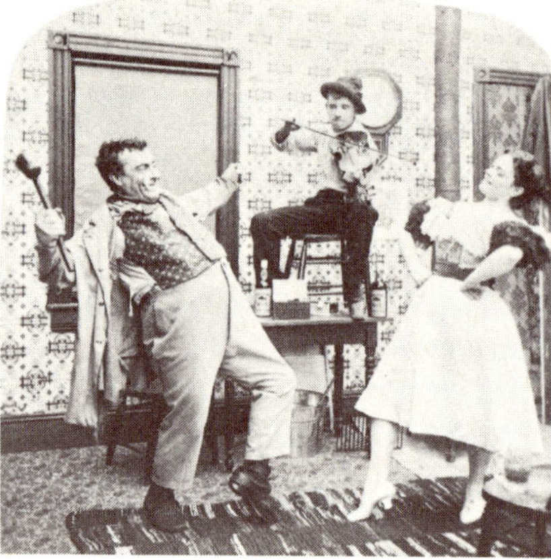

The stereographs taken in America at the turn of the century reflected the need to defuse the menace of alien immigrant groups and to reconcile them to each other by giving them their own 'comic' or 'lovable' characteristics. For example, the Germans have high blood pressure and use exclamation marks a lot, Englishmen are effete and toffee-nosed, etc. Shown here are two examples of type-casting. The French dancing master, for more than a century an alien target, caricatured as effeminate, lascivious and a culture snob, has somehow been resolved into this exquisite young man, the suave darling of refined but slightly saucy girls who long to be *à la mode*. The Irishman clings to the dress and diversions of the Owld Country; he is the life and soul of the wake, and keeps a couple of drops of the hard stuff within easy reach.

(LEFT) *The French Dancing Master*. Photographed and published by Strohmeyer & Wyman, 'sold on' by Underwood & Underwood. 1897. (RIGHT) *The Tipperary Jig*. Photographed and published by Strohmeyer & Wyman.

The Negro has had to wear his stage attributes longer than most: the watermelon and baked-possum image crops up in stereo-views too often for present sensibilities; but among all the 'Rastus' views are some that look unpatronisingly at the Negro condition. *Way Down South in Fields of Cotton* is not sentimentalized, nor is the picture of the Negro family at table in the poverty of their shack. Only the latter's caption strikes an awkward note: 'De breed am small but de flabor am delicious'. J. N. Wilson's plantation scene, opposite, is earlier than the other pictures but seems free of racial emphasis: though it looks like a stage-set, the barn is real.

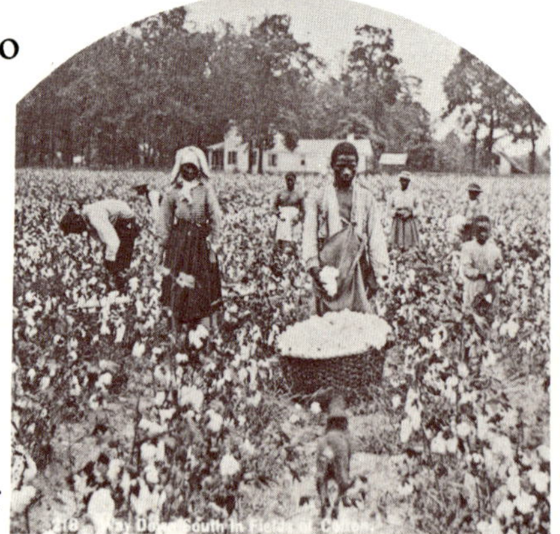 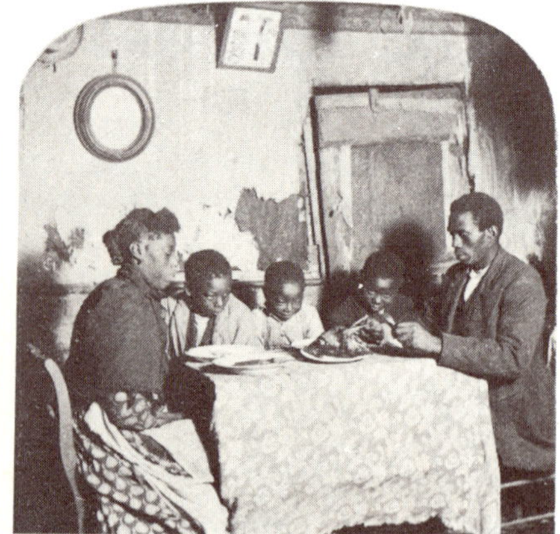

(LEFT) *Way Down South in Fields of Cotton*. Published by the Universal Stereoscopic View Co., New York. (RIGHT) *'De Breed Am Small, But De Flabor Am Delicious.'* Photographed and published by Strohmeyer & Wyman.

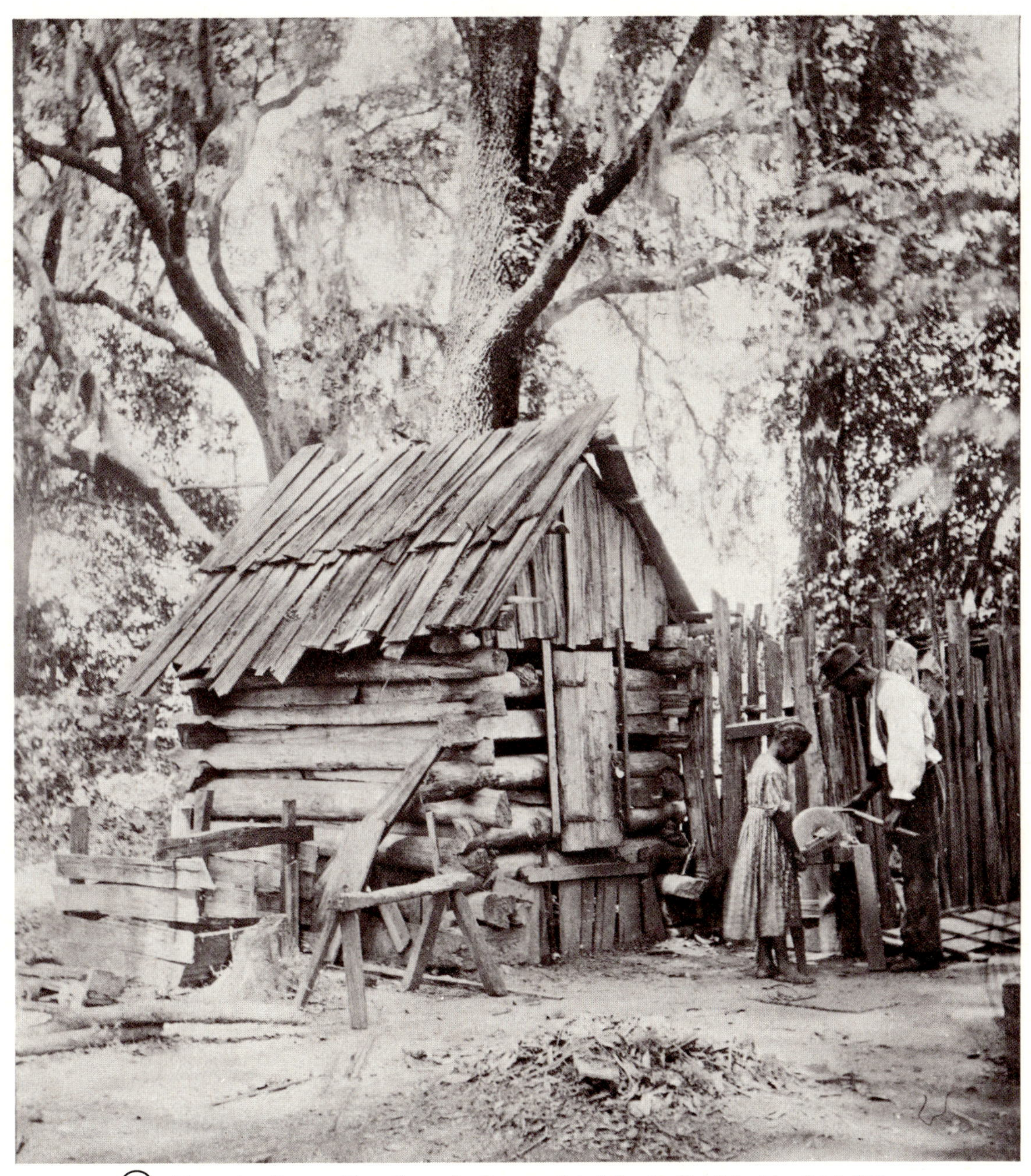

(42) *Plantation Scene: They Go to the Barn to Grind the Ax*. Published by J. N. Wilson, Savannah, Georgia. 1868–78.

ANIMAL LOVERS

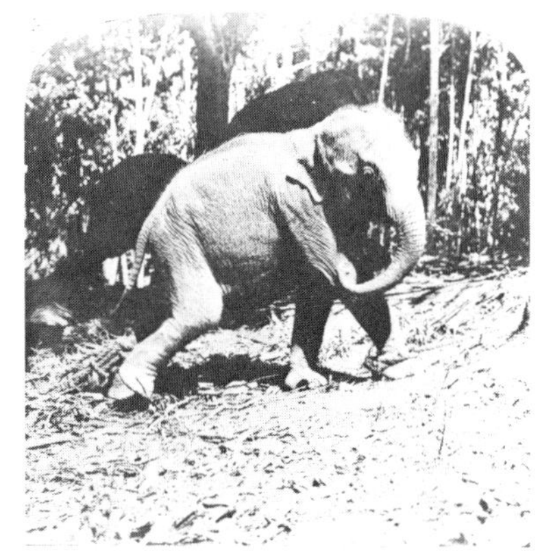

A Tethered Captive in a Frenzy of Rage, Ridgeway Kraal, 1902, Ceylon. Photographed by James Ricalton. Published by Underwood & Underwood.

A significant step forward in photography came with the invention of spools of film. In the 1850s cameras were made which carried magazines of plates; then in 1854 A. J. Melhuish and J. B. Spencer patented a holder from which could be unwound a roll of sensitized waxed paper. As each picture was taken the paper was marked and had to be cut, when the camera was unloaded, to separate the prints.

In 1855–56 Frank Haes used this invention when photographing animals at the London Zoo. Haes found the business of preparing and changing plates complicated enough without also having to keep an eye on the animals, and he later described the 'troubles and difficulties' the project had presented. 'They arose,' reported the *Art Journal*, 'from the natural restlessness of the sitters, who were, in nearly all cases, indisposed to co-operate with the artist.'

Hooker's Sea Bear, opposite, seems unnaturally co-operative, which may also have presented 'troubles and difficulties'. But such problems are not to be compared with those of James Ricalton, travelling in Ceylon for Underwood & Underwood, who made the picture, above left, of the half-grown elephant, recently captured. In Ricalton's words, 'He is ready to demolish everything approaching him; his eyes are bulging and bloodshot with frenzied rage. . . . His friendship for man has yet to be developed, and will require about a year.'

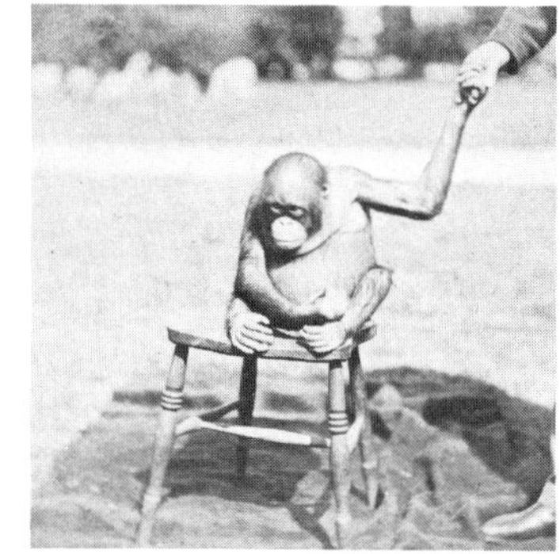

The Orang Utang (*Simia Satyrus*). Photographed by Frank Haes.

Back at the Zoo, while the friendship of Hooker's Sea Bear seems well advanced, that of the Orang Utang, above right, has reached the hand-holding stage.

The preference among Victorian painters, notably Landseer, for endowing animal subjects with 'human' characteristics is not very apparent in photographs, probably because of the animals' reluctance to be posed. With fast film the Edwardians made up for lost time and the cute-ification of the animal kingdom was soon well on its way to the vulgarity of Disney's unconstrained zöophily. Instead of illustrating such kinky sentimentality (cows in skirts, dogs with aprons), here is an unusual example of a human in an animal role – *My Gee-Gee.*

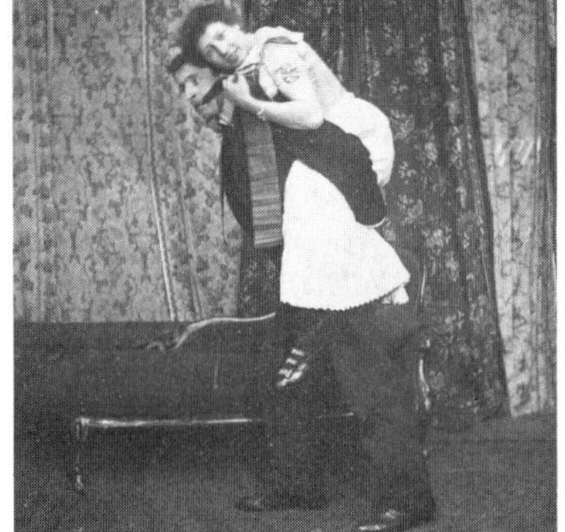

My Gee Gee. Photographer unknown.

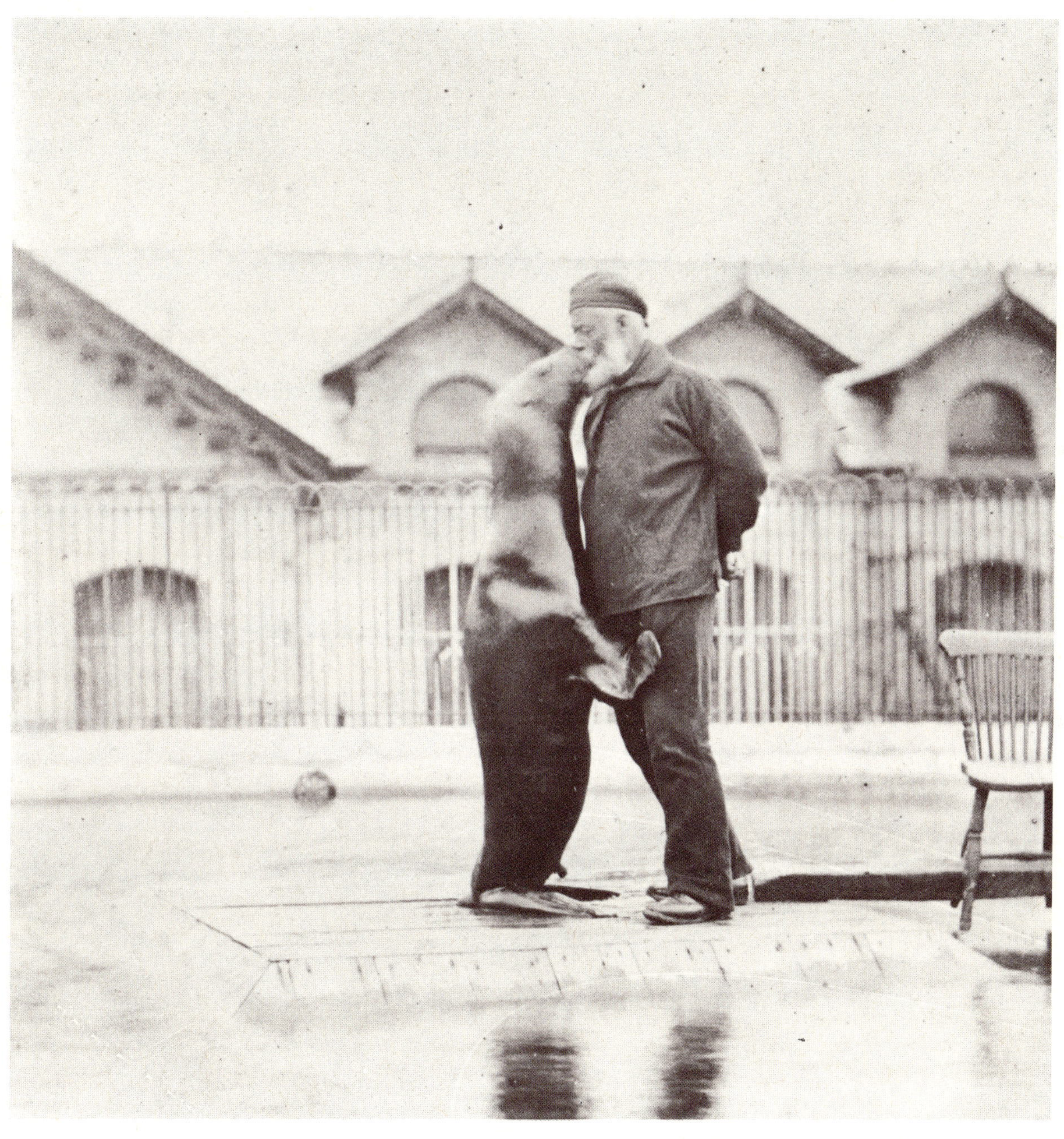

(43) *Hooker's Sea Bear* (*Otaria Hookeri*). Photographed by Frank Haes. Published by Frank Haes & Co. under the auspices of the Council of the Zoological Society of London.

IMAGES OF WAR

A valiant soldier goes off to war in one of the earliest story-telling sets of the London Stereo-scopic Company; he is wounded (in his wife's dream) but returns covered with glory. Forty years later an Underwood set tells the same story, of duty done and a happy end. In both cases the camera never visits the battlefield. In the interim, in fact since the Crimean War (1853–56), photographers had been present at most wars and had tried to fill in the gaps in those discreet tales of valour with images of war's obscene actualities. It is pointless to list the wars and the photographers; the record they brought back was the same one of folly and horror, perhaps because, apart from boredom and discomfort, there is little else in a war to photograph.

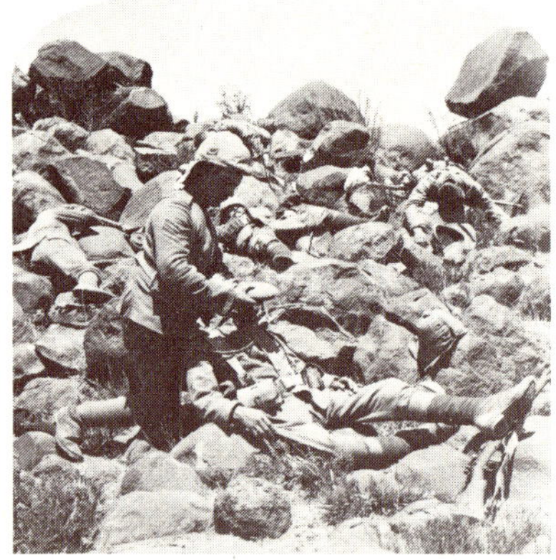

The Last Drop – a Scene on the Battlefield at Dordrecht, South Africa, Dec 30th. Published by Underwood & Underwood. 1900.

The account of the beheading of a condemned Chinese (see plate, opposite) is by James Ricalton. 'Only a few of us had learned the hour of execution and were present, among us an American doctor, who, when this grave was being dug, and the two poor fellows stood nearby, held the hand of one, feeling his pulse. Some one queried, "Normal, Doctor?" "One hundred and twenty-six," replied the physician; and yet the doomed man showed outwardly no mental disturbance. Another, speaking his own language, asked him if he was a Boxer, to which he replied meekly and with mysterious resignation, "I am no Boxer; all the village people hereabouts know me."'

The interrogation and the execution prefigure similar recent events in Vietnam, which were also photographed, and which at the time raised the question of the morality of the photographer's passive role. The question needs to be discussed, it is true, but hardly before one has discussed the role of the principal participants. To direct criticism at the photographer is an evasive device and recalls the primitive habit of killing the messenger who brought news that nobody wanted to hear. Other bringers of bad tidings attended the Boer War and World War I (above and right).

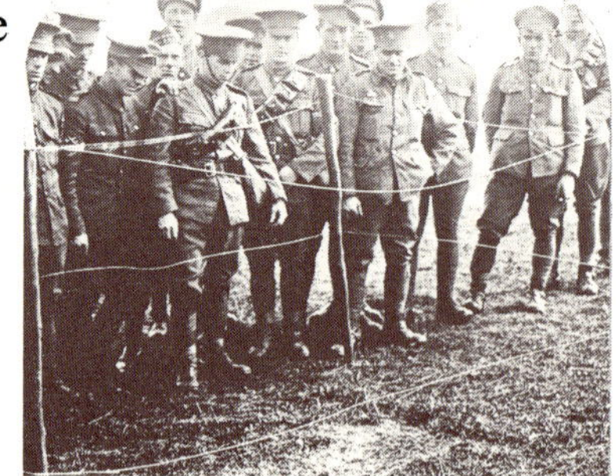

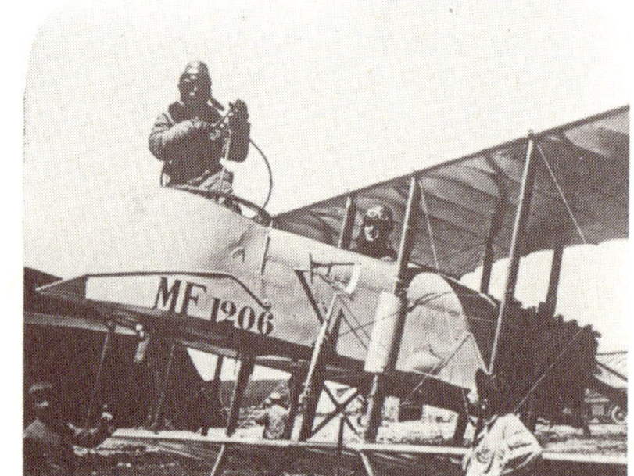

(LEFT) *Impression Made in the Ground by Commander Falling from Burning Zeppelin at Billericay*. World War I scene, published by Realistic Travels. (RIGHT) *About to Start on a Bombing Expedition*. 'War of the Nations' series, published by Underwood & Underwood.

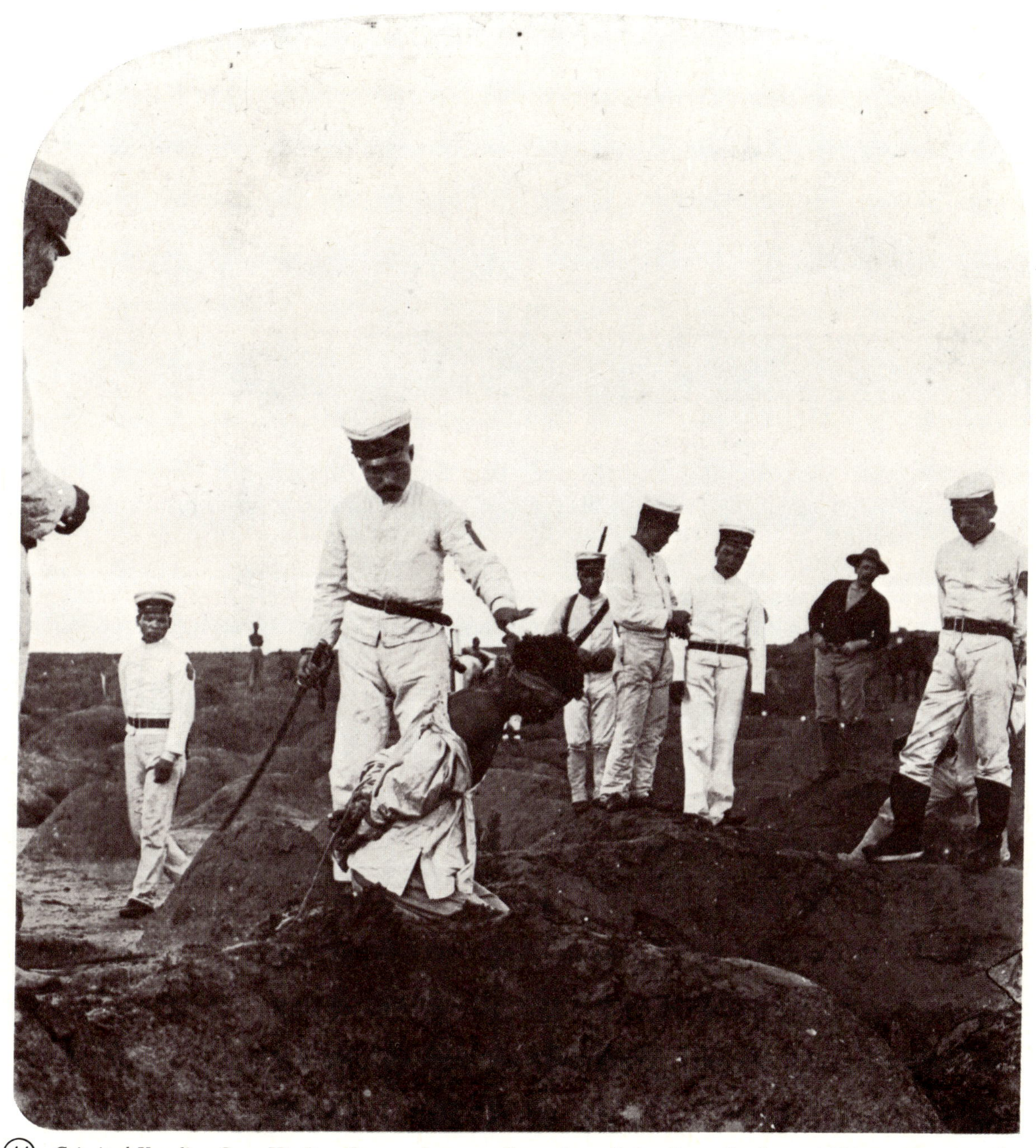

44 *Criminal Kneeling Over His Own Grave – Japanese Executioner Beheading a Condemned Chinese, Tientsin, China.*
Photographed by James Ricalton. Published by Underwood & Underwood. 1904.

TURN OF THE CENTURY

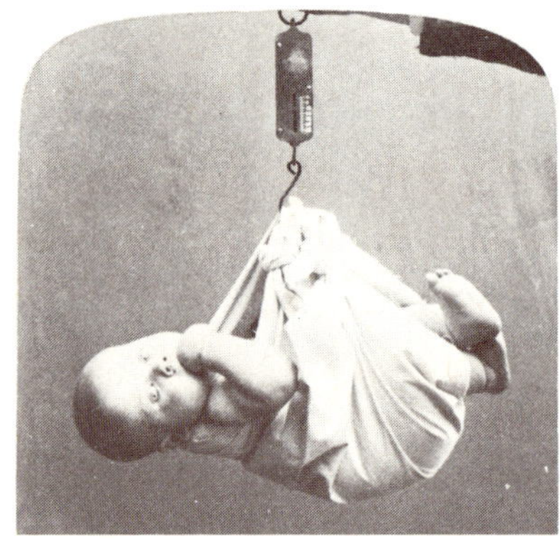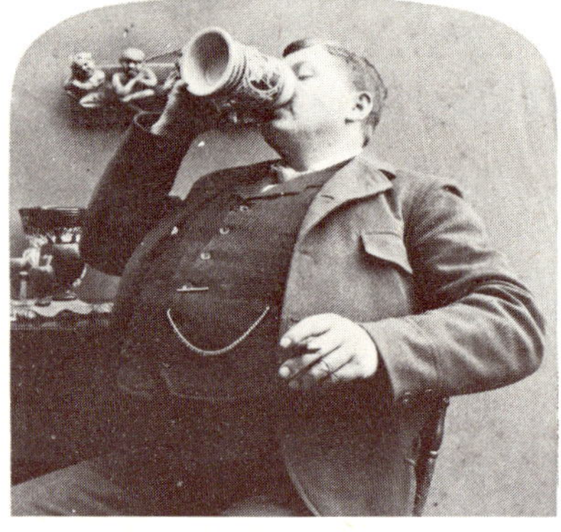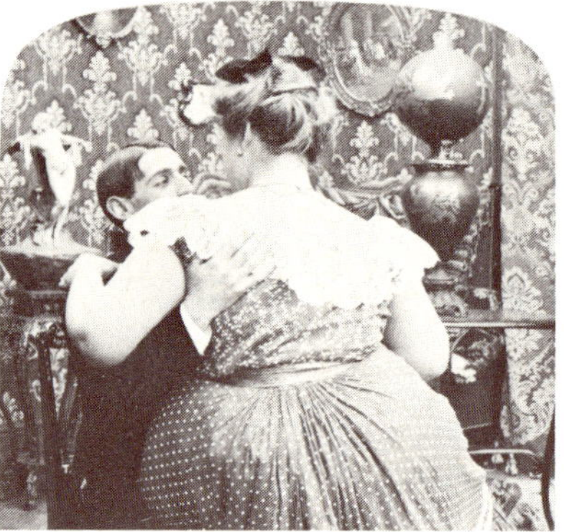

Some Are Born Great . . . Some Achieve Greatness . . . And Some Have Greatness Thrust Upon Them. Sequence of three cards published by Underwood & Underwood. 1901.

The educational policy of the Underwoods and their competitors did not prevent them from keeping alive the stereographic tradition of 'comics', 'sentimentals' and exhibition studies. The stereograph from the Chicago World's Fair, opposite, records the masterpiece of some unsung Claes Oldenburg of the 1890s.

The comic *Greatness* sequence is an Underwood product of 1901. In *You Must Send Her Away Immediately* (1905) the theatrical story-telling tradition is continued. This card is No. 8 of a twelve-part series in which the French cook, 'Dimples', kisses Mr Honeysuckle, the master, but leaves tell-tale hand-prints of flour on the back of his coat; Mrs Honeysuckle sees them, Dimples is replaced by a hag, and the Honeysuckles are reconciled.

In turn-of-the-century 'sentimentals', courting couples were continually disturbed, as ever, by angry parents and small brothers. Eventually, however, the all-important question was asked, and the heaven-directed glance as seen in *Love's Answer* (1900) remained obligatory in sentimental postcards for the next four decades.

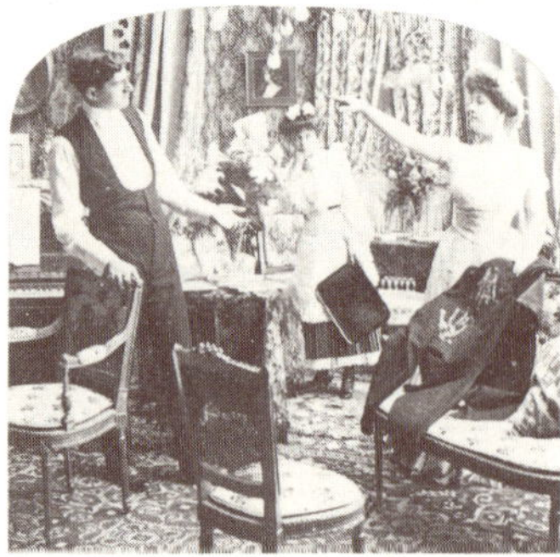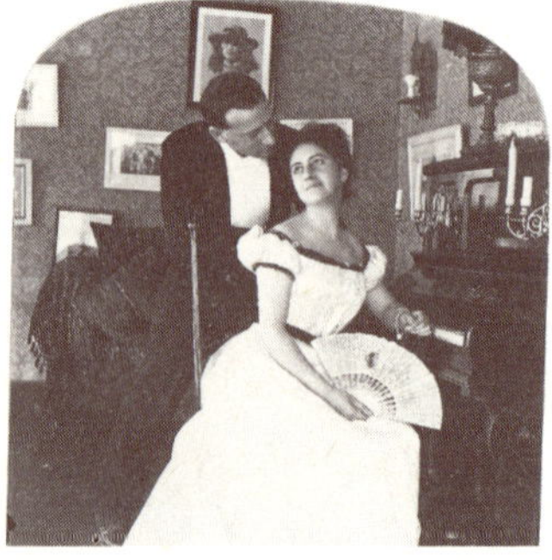

(LEFT) '*You Must Send Her Away Immediately.*' Photographed and published by B. W. Kilburn. 1905.
(RIGHT) *Love's Answer*. Photographed by B. L. Singley. Published by the Keystone View Company. 1900.

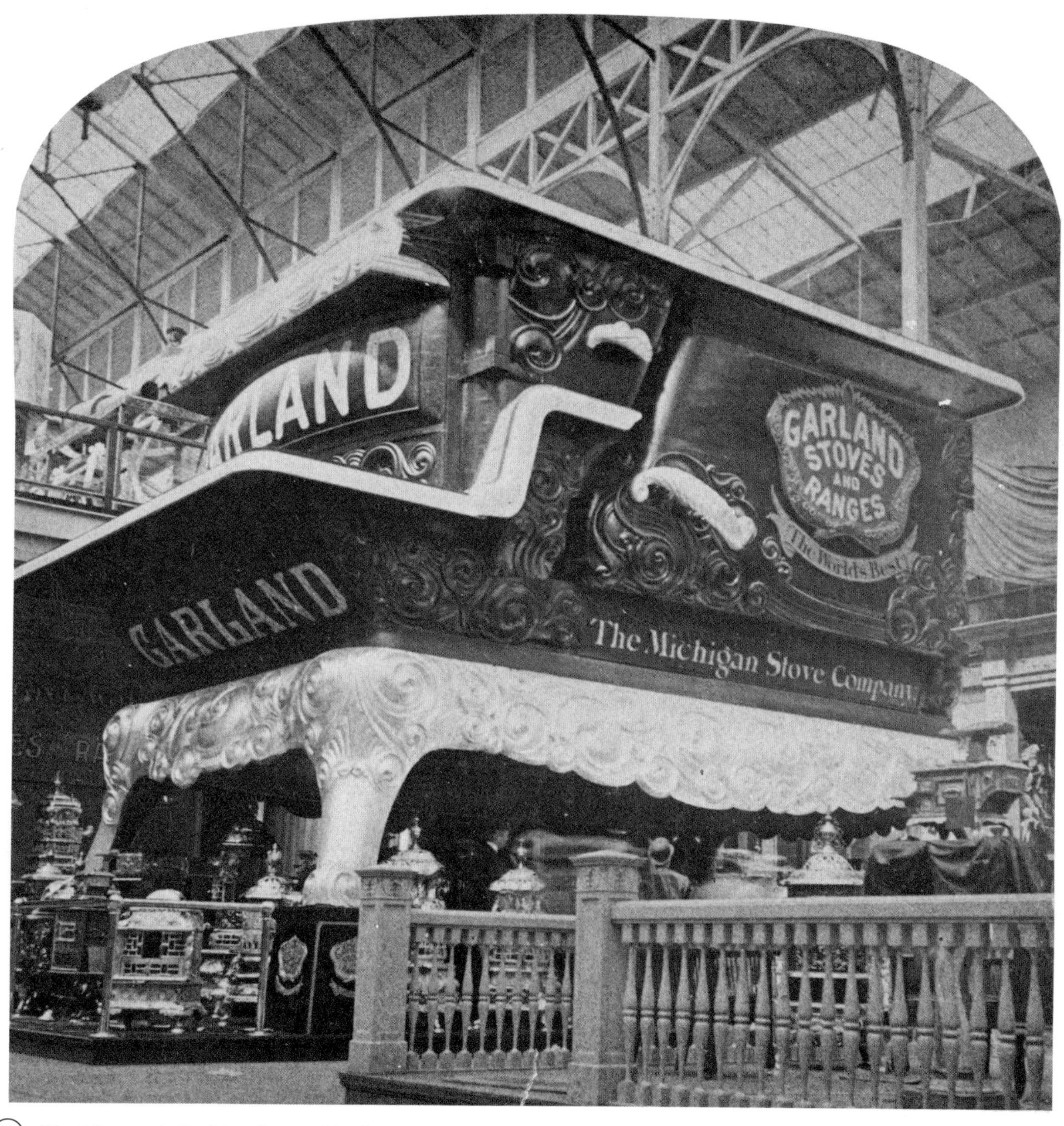

(45) *The Mammoth Cooking Stove of Barbecue Dimensions, World's Fair, Chicago, U.S.A.* Photographed and published by Strohmeyer & Wyman, 'sold on' by Underwood & Underwood. 1892.

PORTRAITURE: THE ART OF THE SUNDAY BEST

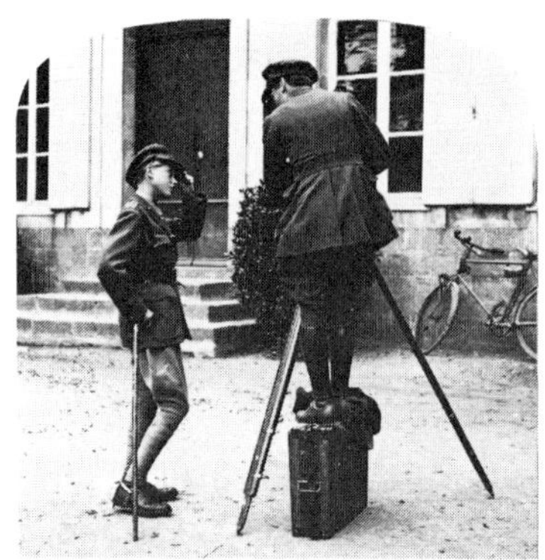

H.R.H. The Prince of Wales Discusses Cinematography with Dr H. D. Girdwood. Published by Realistic Travels.

The enthusiastic first public announcement and description of the daguerreotype, made by the French scientist François Arago on behalf of his Government, included only one note of pessimism:

'In general there is little ground for believing that the same instrument will serve for portraiture, for the problem consists of two apparently irreconcilable conditions. In order to arrive at a short exposure, that is to say, the four or five minutes of immobility that one can expect of a living person, it is necessary to expose the face to full sunshine, but the dazzling light would force even the most insensitive person to blink continually; he would grimace and his usual expression would be gone.'

Arago was not taking into account man's impatient passion to contemplate himself, perhaps the strongest motive behind the tenacious attempts of the pioneers to reduce exposure time.

Portraiture became possible within a few years. Sometimes it required that the sitter's head should be clamped in a vice or the face painted chalk-white to increase its light-reflecting power; but vanity was always a stoic. The moment a photographer had acquired a licence, his first venture was to establish a portrait gallery. The world came flocking.

Cartes de visite, small portraits originally intended to replace the traditional 'calling card', became a universal fad and family albums with pictures of relatives, friends and celebrities were to be found in countless homes. However, unless one is interested in the history of fashion, the parade of Sunday-best facial expressions is enervating. Great beauties, who were famous for their looks, or Tom Thumb, seen here, whom the world paid entrance money to look at, belong in a different category.

Stereographers recorded the appearance of most leaders of state during the latter half of the nineteenth century; but the photographs of monarchs, emperors and presidents are usually formal to the point of masking rather than revealing the sitter. Sometimes tragedy, in the shape of revolution or assassination, can retrospectively invest such stuffy portraits with an enriching irony. In this casual portrait of the Prince of Wales, taken during World War I about twenty years before his brief reign as King Edward VIII and widely publicized abdication, the boyishness of the young prince seems poignantly vulnerable. Famous people's faces are usually well known nowadays, but portraits of some turn-of-the-century figures are rare finds. One such is the author, Henrik Ibsen, opposite, who turned up among fish and fjords in an Underwood set about Norway dated 1905.

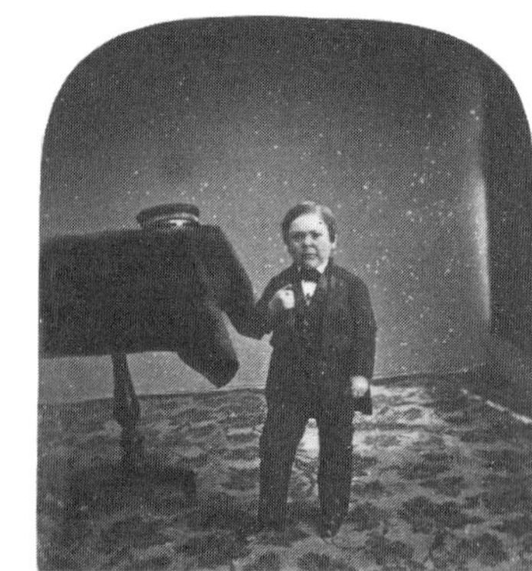

Tom Thumb. Hand-coloured card. Published by the London Stereoscopic Company.

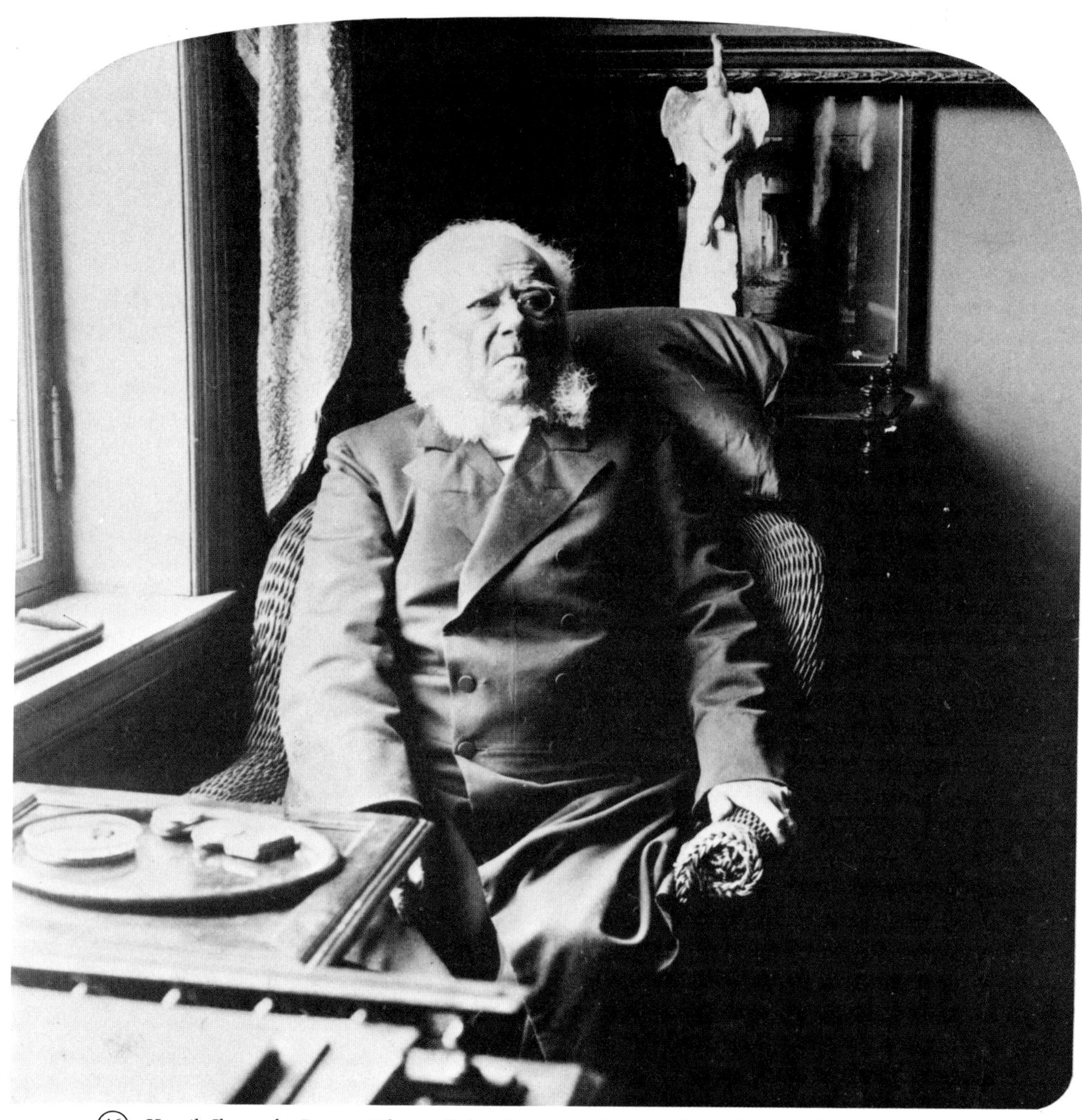

(46) *Henrik Ibsen, the Poet to Whom All the World Pays Homage, in his Home at Christiana, Norway.*
Published by Underwood & Underwood. 1905.

GROUPS

It is said that Rembrandt's so-called *Night Watch* upset his patrons because he forsook the group portrait convention which they had expected by posing his sitters as if they had been 'caught' in the middle of a typical routine, instead of arranging them in a neat row. The group was still posed, but seemed the reverse. Until the camera could take instantaneous pictures, naturalness was always achieved in this unnatural way. Posing, as other examples in this book show, does produce artificial pictures, and many photographers give up the pretence of casualness in favour of the convention that existed before The *Night Watch*. The two extremes are illustrated on this page in the posed *Boatman Somewhat Rattled* and the conventional *Family Cares*.

There are many degrees of compromise between 'living statues' and line-ups like identity parades. Here are two, in which an unusual setting allows the sitter freedom to obey the hardest instruction of all, that is, 'Look natural!' The group of boys on the capstan at Whitby may have been taken in the 1890s by the famous photographer Frank Sutcliffe, while the other, at White Strand Bay in County Donegal, Ireland, may be by William England, taken in 1858. The group of children on holiday in Brighton, opposite, demonstrates that pleasant mixture of luck and timing which the instantaneous photograph made possible.

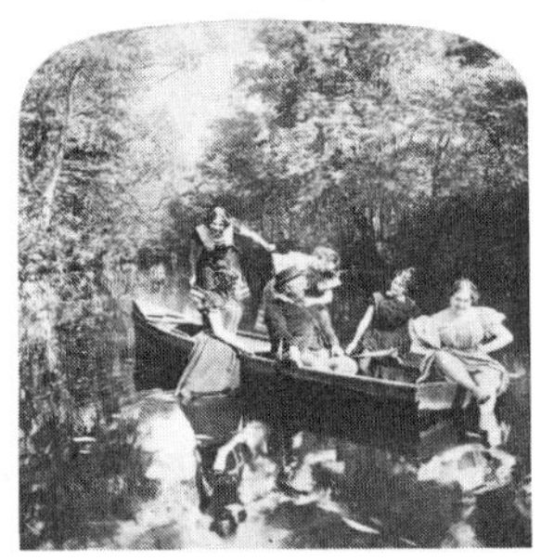
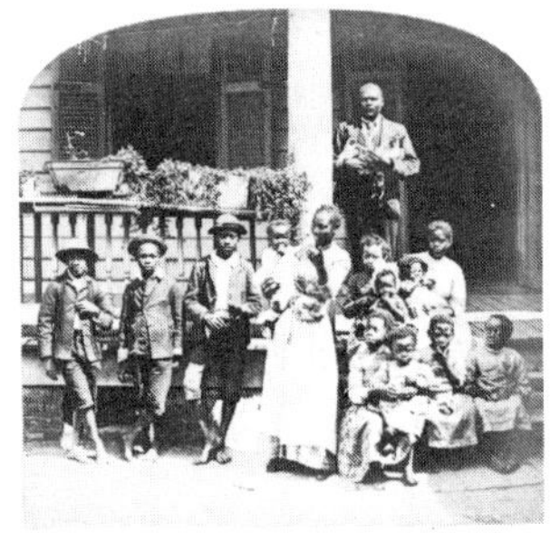
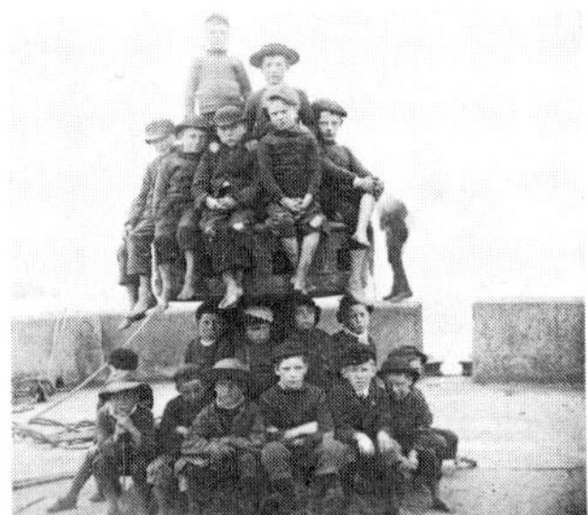
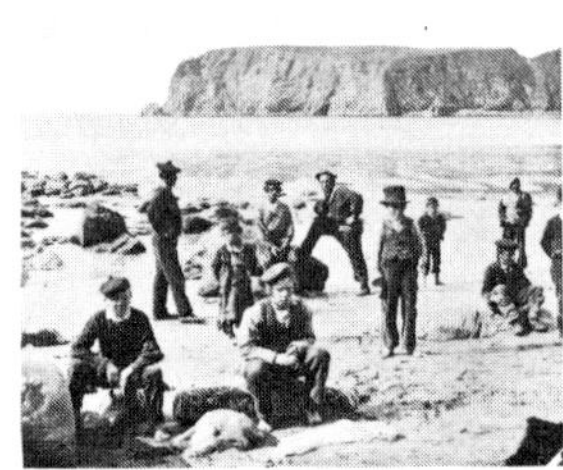

(TOP LEFT) *The Boatman Somewhat Rattled.* Photographed and published by Strohmeyer & Wyman, 'sold on' by Underwood & Underwood. 1899. (TOP RIGHT) *Family Cares.* Photographed and published by B. W. Kilburn. 1891. (BELOW LEFT) *Group of Boys on the 'Capstan'. Whitby.* Possibly by Frank Sutcliffe. Published by Underwood & Underwood. (BELOW RIGHT) *In the White Strand Bay, Malin-Beg, Co. Donegal.* Possibly by William England. *c.* 1858.

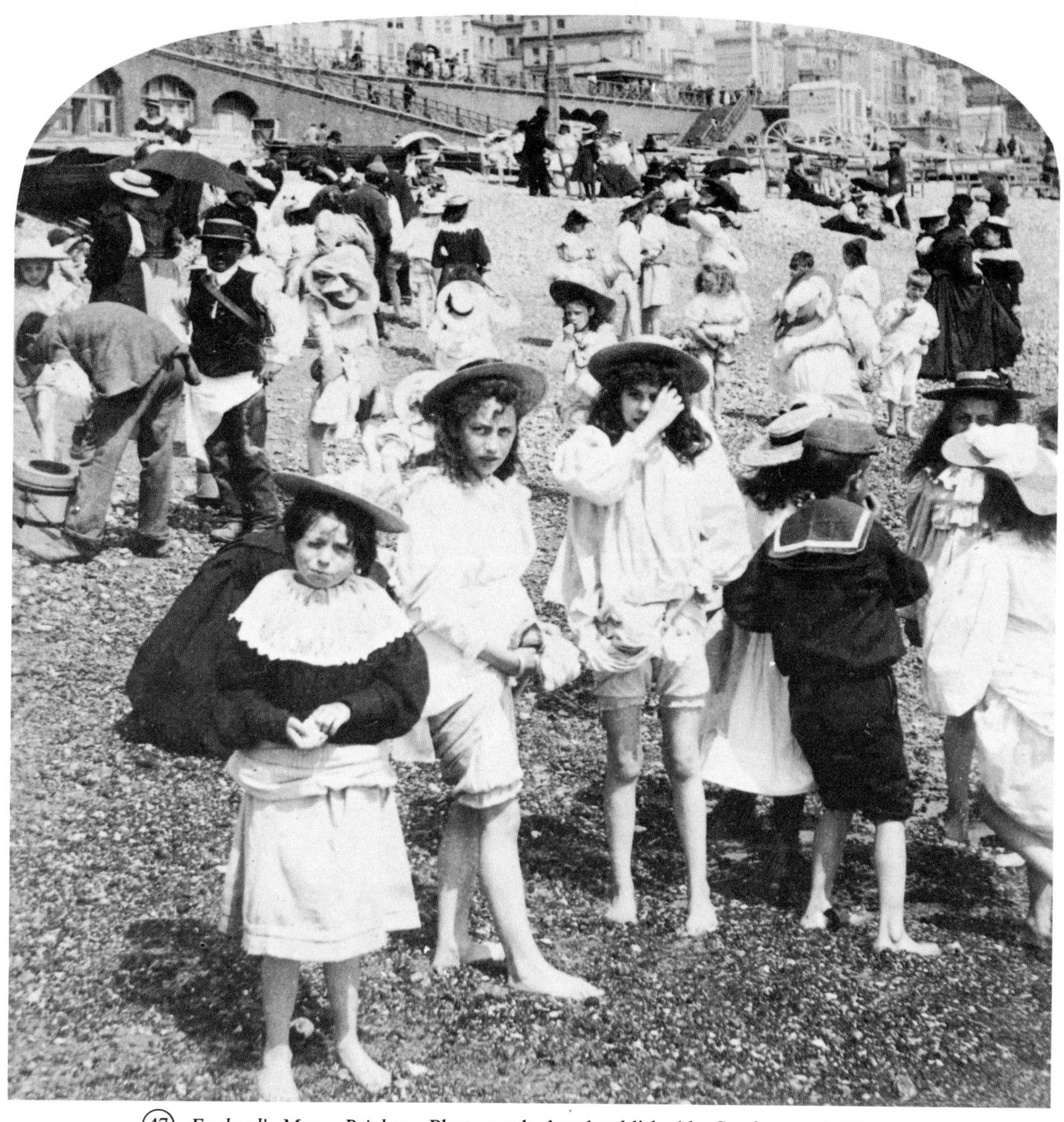

(47) *England's Merry Brighton*. Photographed and published by Strohmeyer & Wyman, 'sold on' by Underwood & Underwood. 1896.

CHILDREN

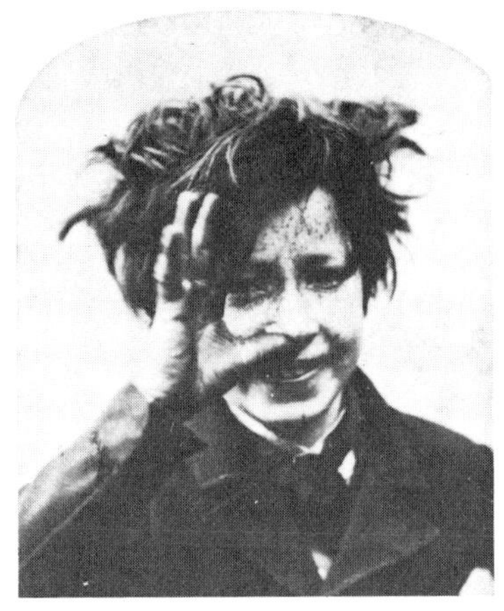

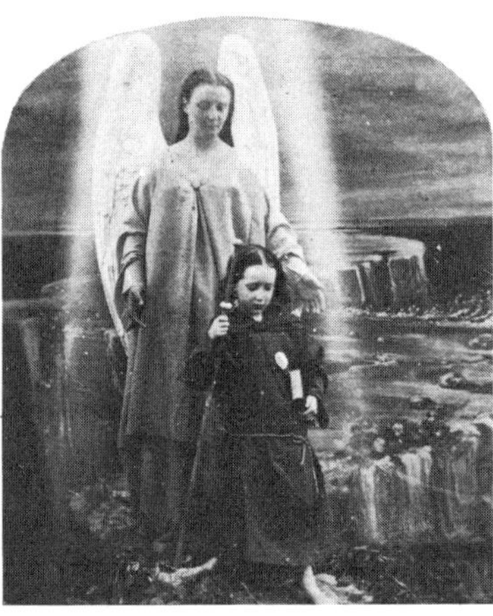

(LEFT) *Impudence.* Published by the London Stereoscopic Company. 1856. (RIGHT) *The Path of Life,* by Alfred Silvester. Hand-coloured card. Published by the London Stereoscopic Company.

Impudence, a portrait of 1856, is not quite our image of the Victorian child. His defiant gesture summarizes twentieth-century reaction to that cruel mixture of harshness and sentimentality which we have come to identify as the 'Victorian' attitude to children.

In the stereoscope the most popular role of the Victorian child, when not seen to be studying or at prayer, is that of the principal injured party in a family bereavement; indeed, if one had only stereographs as evidence, one might be forgiven for assuming that around the 1860s the word 'child' was a synonym for 'orphan'. Even so, apart perhaps from the angels that often lurk ambiguously in its vicinity, vacillating in their duties between bodyguard and kidnapper, the Victorian child is not strikingly different from its grown-up contemporaries.

Turn-of-the-century stereographs are not reassuring. In them the modern child appears, usually at play and frequently depicted with a pen dipped in treacle: *Fast friends Passing the Gates of Sleepy Land,* for example, features the stock cast of the twentieth-century's precious darling set. By 1905, cuteness had replaced quaintness.

Nowadays cards like *She Has Symptoms of Small Pox* (1898) are keenly collected as guides to dating children's toys and dolls. In many such views children are seen imitating grown-ups. In the mirror above the 'Grandma' scene, far right, one can dimly make out the stereographer. He has been sitting there directing the action since the 1850s, when Grandma herself played with dolls.

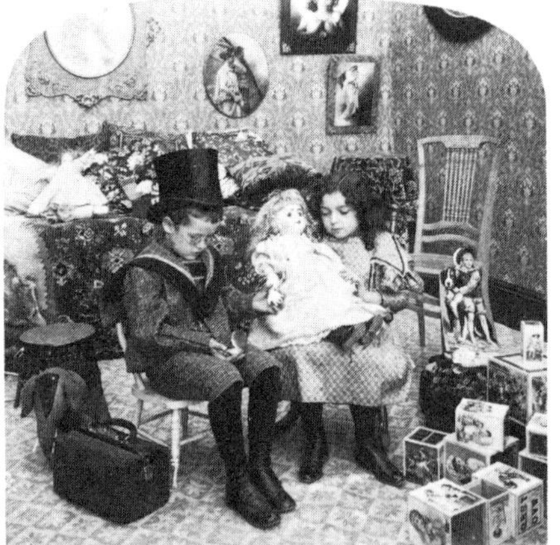

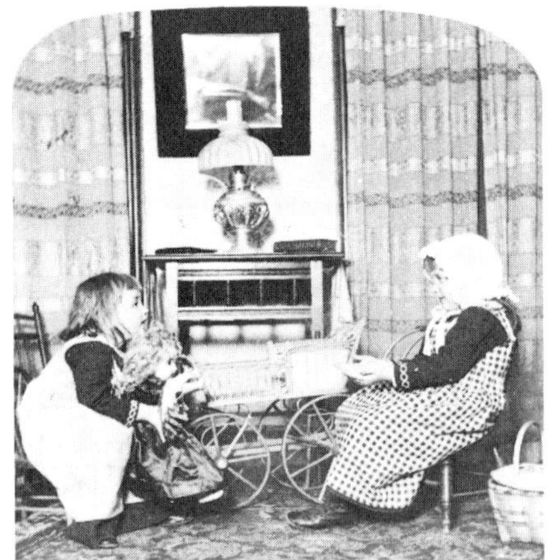

(LEFT) *'She Has Symptoms of Small Pox.'* Photographed and published by Strohmeyer & Wyman, 'sold on' by Underwood & Underwood. 1898. (RIGHT) *'Bless Her Little Heart – Come to Grandma.'* Photographed and published by Strohmeyer & Wyman, 'sold on' by Underwood & Underwood. 1892.

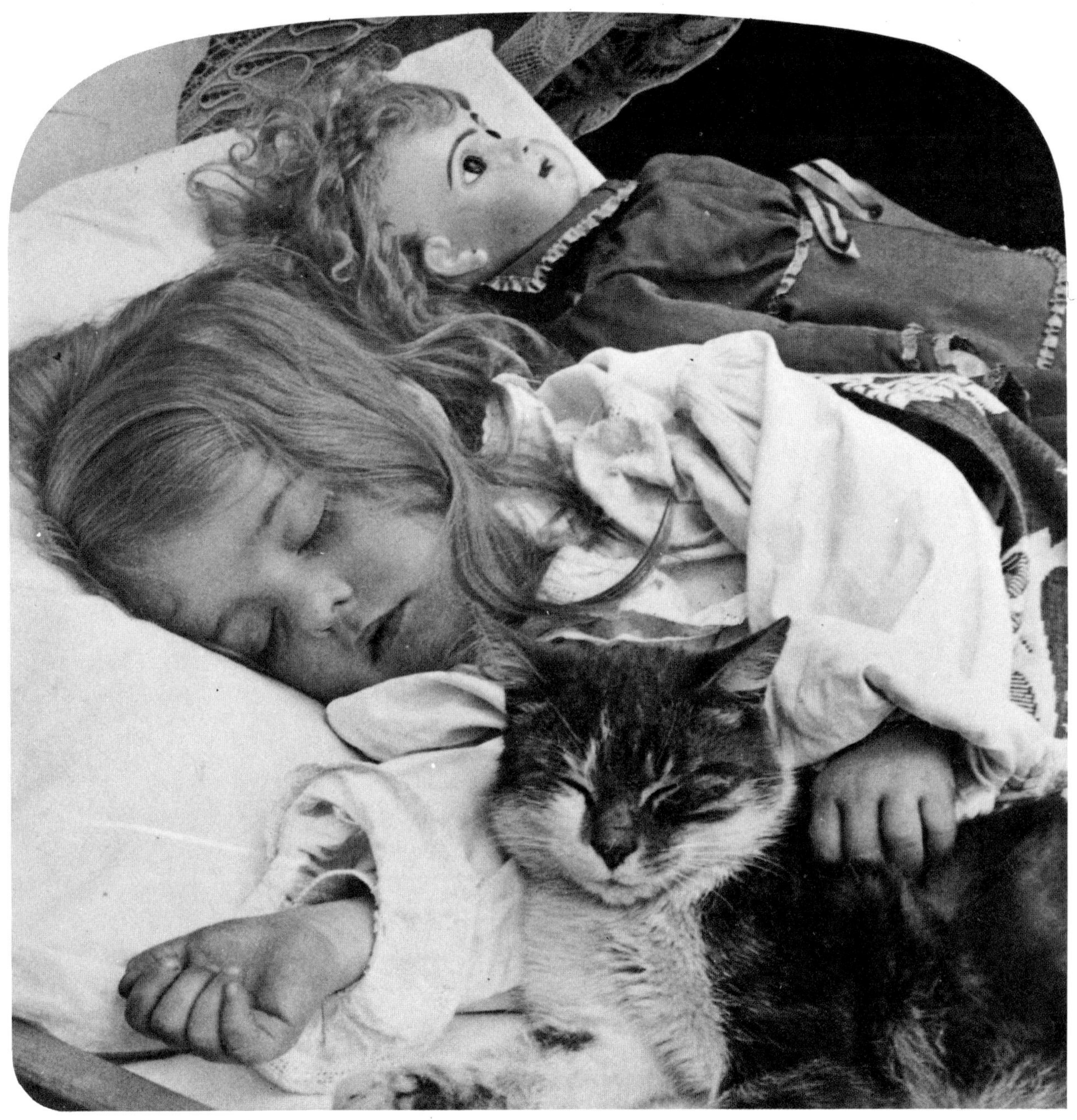

48 *Fast Friends Passing the Gates of Sleepy Land.* Published by Underwood & Underwood. 1905.

119

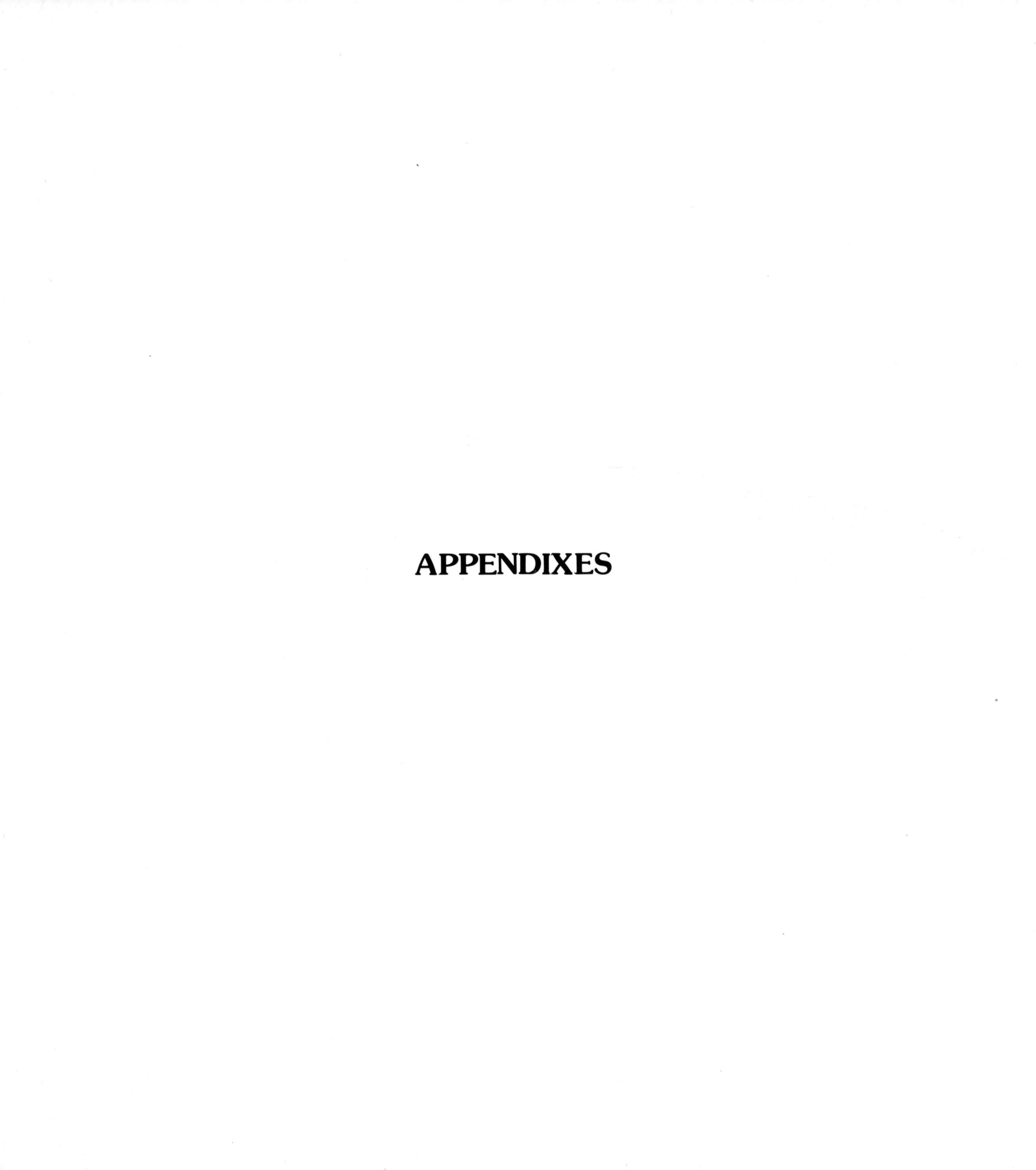

APPENDIXES

APPENDIX I: PHOTOSCULPTURE

An idea that might, at the time, have seemed to realize the stereo-photographer's ambition to duplicate nature's three dimensions, proposed a way of modelling called 'Photosculpture'. In a letter to Claudet,* Ernest Lacan, the editor of *La Lumière* and a keen writer on photography, reported enthusiastically on the success, of the invention, which he had promoted in France, and urged Claudet to help him launch it in Britain where, he said, it would certainly be good business and 'please the vain English aristocracy'.

The process does not now seem so remarkable, nevertheless examples were exhibited by Claudet in 1864 at a *soirée* of the Royal Society at Burlington House and then at his own gallery-studio. The exhibits had been made by their inventor, M. Willème, at an establishment called the Société Générale de Photosculpture de France in the Boulevard de l'Etoile in Paris. The engravings show the two important stages of the procedure.

Photographs were taken simultaneously by twenty-four cameras arranged regularly in a circle round the sitter, well-lit from all sides. These were then projected on to a large screen of ground glass, behind which the sculptor manipulated a modified pantograph. In its original state this simple apparatus, used for copying drawings mechanically, consists of a pencil connected to a pointed object (such as a nail) in such a way that every movement of the point is followed by the pencil; this, placed in contact with a sheet of paper, reproduces its movements exactly. If the point is made to trace a drawing, the pencil automatically duplicates it. In photosculpture the pencil and paper were replaced by a knife and a block of clay. When the sculptor traced the outline of the image projected on the ground glass, the knife cut the clay accordingly. As each of the twenty-four photographs was traced in turn, the clay block was rotated through one twenty-fourth of a circle.

'The bust or statuette', an account in the *Art Journal* of 1864 tells us, 'produced by this means, is a likeness which, although in a somewhat uneven state, no one can mistake. It is now necessary to smooth by hand, or by a tool, all the slight roughness produced by the

Fox Talbot's letter of 25 October 1864, in which he asks Antoine Claudet if he has received a letter written by himself about a month previously on the subject of photosculpture and photoglyphic engraving.

*The letter, in the author's collection, is dated 18 January 1863: this is belied by the envelope which is franked 21 January 1864. Perhaps M. Lacan had simply not adjusted to the New Year.

various cuttings, and to soften down and blend the small intervals between the outlines or profiles.' Several major figures in photography showed interest in photosculpture, perhaps for its commercial potential (see, for example, the letter from Fox Talbot to Claudet), but it seems to have had only a limited success.

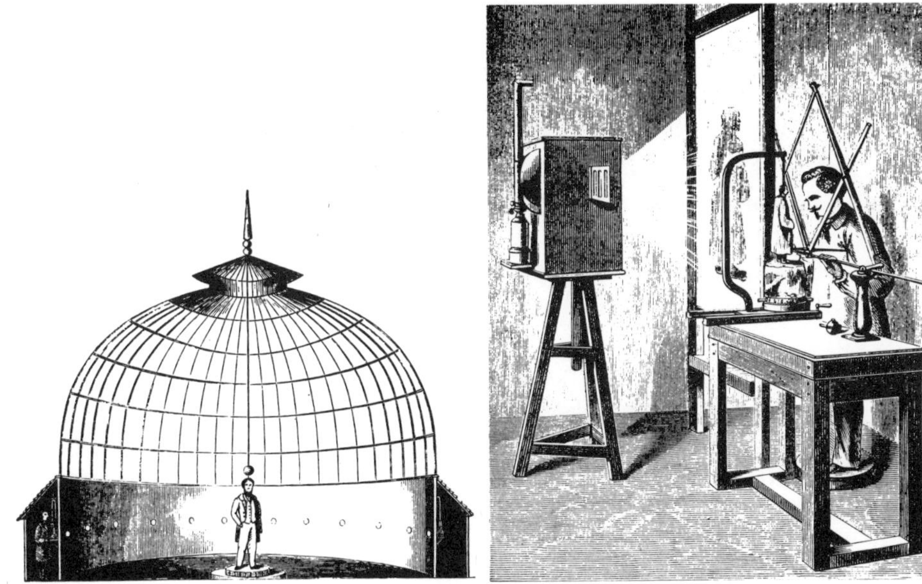

(LEFT) Twenty-four cameras in a circle take simultaneous photographs of the sitter. (RIGHT) The end-product takes shape – a three-dimensional clay statuette.

APPENDIX II: HOLOGRAPHY

In 1947 Dennis Gabor, a Hungarian engineer working in England, invented a way of making three-dimensional pictures which he called 'holograms', for which he was given the Nobel Prize in 1971. Viewing a hologram is exactly like looking through a window at an object placed on the sill outside. As the observer changes viewpoint, the side of the object and things behind it come into view. The three-dimensional effect is uncannily convincing and it is hard to believe one is not looking at a real object.

The image is stored on transparent film, on which the light reflected from all parts of the object has been converted into a complex accumulation of dark and light bands. When a beam of light, made up of pure colour waves in parallel, is projected through the transparency the pattern of bands is converted into an astonishing three-dimensional picture. Nowadays, the required beam of light comes from a laser, invented in 1960. In his early experiments Gabor used the almost-pure light of a mercury lamp, but the perfect hologram was not achieved until Emmett N. Leith and Juris Upatnicks of Michigan University applied the laser to it in 1965.

Making the image on the transparent film also involves the use of a laser. Its beam is split by a semi-transparent mirror which diverts some light straight to the film, the rest bouncing off the surface of the object being holographed, which scatters its orderly waves. These are directed by mirrors to meet the first beam at the film, where the interaction of the two produces the pattern of light bands on the emulsion. An improvement by the American G. Stokes has now made it possible for the hologram to be seen by passing ordinary white light through the transparency, which filters out all waves except those from the laser which originally illuminated the subject.

The sophisticated uses of the hologram are many. Incredible things can be done with holography's potential to 'print' visual information on the atoms of thick 'film'. A one-inch cube can be made to store images of every page of a 30,000-book library, which can be retrieved by laser beams linked to a computer. It is also possible to convert sound waves reflected from the surface of an object into a 3-D picture of it, even when the original is not available to human vision, *ie* in the dark. Another application is to conjure up an image of a still non-existent building or piece of machinery, working solely from the mathematical data on the designer's drawing-board.

The possibilities of this extraordinary invention go far beyond the original stereographers' most daring fantasies, and scientists have hardly begun to realize its utility.

SELECT BIBLIOGRAPHY

The American Museum of Photography. (Published by the AMOP. 1956.)
The Art Journal (1849 onwards). (George Virtue. London.)
Geschichte der Fotographie von Dr Wolfgang Baier. (VEB Fotokinoverlag. Leipzig. 1966.)
Frederick C. Bakewell. *Great Facts*. (Hewlston & Wright. London. 1859.)
Cecil Beaton and Gail Buckland. *The Magic Image*.
Brian Bowers. *Sir Charles Wheatstone, FRS. 1802–1875*. (HMSO. London. 1975.)
Michel F. Braive. *The Era of the Photograph*. Trans. from French by David Butt. (Thames and Hudson. London. 1966.)
Sir David Brewster. *The Stereoscope*. (London. 1856.)
Peter Castle. *Collecting & Valuing Old Photographs*. (Garnstone Press. London. 1973.)
C. W. Ceram. *Archaeology of the Cinema*. (Thames and Hudson. London. 1965.)
W. S. Chadwick. *The Stereoscopic Manual*. 2nd edition. (John Heywood. Manchester and London. *c*. 1890.)
William Culp Darrah. *Stereo Views: A History of Stereographs in America and Their Collection*. (Times & News Publishing Co. 1964.)
'*From Today Painting is Dead*'. *The Beginnings of Photography*. Catalogue of the Arts Council Exhibition at the Victoria and Albert Museum. (London. 1972.)
Helmut and Alison Gernsheim. *A Concise History of Photography*. (Thames and Hudson. London. 1965.)
Helmut and Alison Gernsheim. *The History of Photography*. (Thames and Hudson. London. 1969.)
Helmut and Alison Gernsheim. *L. J. M. Daguerre: The History of the Diorama and the Daguerreotype*. (Dover Publications. New York. 1968; originally Secker & Warburg. 1956.)
Paul N. Harbuck (ed.). *The Book of Photography*. (Cassell. London. 1907.)
B. E. C. Howarth-Loomes. *Victorian Photography: A Collector's Guide*. (Ward Lock. London. 1974.)
The Illustrated Exhibitor. (John Cassell. 1852.)
The Illustrated London News (1843 onwards).
Life Library of Photography. (Time-Life International. 1971–72.)
Oliver Mathews. *Early Photographs and Early Photographers*. (Reedminster Publications. 23 Suffolk Road, London, SW13. 1973.)
Mostra Internazionale della Stereoscopia nella Fotografia e nel cinema. Catalogue. (Museo Nazionale del Cinema, Turin. 1966.)
Beaumont Newhall. *The History of Photography*. 4th edition (Museum of Modern Art. New York. 1964.)
Photographica. Auction catalogues. (Christie's. London. 1972–76.)
Photographic Images and Related Material. Auction catalogues. (Sotheby's. London. 1972–76.)
Peter Pollack. *The Picture History of Photography*. (Thames and Hudson. London. 1964.)
Lake Price. *A Manual of Photographic Manipulations*. (John Churchill. London. 1858.)
Rare Photographic Images, Apparatus and Literature. Auction catalogue. (Parke Bernet. New York. 1970.)
Aaron Scharf. *Art and Photography*. (Allen Lane, the Penguin Press. London. 1968.)
Louis Walton Sipley. *Collector's Guide to American Photography*. (American Museum of Photography. 1957.)
Robert Taft. *Photography and the American Scene*. (Dover Publications. New York. 1964; originally Macmillan. 1938.)
D. B. Thomas. *Cameras: Photographs and Accessories*. (HMSO. London. 1966.)
D. B. Thomas. *The Science Museum Photography Collection*. (HMSO. London. 1969.)
John Werge. *The Evolution of Photography*. (London. 1890.)
C. W. Wilman. *Simplified Stereoscopic Photography*. (Percival Marshall. London. *c*. 1937.)

THE AUTHOR

John Jones is a painter and lecturer in Fine Art at the University of Leeds.
As an art historian he has specialized in twentieth-century painting,
particularly American, and spent a year in the USA interviewing more than a hundred
artists as part of a fellowship from the American Council of Learned Societies.
At Leeds he introduced film studies into the Fine Art course, and while researching
the subject he began to form a collection based on the history of photography.
It is from this collection, which in time spread into related areas such as optics,
Victorian toys and magic lanterns, that the illustrations in this book have been drawn.
John Jones also makes documentary films about art and artists.
His productions include *Matisse, a Sort of Paradise,* co-directed with Lawrence Gowing
for the Arts Council; *Claes Oldenburg Hanging a Picture,* made with Oldenburg in
New York; *Drawing with the Figure,* an Arts Foundation film, and
Kate Barnard and her Work, prepared for the Yorkshire Arts Association.
He is married and has two children.

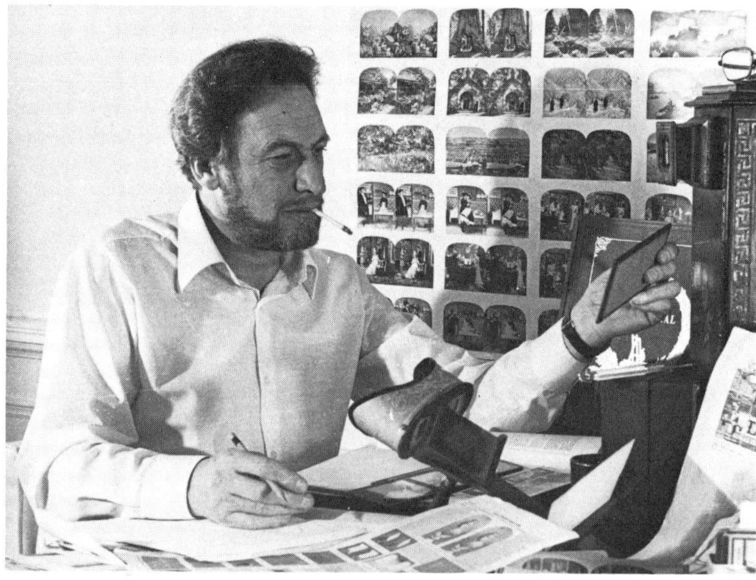

The author, with stereoscope.

A ROXBY PRESS PRODUCTION

This publication was
made in Great Britain by
Roxby Press Productions Ltd,
98 Clapham Common Northside,
London SW4 9SG.

Editorial director Michael Leitch
Designer David Hillman

Volume 1
Printed by Ebenezer Baylis & Son Ltd, Worcester and London
Bound by Webb Son Ltd.
Typesetting by Tradespools Ltd.

Volume 2
Stereoscope designed by David Bristow and John Williamson
Made by Cambridge Moulders Ltd.
Lenses supplied by Combined Optical Industries Ltd.
Technical advisers P. Trevor-Roper, FRCS, and T. W. Davies.

Slipcase made by Petrushkin Ltd.
Assembly by Remploy Ltd.